Creating a World
Without Poverty

Also by Muhammad Yunus
Banker to the Poor

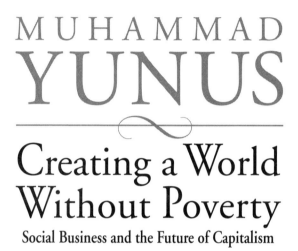

MUHAMMAD
YUNUS

Creating a World
Without Poverty
Social Business and the Future of Capitalism

WITH
KARL WEBER

PublicAffairs

New York

Book Design by Pauline Brown.
Set in Adobe Garamond 11.5 point type by the Perseus Books Group.

Library of Congress Cataloging-in-Publication Data

Yunus, Muhammad, 1940–
Creating a world without poverty : social business and the future of
capitalism / Muhammad Yunus With Karl Weber. — 1st ed.
    p. cm.
    Includes index.
    ISBN–13: 978–1–58648–493–4 (hardcover)
    ISBN–10: 1–58648–493–1 (hardcover)
    1. Social responsibility of business. 2. Industries—Social aspects.
3. Poverty—Prevention. I. Weber, Karl. II. Title.
HD60.Y86   2007
338.7—dc22   2007034545

10 9 8 7 6 5 4 3 2 1

To everyone who wants
to create a world
where not a single person is poor

Contents

Prologue

Starting with
a Handshake

Because the microcredit organization I founded, Grameen Bank, has successfully brought financial services to poor women in Bangladesh, I am often invited to speak with groups that are interested in improving the lot of women. In October 2005, I was scheduled to attend one such conference in the French resort town of Deauville, ninety miles northwest of Paris. I would also be visiting Paris to deliver a lecture at HEC, one of the leading business schools in Europe, where they would honor me with the position of Professor Honoris Causa.

A few days before my trip to France, the coordinator of my schedule in Paris received a message from the office of Franck Riboud, the chairman and CEO of Groupe Danone, a large French corporation (whose American brand name is Dannon). The message read:

> M. Riboud has heard about the work of Professor Yunus in Bangladesh, and he would like very much like to meet him. Since he will be traveling to Deauville shortly, would it be possible for him to have lunch with M. Riboud in Paris?

I am always happy to meet with people interested in my work in general, and in microcredit in particular, especially if they can help in the battle to alleviate and ultimately eliminate global poverty. The chairman of a major multinational corporation would certainly be worth talking to. But I was not sure whether the proposed meeting could be accommodated in my already packed schedule. I told my coordinator that if we could find the time, I would be happy to see M. Riboud.

Don't worry, I was told. The Danone people will make all the arrangements, take you to lunch, and then make sure you're delivered to the HEC campus in plenty of time.

So on October 12, I found myself being whisked from Orly airport in a limousine provided by the Danone corporation to La Fontaine Gaillon, a Parisian restaurant recently opened by the actor Gérard Depardieu, where M. Riboud was waiting for me.

He'd brought along seven of his colleagues—important executives in charge of various aspects of Danone's global business: Jean Laurent, a member of the board of Danone; Philippe-Loïc Jacob, general secretary of Groupe Danone; and Jerome Tubiana, facilitator of Dream Projects in Danone. Also present was Dr. Bénédicte Faivre-Tavignot, professor at HEC in charge of their MBA program in sustainable development.

I was ushered into a private room where I was greeted in a very friendly fashion, served a fine French meal, and invited to tell the group about our work.

I quickly discovered that Franck Riboud and his colleagues were well aware of the work of Grameen Bank. They knew we had helped launch the global movement called microcredit, which helps poor people by offering them small, collateral-free loans—often as little as the equivalent of thirty to forty U.S. dollars—to use in starting tiny businesses. Access to capital, even on a tiny scale, can have a transforming effect on human lives. Over time, many of the poor are able to use the small stake that a microloan provides as the basis for building a thriving business—a tiny farm, a craft workshop, a little store—that can lift them and their families out of poverty. In fact, in the thirty-one years since I began lending money to poor people—especially women—millions of families in Bangladesh alone have improved their economic circumstances with the help of microcredit.

I described to M. Riboud and his colleagues how microcredit has spread to many countries, especially in the developing world, through thousands of microcredit institutions launched by nonprofit organizations, government agencies, and business entrepreneurs seeking to emulate the success of Grameen. "In fact," I told him, "by the end of next year, we hope to announce at the Microcredit Global Summit that 100 million poor people around the world have been the beneficiaries of microcredit—this movement that started from nothing just a few decades ago." (When the summit was held in Halifax, Nova Scotia, in November 2006, we could say that we had in fact reached that goal. We have now set even more ambitious targets for the next ten years, including the most important one: To assist 500 million people around the world in escaping poverty with the help of microcredit.)

Finally, I began to relate how Grameen Bank had expanded its activities into many new areas, all designed to help the poor. We'd launched special lending programs to help poor people pay for housing and higher education. We'd created a program to lend money to beggars, which had already helped free thousands from the necessity to beg and had demonstrated that even the poorest of the poor could be considered "credit-worthy." And we'd developed a series of businesses—some operated on a profit-making basis, some as nonprofits—that were improving economic opportunities for the poor in many other ways. They ranged from bringing telephone and Internet communication services into thousands of remote villages to helping traditional weavers bring their products to market. In these ways, I said, the Grameen idea was reaching more and more families and communities every year.

Once I had completed my brief history of Grameen's progress, I paused and invited Franck Riboud to tell me why he had asked me to lunch. "Now it is your turn," I said, "I've heard of your corporation, but I understand it is not operating in Bangladesh. So tell me something about Groupe Danone."

"I am happy to do so," he replied.

Franck told me about the origins of his corporation. Groupe Danone is one of the world leaders in dairy products; its Danone brand yogurt (known as Dannon in the U.S.) is popular throughout Europe, North America, and in other countries. Danone is also number two in bottled water and biscuits (cookies and crackers) in the world. "This Evian water," Franck said, holding up a blue bottle, "is a Danone product." I'd seen and drunk Evian water in hotels and restaurants around the world. Now I knew a little about the corporation behind the brand.

"This is very interesting," I commented, but I was still at a loss to know what high-end mineral water or yogurt that would be considered luxury products in Bangladesh could have to do with me or Grameen Bank. Franck was ready with an answer. "Danone is an important source of food in many regions of the world. That includes some of the developing nations where hunger is a serious problem. We have major businesses in Brazil, in Indonesia, and in China. Recently we have expanded into India. In fact, more than forty percent of our business is in developing markets.

"We don't want to sell our products only to the well-off people in those countries. We would like to find ways to help feed the poor. It is part of our company's historic commitment to being socially innovative and progressive, which dates back thirty-five years to the work of my father, Antoine Riboud.

"Perhaps this background explains why I asked for this meeting, Professor Yunus. We thought that a man and an organization that have used creative thinking to help so many of the poor might have an idea or two for Groupe Danone."

I had no specific idea what Franck Riboud was looking for. But I could feel he was interested in everything I'd told him so far. Additionally, for some time, I'd been thinking a lot about the role of business in helping the world's poor. Other economic sectors—the volunteer, charitable, and nongovernmental sectors, for instance—devote a great deal of time and energy to dealing with poverty and its consequences. But business—the most financially innovative and efficient sector of all—has no direct mechanism to apply its practices to the goal of eliminating poverty.

The work of Grameen Bank and its sister companies had helped to bring millions of people into the local, regional, and world economies, enabling them to participate in markets, earn money, and support themselves and their families. It seemed to me that there were many opportunities for other kinds of businesses to bring similar benefits to the poor. So when, over lunch in a fine Paris restaurant, one such opportunity seemed to be presenting itself, I decided to seize it if I could.

It was a spur-of-the-moment impulse, not the kind of carefully planned business proposal that most executives prefer. But over the years, I've found that some of my best projects have been started, not on the basis of rigorous prior analysis and planning, but simply from an impulse that says, "Here is a chance to do something good."

I made a suggestion to Franck and his colleagues: "As you know, the people of Bangladesh are some of the poorest in the world. Malnutrition is a terrible problem, especially among children. It leads to awful health consequences as the children grow up.

"Your company is a leading producer of nutritious foods. What would you think about creating a joint venture to bring some of your products to the villages of Bangladesh? We could create a company that we own together and call it Grameen Danone. It could manufacture healthful foods that will improve the diet of rural Bangladeshis—especially the children. If the products were sold at a low price, we could make a real difference in the lives of millions of people."

I was about to learn that Franck Riboud, CEO of one of the world's best-known companies, could be just as impulsive as a "banker to the poor" from Bangladesh. He rose from his chair at the opposite side of the table from me, reached toward me, and extended his hand. "Let's do it," he said, and we shook hands.

I was as elated as I was incredulous. "Can this really be happening so quickly?" I wondered. "What have we agreed to do here? Perhaps he doesn't understand my Bangladeshi accent." We sat back down, and I decided I'd better make sure that Franck knew what he was getting himself—and his company—into.

"Maybe I haven't been quite clear," I said gently. "I am proposing a new company, a joint venture between your company and Grameen. I am calling it Grameen Danone, with our name, Grameen, to come first, since it is better known in Bangladesh than yours."

Franck nodded. "No, I got it!" he assured me. "Your plan is quite clear to me. I shook hands with you because you told me that, in Grameen Bank, you rely on mutual trust between the bank and the borrowers, making loans on the basis of a handshake rather than legal papers. So I am following your system. We shook hands, and as far as I am concerned, the deal is final."

I was pleased and excited by Franck's response. Then I told him something else. "I am not done with my proposal yet. Our joint venture will be a social business."

This time he looked a bit puzzled, as though he had heard a phrase that he could not immediately translate. "A social business? What is that?"

"It's a business designed to meet a social goal. In this case, the goal is to improve the nutrition of poor families in the villages of Bangladesh. A social business is a business that pays no dividends. It sells products at prices that make it self-sustaining. The owners of the company can get back the amount they've invested in the company over a period of time, but no profit is paid to investors in the form of dividends. Instead, any profit made stays in the business—to finance expansion, to create new products or services, and to do more good for the world.

"This is an idea of my own—something I've been thinking about for a long time. I believe that many kinds of enterprises can be created as social businesses in order to serve the poor. I've been looking for a chance to put the idea into practice. We've already made a beginning in Bangladesh, setting up eye-care hospitals as social businesses. But Grameen Danone will be a powerful new example of the idea—that is, if you agree."

Franck smiled. "This is extremely interesting," he said. He stood up again, extended his hand toward me across the table. I stood up and reached for his hand. As we shook hands, he said, "Let's do it."

I was so stunned, even more convinced that my ears were deceiving me, that, a couple of hours later, on the road to the HEC campus, I quickly sent Franck an email. In it, I summarized my understanding of our discussion and asked him to confirm, clarify, or correct my impressions. If he was seriously pledging himself to create the world's first multinational social business as a partnership between Grameen and Danone, I wanted to make sure he understood what was involved. And if there had been some confusion between us—or if he had simply had second thoughts, or been dissuaded by his colleagues—I wanted to give him an opportunity to say "no" quickly and easily, with no hard feelings.

But Franck and his team at Danone were fully committed to the project. While I was at HEC, I received a call from Emmanuel Faber, the chief of Danone's operation in Asia. Franck had mentioned Emmanuel during our meeting, explaining that he would be the logical person to direct Danone's end of our joint project. Now Emmanuel called from his Shanghai office.

"Professor Yunus," he told me, "I am thrilled that a concrete idea has emerged from your lunch. I'm looking forward to meeting you and talking about the project. Meanwhile, please send me your initial thoughts about it." I promised I would.

Not only were Franck Riboud and Danone committed to the project, they wanted to move ahead at a rapid pace to make our new business into a reality. I discovered this during the whirlwind of the next several months, as Groupe Danone and Grameen worked together to create something new under the sun: the world's very first consciously designed multinational social business.

Creating a World
Without Poverty

ONE

The Promise of
Social Business

1

A New Kind of Business

Since the fall of the Soviet Union in 1991, free markets have swept the globe. Free-market economics has taken root in China, Southeast Asia, much of South America, Eastern Europe, and even the former Soviet Union. There are many things that free markets do extraordinarily well. When we look at countries with long histories under capitalist systems—in Western Europe and North America—we see evidence of great wealth. We also see remarkable technological innovation, scientific discovery, and educational and social progress. The emergence of modern capitalism three hundred years ago made possible material progress of a kind never before seen. Today, however—almost a generation after the Soviet Union fell—a sense of disillusionment is setting in.

To be sure, capitalism is thriving. Businesses continue to grow, global trade is booming, multinational corporations are spreading into markets in the developing world and the former Soviet bloc, and technological advancements continue to multiply. But not everyone is benefiting. Global income distribution tells the story: Ninety-four percent of world income goes to 40 percent of the people, while the other 60 percent must live on only 6 percent of world income. Half of the world lives on two dollars a day or less, while almost a billion people live on less than one dollar a day.

Poverty is not distributed evenly around the world; specific regions suffer its worst effects. In sub-Saharan Africa, South Asia, and Latin America, hundreds of millions of poor people struggle for survival. Periodic disasters, such as the 2004 tsunami that devastated regions on the Indian Ocean, continue to kill hundreds of thousands of poor and vulnerable people. The divide between the global North and South—between the world's richest and the rest—has widened.

Some of the countries that have enjoyed economic success over the past three decades have paid a heavy price, however. Since China introduced economic reforms in the late 1970s, it has experienced rapid economic growth, and, according to the World Bank, over 400 million Chinese have escaped poverty. (As a result, India has now become the nation with the largest population of poor people, even though China has a bigger overall population.)

But all of this progress has brought with it a worsening of social problems. In their rush to grow, Chinese officials have looked the other way when companies polluted the water and air. And despite the improved lot of many poor, the divide between the haves and have-nots is widening. As measured by technical indicators such as the Gini coefficient, income inequality is worse in China than in India.

Even in the United States, with its reputation as the richest country on earth, social progress has been disappointing. After two decades of slow progress, the number of people living in poverty has increased in recent years.[1] Some forty-seven million people, nearly a sixth of the population, have no health insurance and have trouble getting basic medical care. After the end of the Cold War, many hoped for a "peace dividend"—defense spending could decline, and social programs for education and medical care would increase. But especially since September 11, 2001, the U.S. government has focused on military action and security measures, ignoring the poor.

These global problems have not gone unnoticed. At the outset of the new millennium, the entire world mobilized to address them. In 2000, world leaders gathered at the United Nations and pledged, among other goals, to reduce poverty by half by 2015. But after half the time has elapsed, the results are disappointing, and most observers think the Millennium Goals will not be met. (My own country of Bangladesh, I'm happy to say, is an exception. It is moving steadily to meet the goals and is clearly on track to reduce poverty by half by 2015.)

What is wrong? In a world where the ideology of free enterprise has no real challenger, why have free markets failed so many people? As some nations march toward ever greater prosperity, why has so much of the world been left behind?

The reason is simple. Unfettered markets in their current form are not meant to solve social problems and instead may actually exacerbate poverty, disease, pollution, corruption, crime, and inequality.

I support the idea of globalization—that free markets should expand beyond national borders, allowing trade among nations and a continuing flow of capital, and with governments wooing international companies by offering them business facilities, operating conveniences, and tax and regulatory advantages. Globalization, as a general business principle, can bring more benefits to the poor than any alternative. But without proper oversight and guidelines, globalization has the potential to be highly destructive.

Global trade is like a hundred-lane highway criss-crossing the world. If it is a free-for-all highway, with no stoplights, speed limits, size restrictions, or even lane markers, its surface will be taken over by the giant trucks from the world's most powerful economies. Small vehicles—a farmer's pickup truck or Bangladesh's bullock carts and human-powered rickshaws—will be forced off the highway.

In order to have win-win globalization, we must have fair traffic laws, traffic signals, and traffic police. The rule of "the strongest takes all" must be replaced by rules that ensure that the poorest have a place on the highway. Otherwise the global free market falls under the control of financial imperialism.

In the same way, local, regional, and national markets need reasonable rules and controls to protect the interests of the poor. Without such controls, the rich can easily bend conditions to their own benefit. The negative impact of unlimited single-track capitalism is visible every day—in global corporations that locate factories in the world's poorest countries, where cheap labor (including children) can be freely exploited to increase profits; in companies that pollute the air, water, and soil to save money on equipment and processes that protect the environment; in deceptive marketing and advertising campaigns that promote harmful or unnecessary products.

Above all, we see it in entire sectors of the economy that ignore the poor, writing off half the world's population. Instead, businesses in these sectors focus on selling luxury items to people who don't need them, because that is where the biggest profits are.

I believe in free markets as sources of inspiration and freedom for all, not as architects of decadence for a small elite. The world's richest countries, in North America, Europe, and parts of Asia, have benefited enormously from the creative energies, efficiencies, and dynamism that free markets produce. I have devoted my life to bringing those same benefits to the world's most neglected people— the very poor, who are not factored in when economists and business people speak about the market. My experience has shown me that the free market—powerful and useful as it is—could address problems like global poverty and environmental degradation, but not if it must cater solely and relentlessly to the financial goals of its richest shareholders.

Is Government the Answer?

Many people assume that if free markets can't solve social problems, government can. Just as private businesses are devoted to individual profit, government is supposed to represent the interests of society as a whole. Therefore, it seems logical to believe that large-scale social problems should be the province of government.

Government can help create the kind of world we all want to live in. There are certain social functions that can't be organized by private individuals or private organizations—national defense, a central bank to regulate the money supply and the banking business, a public school system, and a national health service to ensure medical care for all and minimize the effects of epidemics. Equally important, government establishes and enforces the rules that control and limit capitalism—the traffic laws. In the world economy, rules and regulations concerning globalization are still being debated. An international economic regulatory regime has yet to fully emerge. But on the national and local levels, many governments do a good job of policing free markets. This is especially true in the industrialized world, where capitalism has a long history and where democratic governments have gradually implemented reasonable regulatory systems.

The traffic laws for free markets oversee inspection of food and medicine and include prohibitions against consumer fraud, against selling dangerous or defective products, against false advertising and violation of contracts, and against polluting the environment. These laws also create and regulate the information framework within which business is conducted—the operation of stock markets, disclosure of company financial information, and standardized accounting and auditing practices. These rules ensure that business is conducted on a level playing field.

The traffic laws for business are not perfect, and they are not always enforced well. Thus some companies still deceive consumers, foul the environment, or defraud investors. These problems are especially serious in the developing world, with its often weak or corrupt governments. In the developed world, governments usually perform their regulatory tasks reasonably well, although starting in the 1980s, conservative politicians have taken every opportunity to undermine government regulations.

However, even an excellent government regulatory regime for business is not enough to ensure that serious social problems will be confronted, much less solved. It can affect the way business is done, but it cannot address the areas that business neglects. Business cannot be mandated to fix problems; it needs an incentive to want to do so. Traffic rules can make a place for small cars and trucks and even rickshaws on the global economic highway. But what about the millions of people who don't own even a modest vehicle? What about the millions of women and children whose basic human needs go unmet? How can the bottom half of the world's population be brought into the mainstream world economy and given the capability to compete in the free market? Economic stop signs and traffic police can't make this happen.

Governments have long tried to address these problems. During the late Middle Ages, England had Poor Laws to help those who might otherwise starve. Modern governments have programs that address social problems and employ doctors, nurses, teachers, scientists, social workers, and researchers to try to alleviate them.

In some countries, government agencies have made headway in the battle against poverty, disease, and other social ills. Such is the case with overpopulation in Bangladesh, which is one of the world's most densely populated countries, with 145 million people in a land area the size of Wisconsin. Or, to put it another way, if the *entire population of the world* were squeezed into the area of the United States of America, the resulting population density would be *slightly less* than exists in Bangladesh today! However, Bangladesh has made genuine progress in alleviating population pressure. In the last three decades, the average number of children per mother has fallen from 6.3 in 1975 to 3.3 in 1999, and the decline continues. This remarkable improvement is largely due to government efforts, including the provision of family planning products, information, and services through clinics around the country. Development and poverty-alleviation efforts by nongovernmental organizations, or NGOs, as well as Grameen Bank have also played an important role.

Governments can do much to address social problems. They are large and powerful, with access to almost every corner of society, and through taxes they can mobilize vast resources. Even the governments of poor countries, where tax revenues are modest, can get international funds in the form of grants and low-interest loans. So it is tempting to simply dump our world's social problems into the lap of government and say, "Here, fix this."

But if this approach were effective, the problems would have been solved long ago. Their persistence makes it clear that government alone does not provide the answer. Why not?

There are a number of reasons. One is that governments can be inefficient, slow, prone to corruption, bureaucratic, and self-perpetuating. These are all side effects of the advantages governments possess: Their vast size, power, and reach almost inevitably make them unwieldy as well as attractive to those who want to use them to amass power and wealth for themselves.

Government is often good at creating things but not so good at shutting them down when they are no longer needed or become burdens. Vested interests—especially jobs—are created with any new institution. In Bangladesh, for example, workers whose sole job was to wind the clocks on the mantelpieces of government administrators retained their positions, and their salaries, for many years after wind-up clocks were superseded by electrical timepieces.

Politics also stands in the way of efficiency in government. Of course, "politics" can mean "accountability." The fact that groups of people demand that government serve their interests and put pressure on their representatives to uphold those interests is an essential feature of democracy.

But this same aspect of government sometimes means that progress is thwarted in favor of the interests of one or more powerful groups. For example, look at the illogical, jerry-rigged, and inefficient health-care system in the United States, which leaves tens of millions of people with no health insurance. Reform of this system has so far been impossible because of powerful insurance and pharmaceutical companies.

These inherent weaknesses of government help to explain why the state-controlled economies of the Soviet era ultimately collapsed. They also explain why people around the world are dissatisfied with state-sponsored solutions to social problems.

Government must do its part to help alleviate our worst problems, but government alone cannot solve them.

The Contribution of Nonprofit Organizations

Frustrated with government, many people who care about the problems of the world have started nonprofit organizations. Nonprofits may take various forms and go under many names: not-for-profits, nongovernmental organizations, charitable organizations, benevolent societies, philanthropic foundations, and so on.

Charity is rooted in basic human concern for other humans. Every major religion requires its followers to give to the needy. Especially in times of emergency, nonprofit groups help get aid to desperate people. Generous assistance from people within the country and around the world has saved tens of thousands of lives in Bangladesh after floods and tidal waves.

Yet nonprofits alone have proven to be an inadequate response to social problems. The persistence and even worsening of global poverty, endemic disease, homelessness, famine, and pollution are sufficient evidence that charity by itself cannot do the job. Charity too has a significant built-in weakness: It relies on a steady stream of donations by generous individuals, organizations, or government agencies. When these funds fall short, the good works stop. And as almost any director of a nonprofit organization will tell you, there is never enough money to take care of all the needs. Even when the economy is strong and people have full purses, there is a limit to the portion of their income they will donate to charity. And in hard times, when the needs of the unfortunate are greatest, giving slows down. Charity is a form of trickle-down economics; if the trickle stops, so does help for the needy.

Relying on donations creates other problems. In countries where the social needs are greatest—Bangladesh, elsewhere in South Asia, and in large parts of Latin America and sub-Saharan Africa—the resources available for charity are usually very small. And it is often difficult to get donors from the richest countries to take a sustained interest in giving to distant countries they may never have visited, to benefit people they will never know. This is understandable, but it leaves serious social problems in those countries unaddressed.

The problems become even greater in times of crisis—when a natural disaster strikes, when war causes population upheavals and suffering, when an epidemic strikes, or when environmental collapse makes whole districts unlivable. The demand for charity quickly outpaces the supply. And today, with news and information constantly coming in from around the world, the demands for our attention and concern have never been greater. Dramatic disasters reported on television absorb the lion's share of charitable giving, while less publicized calamities that may be equally destructive are ignored. And eventually, "compassion fatigue" sets in, and people simply stop giving.

As a result, there is a built-in ceiling to the reach and effectiveness of nonprofit organizations. The need to constantly raise funds from donors uses up the time and energy of nonprofit leaders, when they should be planning the growth and expansion of their programs. No wonder they don't make much progress in their battles against social problems.

For all the good work that nonprofits, NGOs, and foundations do, they cannot be expected to solve the world's social ills. The very nature of these organizations as defined by society makes that virtually impossible.

Multilateral Institutions—
The Development Elite

There is another category of organizations known as *multilateral institutions.* These are sponsored and funded by governments. Their mission is to eliminate poverty by promoting economic development in countries and regions that are lagging behind the prosperous nations of the northern hemisphere. Among the multilateral institutions, the World Bank leads the way. The World Bank has a private sector window called the International Finance Corporation. There are also four regional development banks, which closely follow the lead of the World Bank.

Unfortunately, in practice, the multilaterals have not achieved much in attaining their professed social goals either. Like governments, they are bureaucratic, conservative, slow-moving, and often self-serving. Like nonprofits, they are chronically underfunded, difficult to rely upon, and often inconsistent in their policies. As a result, the hundreds of billions of dollars they have invested over the past several decades have been largely ineffective—especially when measured against the goal of alleviating problems like global poverty.

Multilateral institutions like the World Bank name elimination of poverty as their overarching goal. But they focus exclusively on pursuing this goal through large-scale economic growth. This means that, as long as gross domestic product (GDP) is increasing in a country or a region, the World Bank feels that it is achieving its mission. This growth may be excruciatingly slow; it may be occurring without any benefits to the poor; it may even be occurring at the expense of the poor—but none of this persuades the World Bank to change its policies.

Growth is extremely important in bringing down poverty—there is no doubt about it. But to think that the only way to reduce poverty is to promote growth drives the policymaker to a straight theoretical path of building infrastructure to promote industrialization and mechanization.

There is a debate about the type of growth we should pursue based on serious concerns about the hazards of the World Bank's approach. "Pro-poor growth" and "anti-poor growth" are often treated as separate policy options. But my concern is different. Even if the policymaker identifies and works only for pro-poor growth, he is still missing the real issue. The objective of the policymaker is obviously to generate a spin in the economy so that the poor people are drawn into the spin. But in this conceptualization, the poor people are looked at as objects. In this frame of mind, policymakers miss the tremendous potential of the poor, particularly poor women and the children of poor families. They cannot see the poor as independent actors. They worry about the health, the education, and the jobs of the poor. They cannot see that the poor people can be actors themselves. The poor can be self-employed entrepreneurs and create jobs for others.

Furthermore, in their pursuit of growth, policymakers are focusing on efforts to energize well-established institutions. It never occurs to them that these institutions themselves may be contributing to creating or sustaining poverty. Institutions and policies that created poverty cannot be entrusted with the task of eliminating it. Instead, new institutions designed to solve the problems of the poor need to be created.

Another problem arises from the channel that donors use for the selection and implementation of projects. Both bilateral and multilateral donors work almost exclusively through the government machine. To make a real impact, they should be open to all segments of society and be prepared to utilize the creative capacity that is lying outside the government. I am sure that once donors begin to reach beyond the government, they'll come up with many exciting innovations. They can start with small projects and then let them grow if they see positive results.

Over the years, I have been watching the difference between the business styles of the World Bank and Grameen Bank. Theoretically, we are in the same business—helping people get out of poverty. But the ways in which we pursue this goal are very different.

Grameen Bank has always believed that if a borrower gets into trouble and cannot pay back her loan, it is our responsibility to help her. If we have a problem with our borrower, we tell ourselves that she is right—that we must have made some mistake in our policies or in our implementation of those policies. So we go back and fix ourselves. We make our rules very flexible so that they can be adjusted to the requirements of the borrower.

We also encourage our borrowers to make their own decisions about how to use the loans. If a borrower asks a Grameen staff member, "Please tell me what would be a good business idea for me," the staff member is trained to respond this way: "I am sorry, but I am not smart enough to give you a good business idea. Grameen has lots of money, but no business ideas. That's why Grameen has come to you. You have the idea, we have the money. If Grameen had good business ideas, instead of giving the money to you, it would use the money itself and make more money."

We want our borrowers to feel important. When a borrower tries to shy away from a loan offer, saying that she has no business experience and does not want to take money, we work to convince her that she can come up with an idea for a business of her own. Will this be her very first experience of business? That is not a problem. Everything has to have a beginning somewhere, we tell her.

It is quite different with the World Bank. If you are lucky enough to be funded by them, they give you money. But they also give you ideas, expertise, training, plans, principles, and procedures. Your job is to follow the yellow lines, the green lines, and the red lines—to read the instructions at each step and obey them precisely. Yet, despite all this supervision, the projects don't always work out as planned. And when this happens, it is the recipient country that usually seems to bear the blame and to suffer the consequences.

There are also big differences in the incentive systems in the two organizations. In Grameen Bank, we have a five-star evaluation and incentive system for our staff and our branches. If a staff member maintains a 100 percent repayment record for all his borrowers (usually 600), he gets a green star. If he generates profit through his work, he gets another star—a blue star. If he mobilizes more in deposits than the amount of his outstanding loans, he gets a third star—a violet star. If he makes sure all the children of all his borrowers are in school, he gets a brown star. Finally, if all his borrowers move out of poverty, he gets a red star. The staff member can display the stars on his chest. He takes tremendous pride in this accomplishment.

By contrast, in the World Bank, a staff member's success is linked to the amount of the loans he has successfully negotiated, not the impact his work has made. We don't even consider the amount of loans made by a staff member in our reward system.

There have been campaigns to close down the World Bank and the International Monetary Fund. I have always opposed such campaigns. These are important global institutions created for very good causes. Rather than close them down, we should overhaul them completely. The world has changed so much since the time they were created, it is time to revisit them. It is obvious that the present architecture and work procedures are not adequate to do the job. If I were asked about my ideas, I'd emphasize the following:

- A new World Bank should be open to both government and private investors, with private investment following the social business model I will describe.
- It should work through governments, NGOs, and the new type of organization I am proposing in this book— social businesses.
- Instead of the International Finance Corporation, the World Bank should have another window—a social business window.
- The president of the World Bank should be selected by a search committee that will consider qualified candidates from anywhere in the world.
- The World Bank should work through semi-autonomous national branches, each with its own board of advisors, rather than powerless country offices.
- Evaluation of the staff should be related to the quality of their work and the impact it has made, not the volume of loans negotiated. If a project fails or performs poorly,

the staff member involved in designing and promoting it should be held responsible.

- The World Bank should grade all projects each year on the basis of their impact on poverty reduction, and each country office should be graded on the same basis.

Corporate Social Responsibility

Still another response to the persistence of global poverty and other social ills has been a call for social responsibility on the part of business. NGOs, social activists, and politicians have put pressure on corporations to modify their policies in regard to labor, the environment, product quality, pricing, and fair trade.

To their credit, many businesses have responded. Not so long ago, many executives managed corporations with a "public be damned" attitude. They exploited their workers, polluted the environment, adulterated their products, and committed fraud—all in the name of profit. In most of the developed world, those days are long gone. Government regulation is one reason for this, and another is the movement for corporate social responsibility (CSR).

Millions of people are now better informed than ever about both the good and the bad things that corporations can do. Newspapers, magazines, television, radio, and the Internet investigate and publicize episodes of business wrongdoing. Many customers will avoid patronizing companies that harm society. As a result, most corporations are eager to create a positive image. And this has given a strong push to CSR.

CSR takes two basic forms. One, which might be called "weak CSR," has the credo: *Do no harm to people or the planet (unless that means sacrificing profit)*. Companies that practice weak CSR are supposed to avoid selling defective goods, dumping factory wastes into rivers or landfills, or bribing government officials.

The second form, "strong CSR," says: *Do good for people and the planet (as long as you can do so without sacrificing profit)*. Companies that practice strong CSR actively seek out opportunities to benefit others as they do business. For example, they may work to develop

green products and practices, provide educational opportunities and
health plans for their employees, and support initiatives to bring
transparency and fairness to government regulation of business.

Is CSR a force that is leading to positive change among business
leaders? Could it be that CSR is the mechanism we have been searching for, the tool with which at least some of the problems of society
can be fixed?

Unfortunately, the answer is no. There are several reasons why.

The concept of socially responsible business is built on good intentions. But some corporate leaders misuse the concept to produce
selfish benefits for their companies. Their philosophy seems to be:
Make as much money as you can, even if you exploit the poor to do
so—but then donate a tiny portion of the profits for social causes or
create a foundation to do things that will promote your business interest. And then be sure to publicize how generous you are!

For companies like these, CSR will always be mere window dress-
ing. In some cases, the same company that devotes a penny to CSR
spends 99 cents on moneymaking projects that make social problems
worse. This is not a formula for improving society!

There are a few companies whose leaders are sincerely interested
in social change. Their numbers are growing, as a younger generation
of managers rises to the top. Today's young executives, raised on television and the Internet, are more aware of social problems and more
attuned to global concerns than any previous generation. They care
about issues like climate change, child labor, the spread of AIDS, the
rights of women, and world poverty. As these young people become
corporate vice presidents, presidents, and CEOs, they bring these
concerns into the boardroom. These new leaders are trying to make
CSR into a core part of their business philosophy.

This is a well-intended effort. But it runs up against a basic
problem. Corporate managers are responsible to those who own the
businesses they run—either private owners or shareholders who invest through the stock market. In either case, those owners have only
one objective: *To see the monetary value of their investment grow.*
Thus, the managers who report to them must strive for one result:
To increase the value of the company. And the only way to achieve this

is by increasing the company's profits. In fact, maximizing profit is their legal obligation to their shareholders unless the shareholders mandate otherwise.

Companies that profess a belief in CSR always do so with this proviso, spoken or unspoken. In effect, they are saying, "We will do the socially responsible thing—so long as it doesn't prevent us from making the largest possible profit." Some proponents of CSR say that pursuit of profit and social responsibility need not be in conflict. Sometimes this is true. Occasionally, through a happy accident, the needs of society and opportunities for high profits happen to coincide.

But what happens when profit and CSR do *not* go together? What about when the demands of the marketplace and the long-term interests of society conflict? What will companies do? Experience shows that profit always wins out. Since the managers of a business are responsible to the owners or shareholders, they *must* give profit the highest priority. If they were to accept reduced profits to promote social welfare, the owners would have reason to feel cheated and consider corporate social responsibility as corporate financial *irresponsibility*.

Thus, although advocates of CSR like to talk about the "triple bottom line" of financial, social, and environmental benefits by which companies should be measured, ultimately only one bottom line calls the shots: financial profit.

Throughout the 1990s and into the new century, American auto companies have produced gas-guzzling, super-sized SUVs, which demand enormous resources to manufacture, use huge amounts of fuel, and create terrible pollution. But they are very popular—and very profitable—and car makers continue to build and sell them by the millions. SUVs are bad for society, for the environment, and for the world, but the big auto companies' primary goal is to make profits, so they keep on doing something very socially irresponsible.

This example illustrates the most fundamental problem with CSR. By their nature, corporations are not equipped to deal with social problems. It's not because business executives are selfish, greedy, or bad. The problem lies with the very nature of business. Even more profoundly, it lies with the concept of business that is at the center of capitalism.

Capitalism Is a
Half-Developed Structure

Capitalism takes a narrow view of human nature, assuming that people are one-dimensional beings concerned only with the pursuit of maximum profit. The concept of the free market, as generally understood, is based on this one-dimensional human being.

Mainstream free-market theory postulates that you are contributing to the society and the world in the best possible manner if you just concentrate on getting the most for yourself. When believers in this theory see gloomy news on television, they should begin to wonder whether the pursuit of profit is a cure-all, but they usually dismiss their doubts, blaming all the bad things in the world on "market failures." They have trained their minds to believe that well-functioning markets simply cannot produce unpleasant results.

I think things are going wrong not because of "market failures." The problem is much deeper than that. Mainstream free-market theory suffers from a "conceptualization failure," a failure to capture the essence of what it is to be human.

In the conventional theory of business, we've created a one-dimensional human being to play the role of business leader, the so-called entrepreneur. We've insulated him from the rest of life, the religious, emotional, political, and social. He is dedicated to one mission only—maximize profit. He is supported by other one-dimensional human beings who give him their investment money to achieve that mission. To quote Oscar Wilde, they know the price of everything and the value of nothing.

Our economic theory has created a one-dimensional world peopled by those who devote themselves to the game of free-market competition, in which victory is measured purely by profit. And since we are persuaded by the theory that the pursuit of profit is the best way to bring happiness to humankind, we enthusiastically imitate the theory, striving to transform ourselves into one-dimensional human beings. Instead of theory imitating reality, we force reality to imitate theory.

And today's world is so mesmerized by the success of capitalism it does not dare doubt that system's underlying economic theory.

Yet the reality is very different from the theory. People are not one-dimensional entities; they are excitingly multi-dimensional. Their emotions, beliefs, priorities, and behavior patterns can best be compared to the millions of shades we can produce from the three primary colors. Even the most famous capitalists share a wide range of interests and drives, which is why tycoons from Andrew Carnegie and the Rockefellers to Bill Gates have ultimately turned away from the game of profit to focus on higher objectives.

The presence of our multi-dimensional personalities means that not every business should be bound to serve the single objective of profit maximization.

And this is where the new concept of social business comes in.

Note

1 There are almost as many definitions of poverty as there are individuals and groups studying the problem. A recent World Bank study mentions thirty-three different poverty lines developed and used by particular countries in addressing the needs of their own poor people. Earlier in this chapter, I mentioned the widely used poverty benchmark of an income equivalent to one dollar a day or less. In the remainder of this book, whenever I refer to "poverty" with no more specific explanation, this dollar-a-day definition may be assumed.

2

Social Business:
What It Is and What It Is Not

To make the structure of capitalism complete, we need to introduce another kind of business—one that recognizes the multi-
dimensional nature of human beings. If we describe our existing
companies as profit-maximizing businesses (PMBs), the new kind of
business might be called social business. Entrepreneurs will set up
social businesses not to achieve limited personal gain but to pursue
specific social goals.

To free-market fundamentalists, this might seem blasphemous.
The idea of a business with objectives other than profit has no place
in their existing theology of capitalism. Yet surely no harm will be
done to the free market if not all businesses are PMBs. Surely capitalism is amenable to improvements. And surely the stakes are too high
to go on the way we have been going. By insisting that all businesses,
by definition, must necessarily be PMBs and by treating this as some
kind of axiomatic truth, we have created a world that ignores the multi-
dimensional nature of human beings. As a result, businsses remain incapable of addressing many of our most pressing social problems.

We need to recognize the real human being and his or her multi-
faceted desires. In order to do that, we need a new type of business
that pursues goals other than making personal profit—a business that
is totally dedicated to solving social and environmental problems.

In its organizational structure, this new business is basically the
same as the existing PMB. But it differs in its objectives. Like other
businesses, it employs workers, creates goods or services, and provides

these to customers for a price consistent with its objective. But its underlying objective—and the criterion by which it should be evaluated—is to create social benefits for those whose lives it touches. The company itself may earn a profit, but the investors who support it do not take any profits out of the company except recouping an amount equivalent to their original investment over a period of time. A social business is a company that is cause-driven rather than profit-driven, with the potential to act as a change agent for the world.

A social business is not a charity. It is a business in every sense. It has to recover its full costs while achieving its social objective. When you are running a business, you think differently and work differently than when you are running a charity. And this makes all the difference in defining social business and its impact on society.

There are many organizations in the world today that concentrate on creating social benefit. Most do *not* recover their total costs. Nonprofit organizations and nongovernmental organizations rely on charitable donations, foundation grants, or government support to implement their programs. Most of their leaders are dedicated people doing commendable work. But since they do not recover their costs from their operations, they are forced to devote part of their time and energy, sometimes a significant part, to raising money.

A social business is different. Operated in accordance with management principles just like a traditional PMB, a social business aims for full cost recovery, or more, even as it concentrates on creating products or services that provide a social benefit. It pursues this goal by charging a price or fee for the products or services it creates.

How can the products or services sold by a social business provide a social benefit? There are countless ways. For a few examples, imagine:

- A social business that manufactures and sells high-quality, nutritious food products at very low prices to a targeted market of poor and underfed children. These products can be cheaper because they do not compete in the luxury market and therefore don't require costly packaging or advertising, and because the company that sells them is not compelled to maximize its profit.
- A social business that designs and markets health insurance policies that provide affordable medical care to the poor.

- A social business that develops renewable-energy systems and sells them at reasonable prices to rural communities that otherwise can't afford access to energy.
- A social business that recycles garbage, sewage, and other waste products that would otherwise generate pollution in poor or politically powerless neighborhoods.

In each of these cases, and in the many other kinds of social businesses that could be imagined, the company is providing a product or service that generates sales revenue even as it benefits the poor or society at large.

A social-objective-driven project that charges a price or fee for its products or services but cannot cover its costs fully does not qualify as a social business. As long as it has to rely on subsidies and donations to cover its losses, such an organization remains in the category of a charity. But once such a project achieves full cost recovery, on a sustained basis, it graduates into another world—the world of business. Only then can it be called a social business.

The achievement of full cost recovery is a moment worth celebrating. Once a social-objective-driven project overcomes the gravitational force of financial dependence, it is ready for space flight. Such a project is self-sustaining and enjoys the potential for almost unlimited growth and expansion. And as the social business grows, so do the benefits it provides to society.

Thus, a social business is designed and operated as a business enterprise, with products, services, customers, markets, expenses, and revenues—but with the profit-maximization principle replaced by the social-benefit principle. Rather than seeking to amass the highest possible level of financial profit to be enjoyed by the investors, the social business seeks to achieve a social objective.

Social Business Profits
Stay within the Business

A social business differs from a charity or an NGO or a nonprofit group in another important way. Unlike those organizations, but like a traditional PMB, a social business has owners who are entitled to recoup their investments. It may be owned by one or more individuals, either as a sole proprietorship or a partnership, or by one or more investors, who pool their money to fund the social business and hire professional managers to run it. It may be also owned by government or a charity, or any combination of different kinds of owners.

Like any business, a social business cannot incur losses indefinitely. But any profit it earns does not go to those who invest in it. Thus, a social business might be defined as a *non-loss, non-dividend business*. Rather than being passed on to investors, the surplus generated by the social business is reinvested in the business. Ultimately, it is passed on to the target group of beneficiaries in such forms as lower prices, better service, and greater accessibility.

Profitability is important to a social business. Wherever possible, without compromising the social objective, social businesses should make profit for two reasons: First, to pay back its investors; and second, to support the pursuit of long-term social goals.

Like a traditional PMB, a social business needs to have a long-term road map. Generating a surplus enables the social business to expand its horizons in many ways—by moving into new geographic areas, improving the range or quality of goods or services offered, mounting research and development efforts, increasing process efficiencies, introducing new technologies, or making innovations in marketing or service delivery so as to reach deeper layers of low-income people.

However, the bottom line for the social business is to operate without incurring losses while serving the people and the planet—and in particular those among us who are most disadvantaged—in the best possible manner.

How long will it take for investors to get back their investment in a social business? That is up to the management of the social business and the investors themselves. The proposed payback period would be specified in the investment prospectus: It might be five years, ten, or twenty. Investors could choose the appropriate social business in which to invest partly on the basis of this time frame and on their own anticipated needs, as well as their preference for a particular social objective.

Once the initial investment funds are recouped, investors can decide what to do with those funds. They might reinvest in the same social business, invest in another social business or a PMB, or use the money for personal purposes. In any case, they remain as much own-ers of the social business as before, and have as much control over the company as before.

Why would investors put their money into a social business? Gen-erally speaking, people will invest in a social business for the same kind of personal satisfaction that they can get from philanthropy. The satisfaction may be even greater, since the company they have created will continue to work for the intended social benefit for more and more people without ever stopping. The many billions of dollars that people around the world donate to charitable causes every year demonstrate that they have a hunger to give money in a way that will benefit other human beings. But investing in a social business has sev-eral enormous differences from philanthropy.

First, the business one creates with social business is self-sustaining. There is no need to pump in money every year. It is self-propelling, self-perpetuating, and self-expanding. Once it is set up, it continues to grow on its own. You get more social benefits for your money.

Second, investors in a social business get their money back. They can reinvest in the same or a different social business. This way, the same money can bring more social benefits.

Since it is a business, businesspeople will find this as an exciting opportunity not only to bring money to social business but to lever-age their own business skills and creativity to solve social problems. Not only does the investor get his money back, he still remains an owner of the company and decides its future course of action. That's a very exciting prospect on its own.

Broadening the Landscape of Business

With the entry of social businesses, the marketplace suddenly finds itself with some new and exciting options, and becomes a more inter-esting, engaging, and competitive place. Social concerns enter the marketplace on an equal footing, not through the public relations window.

Social businesses will operate in the same marketplace with PMBs. They will compete with them, try to outmaneuver them, and seek to capture market share from them, just as other businesses do. If a social business is offering a particular product or service that is also available from a PMB, consumers will decide where to buy, just as they now choose among competing PMBs. They will consider price, quality, convenience, availability, brand image, and all the other traditional factors that influence consumer choices today.

Perhaps for some consumers, the social benefits created by the social business will be an additional reason to buy from it—just as some consumers today prefer to patronize companies with a reputation for being worker-friendly, environmentally conscious, or socially responsible. But for the most part, social businesses will compete with PMBs on the same terms as we see in traditional capitalist competition—and may the best company win.

Social businesses will also compete with one another. If two or more social businesses are operating in the same market, consumers will have to decide which one to patronize. Again, product and service quality will probably be the main determining factor for most customers.

Social businesses will also compete for potential investors, just as PMBs do. Of course, this will be a different kind of competition than we see among PMBs.

Consider two profit-maximizing businesses that are competing for investment dollars—two auto makers, for example. The competition here will turn on which PMB is perceived as having a greater future profit potential. If most investors believe that company A is likely to be more profitable than company B, they will rush to buy shares of company A stock, because they expect to earn higher dividends in the future, and they also expect to benefit from continuing growth in the overall value (or *equity*) of the company. This launches a positive cycle in which company A stock rises in price, making investors happy.

By contrast, when two social businesses compete for investors, the competition is based not on future profit maximization but on social benefits achieved. Each social business will claim that it is better positioned to serve the people and the planet than its rival, and it will develop and publicize a business plan to support that claim. Would-be social investors will scrutinize those claims carefully. After all, they are planning to invest their money with the goal of benefiting society, and they will want to be sure that their investment does the greatest possible good. Just as a profit-minded investor seeks to maximize expectations of future dividends and equity growth, a social investor wants to find out how close the company is getting in solving the social problem it is addressing.

Thus, competing social businesses will push each other to improve their efficiency and to serve the people and the planet better. This is one of the great powers of the social-business concept: It brings the advantages of free-market competition into the world of social improvement.

Competition in the marketplace of ideas almost always has a powerful positive impact. When a large number of people are vying to do the best possible job of developing and refining an idea—and when the flow of money toward them and their company depends on the outcome of the competition—the overall level of everyone's performance rises dramatically. We see this beneficial effect of competition in many arenas. Intense competition among makers of personal computers, for example, has caused the price of PCs to fall dramatically even as their speed, power, and other features have improved. The rise of Japanese manufacturers of cars and electronic products forced U.S. and European companies to improve the quality of their goods so as to compete for both customers and investors.

By creating a competitive marketplace for social-benefit investing, the concept of social business brings the same kind of positive pressure to bear among those who seek to serve the disadvantaged people of the world.

Competition among social businesses will be different in quality than competition among PMBs. PMB competition is about making more money. If you lose, you get financially hurt. Social business competition will be about pride, about establishing which team is best able to achieve the social objective. Competitors will remain friends. They will learn from each other. They can merge with each other at any time to become a stronger social force. And they will feel happy to see another social business entering the same area of business, rather than getting worried.

To attract investors, I propose the creation of a separate stock market, which could be called the social stock market. Only social businesses will be listed there. (See chapter 8 for a detailed description of this concept.) The existence of a public marketplace for trading shares in social businesses will have many benefits. It will create liquidity, making it easy for shareholders to move in and out of social investments, just as they currently do with investments in PMBs. It will generate public scrutiny and evaluation of social businesses, providing a layer of "natural regulation" to supplement any government regulation that will need to be created to avoid the usual problems of the marketplace: deception, false reporting, inflated claims, disguised businesses, and so on. And it will raise the public profile of the social-business concept, attracting even more money and energy from investors and entrepreneurs alike.

Two Kinds of Social Businesses

At this stage in the development of the concept of social business, we can only glimpse its general outlines. In the years to come, as social businesses begin to spring up around the world, new features and forms of social business will undoubtedly be developed. But from today's vantage point, I propose two possible kinds of social businesses.

The first I have already described: Companies that focus on providing a social benefit rather than on maximizing profit for the owners, and that are owned by investors who seek social benefits such as poverty reduction, health care for the poor, social justice, global sustainability, and so on, seeking psychological, emotional, and spiritual satisfactions rather than financial reward.

The second operates in a rather different fashion: Profit-maximizing businesses that are owned by the poor or disadvantaged. In this case, the social benefit is derived from the fact that the dividends and equity growth produced by the PMB will go to benefit the poor, thereby helping them to reduce their poverty or even escape it altogether.

Notice the differences between these two kinds of social businesses. In the first case, it is the nature of the products, services, or operating systems of the business that creates the social benefit. This kind of social business might provide food, housing, health care, education, or other worthwhile goods to help the poor; it might clean up the environment, reduce social inequities, or work to alleviate ills such as drug and alcohol abuse, domestic violence, unemployment, or crime. Any business that can achieve objectives like these while covering its costs through the sales of goods or services *and* that pays no financial dividend to its investors can be classified as a social business.

With the second type of social business, goods or services produced might or might not create a social benefit. The social benefit created by this kind of company comes from its ownership. Because the ownership of shares of the business belongs to the poor or disadvantaged (as defined by specific, transparent criteria developed and enforced by the company directors), any financial benefit generated by the company's operations will go to help those in need.

Imagine that a poor rural region of a country is separated from the main commercial centers by a river too deep, wide, and wild to be forded by pedestrians or ordinary vehicles. The only way to cross this river is by ferry, which provides expensive, slow, and intermittent service. As a result, the area's poor and low-income residents face economic and social handicaps that depress their incomes, reduce availability of affordable goods, and lower their access to education, health care, and other vital services. In our example, we assume that the national and local governments are unable to address the problem because of lack of funds, political indifference, or other shortcomings. (Although this is a hypothetical example, it accurately describes conditions in much of the developing world.)

Now suppose a private company is formed to build a new highway and a safe, modern bridge to connect the rural area with the commercial center of the country. This company could be structured as a social business in two ways.

First, it could provide access to poor and low-income residents at a discounted toll, while charging a commercial toll to middle- and upper-class residents and to large commercial organizations. (Obviously some kind of means-testing procedure would be needed to verify the eligibility of poor people for the discounted toll; perhaps the same kind of ID card that is used to indicate eligibility for government welfare could be accepted by the toll-takers.) The toll revenues would cover the costs of building, operating, and maintaining the bridge and highway, and, over time, they could be used to repay the funds initially provided by investors. However, those investors would receive no further profits. If profits beyond this are generated by the tolls, they could be used to build additional infrastructure to benefit the rural community—more roads and bridges, for example, or perhaps some social businesses to stimulate the local economy and create jobs.

Second, ownership of the bridge-and-highway company could actually be put in the hands of the poor and lower-income residents of the rural area. This could be done through the sale of low-priced shares, purchased by them with loans provided by microcredit organizations or through credit that is later recouped from the profit of the company. Further profits generated by tolls could *either* be invested in new infrastructure projects or paid in the form of dividends to the poor and lower-income residents who own the company, thereby benefiting them in direct financial fashion.

Grameen Bank makes small loans available without collateral and at a reasonable cost to the poor, thereby enabling them to start or expand tiny businesses and ultimately lift themselves out of poverty. Grameen Bank would be a regular PMB if it were owned by well-off investors. But it is not. Grameen Bank is owned by the poor: Ninety-four percent of the ownership shares of the institution are held by the borrowers themselves.

Thus, Grameen Bank is a social business by virtue of its ownership structure. If a big bank like Grameen can be owned by poor women in Bangladesh, any big company can be owned by poor people, if we seriously come up with practical ownership-management models.

And yes, a social business could also combine *both* forms of benefit to the poor: It could follow a business plan designed to produce social benefits through the nature of the goods and services it creates and sells *and also* be owned by the poor or disadvantaged.

The Difference between Social Business
and Social Entrepreneurship

Some people are puzzled when they hear about social business for the first time. Most often, social business is equated with *social entrepreneurship*. My friend Bill Drayton has built a global movement around the concept of social entrepreneurship through his Ashoka Foundation.

Decades ago, Bill became convinced that creative, innovative thinking could be applied to solve seemingly intractable social problems. He was excited to see that many people around the world are doing just that, some of them without even realizing that they fall into a very special group of people. One of the first initiatives Bill undertook was to find these people and to give them recognition by calling them Ashoka Fellows. Then he upgraded his initiatives by organizing conferences, meetings, and workshops to bring social entrepreneurs together, helping them learn from each other, supporting them with small grants, introducing them to donors, documenting their activities, and producing videos that portrayed their work and philosophies.

Today, social entrepreneurship has become a recognized movement. Besides Ashoka, there are several other foundations dedicated to promoting social entrepreneurship, including the Skoll Foundation, founded by Jeff Skoll (the first employee and CEO of eBay), and the Schwab Foundation for Social Entrepreneurship, founded by Klaus Schwab (the founder of the World Economic Forum). They have made it their mission to find, support, and encourage social entrepreneurs around the world.

Social entrepreneurship has become a popular concept among both business people and the general public. The American business magazine *Fast Company* publishes a list of the twenty-five best social entrepreneurs every year, bringing attention and funding to some of today's most effective social service organizations. Social entrepreneurship has even become an academic discipline, having found its way into the curricula of some thirty U.S. business schools since the first course in the subject was offered at Harvard in 1995 by Dr. J. Gregory Dees, now at Duke University's Fuqua School of Business.

The concept of social entrepreneurship is very important. It brings out the power of yearning in people to do something about problems that are not currently being addressed with the efficiency and urgency they deserve. Because of the movement built around this concept today, we can see an enormous range of people around the world doing exciting things to help others. Grameen Bank and the Grameen sister organizations are often cited as being significant symbols of this movement.

But social business and social entrepreneurship are not the same thing. Social entrepreneurship is a very broad idea. As it is generally defined, any innovative initiative to help people may be described as social entrepreneurship. The initiative may be economic or non-economic, for-profit or not-for-profit. Distributing free medicine to the sick can be an example of social entrepreneurship. So can setting up a for-profit health-care center in a village where no health facility exists. And so can launching a social business.

In other words, social business is a subset of social entrepreneurship. All those who design and run social businesses are social entrepreneurs. But not all social entrepreneurs are engaged in social businesses.

Until very recently, the movement around social entrepreneurship has not showcased the issue of social business because that concept did not exist. Now that the concept has been introduced and is being translated into reality, I am sure that many in the social-entrepreneurship movement will be attracted to it.

The social-entrepreneurship movement can start giving special attention to the creation and promotion of social businesses by devising and sharpening appropriate tools and institutional facilities needed to support this new type of enterprise. Some social entrepreneurs may be encouraged to move in the direction of social business because they can achieve much more in terms of social benefits than is possible through traditional structures.

What about a "Hybrid"?

Some of those who learn about social business wonder whether a hybrid version—combining characteristics of a PMB with those of a social business—is possible.

PMBs are driven by the profit motive—that is, the desire for personal gain. Social business is driven by the desire to do good for people and the planet—that is, selfless concern for others. Can there be a business that mixes both, including some elements of self-interest and some elements of selflessness?

Of course, this can happen—it can happen in limitless ways. One can imagine a business driven by, say, 60 percent social-benefit objectives and 40 percent personal-benefit objectives, or the other way around. There can be innumerable such combinations.

But in the real world, it will be very difficult to operate businesses with the two conflicting goals of profit maximization and social benefits. The executives of these hybrid businesses will gradually inch toward the profit-maximization goal, no matter how the company's mission is designed. For example, suppose we instruct the CEO of a food company to "maximize profit *and* make sure that poor children benefit nutritionally by providing them with high-quality meals at the lowest possible price." The CEO will be confused as to which part of the instruction is the real instruction. How will his success be judged—on the basis of the money he earns for the investors or on the basis of the social goals he achieves?

Making matters worse, the existing business environment is exclusively focused on profit maximization. All current tools of business are related to judging whether or not a business is maximizing profit. Accounting practices and standards are clearly established for that purpose; profit can be measured in precise financial terms. But measuring the achievement of social objectives has conceptual complications. If the goal is to improve the nutrition of poor children, who exactly is "poor"? What biological standards will be used to measure their nutritional status before and after? How reliable will the information be? These are difficult questions to answer precisely. Furthermore, since social problems are inherently complex, information related to social goals would generally suffer from a greater time lag than profitability data.

For all these reasons, our CEO will find it much easier to run the company basically as a PMB and be judged in the company of other PMBs. And so, it is more realistic to think in terms of two pure models: the profit-maximizing model and the social-business model.

One big advantage of pure models is that it is difficult to add gimmicks to them to create a false impression in people's minds. If you are a social business, you are a social business, and investors will not expect any return from your revenues. But if you are a profit-maximizing company, you are in the business of making money, and no one will be deceived into thinking that you are in business for social reasons.

Past Attempts to Combine Social Goals with Traditional Business

Social business is not just a theoretical concept. There are social businesses around the world, including the Grameen Bank and such Grameen-affiliated companies as Grameen Danone. Other fledgling social businesses are beginning to pop up, embodying the potential for social good and economic development latent in this new form of business.

Social businesses can become powerful players in the national and international economy, but we have a long way to go to achieve that goal. Today the assets of all the social businesses of the world wouldn't add up to even an ultra-thin slice of the global economy. It is not because they lack growth potential, but because conceptually people neither recognize their existence nor make any room for them in the market. They are considered freaks and are kept outside the mainstream economy. People do not pay attention to them—in fact, they literally *cannot see them*—because their eyes are blinded by the theories taught in our schools. Once we recognize social business as a valid economic structure, supportive institutions, policies, regulations, norms, and rules will come into being to help it become mainstream.

Over the past three centuries, since modern capitalism began its ascent to world dominance, many people around the world have recognized the shortcomings of the current, incomplete form of capitalism. They have experimented with various ways of remedying the problem. However, the full structure of social business as I envision it has not emerged, even as a concept, until our time. As a result, none of the existing modes by which people have tried to adapt businesses to serve social goals has been very effective. Only social business offers the full solution for which thousands of people have been searching.

One attempt to bring humane, enlightened thinking into business organizations is the cooperative movement, in which workers and consumers join forces in owning businesses and managing those businesses for the benefit of all.

Robert Owen (1771–1858), a Welshman who owned and operated cotton mills in England and Scotland, is often considered the pioneer of this movement. Owen was appalled by the exploitation of workers in the earliest decades of the industrial revolution. In particular, he deplored the widespread English practice of paying mill workers not in common currency but in scrip that could be used only in company-owned stores, which, in turn, charged inflated prices for shoddy goods.

This vicious cycle of oppression was reminiscent of the near-enslavement of poor Bangladeshis by moneylenders that I discovered in Jobra when I first began the work that led to the founding of Grameen Bank. It also recalls the exploitation of sharecroppers in the American South by landowners who used the indebtedness of their farm laborers to force them into doing business with overpriced company stores, creating a closed economic loop in which capital flowed only into the pockets of the owners and never went to benefit the working people.

Owen took practical steps to deal with this problem. At his own mills in New Lanark, Scotland, he opened stores where high-quality goods were sold at prices just above cost, with the savings from bulk purchases passed on to his employees. This was the germ from which the cooperative movement sprang. This movement is built around the concept of having businesses owned by their customers and operated primarily for the benefit of those customers rather than to generate profits for merchants. Shops that are operated on Owen's plan are common to this day throughout Britain and elsewhere in Europe.

The cooperative movement began as a response to the exploitation of the poor by rapacious company owners. However, the cooperative concept is not inherently oriented toward helping the poor or producing any other specific social benefit. Depending on the goals and interests of the people who band together to create and share ownership of a cooperative business, such a business can be structured to benefit the middle class as well as those who are needy. If they fall into selfish hands, cooperatives can even become a means for controlling the economy for purposes of individual or group gain rather than to help everyone in society. When a cooperative business loses sight of its original social objectives, it becomes, in practice, a profit-maximizing company almost the same as any other.

Another way in which some people have tried to combine the dynamism and self-sufficiency of business with the pursuit of worthy social goals has been through the creation of nonprofit organizations that sell socially beneficial products and services. These companies are not true social businesses as I define them. They generally achieve only partial cost recovery, which means that they do not attain the "lift-off velocity" that would enable them to escape the gravitational pull of dependence on charity. Also, they do not have the investor-owner feature that distinguishes social business, creating a source of funds with an interest in ensuring both the efficiency and effectiveness of the social benefits generated by the business.

There have also been attempts by managers of traditional PMBs to manage companies in a socially responsible fashion. That includes the occasional launch of a PMB that offers some social benefits alongside the pursuit of profit. Corporations may take this step for any number of reasons:

- To support the personal goals or values of a powerful or respected corporate leader
- To earn favorable publicity for the company, or to deflect criticism over past ethical and business lapses
- To attract customers who may prefer to do business with a company they perceive as "good guys"
- To win the friendship and support of government regulators or legislators who are considering laws that might affect the company
- To reduce opposition from community organizations or public-interest groups that might otherwise try to block company plans for expansion
- To gain a foothold in a new market that holds promise for the future but is currently unprofitable—while also earning points in the court of public opinion

It can be difficult to tell, in a particular instance, what combination of motives drives a particular company decision. In some cases, even the company executives may not be able to accurately describe the precise blend of motives that impel them. However, because they are PMBs, these businesses will ultimately be subject to the same financial pressures as all other for-profit companies. And this means that any social goals their managers may want to pursue will be set aside whenever they conflict with the maximization of profit.

In the end, none of the organizational structures I've described here—the cooperative, the nonprofit enterprise, or the socially responsible PMB—offers the powerful advantages of the true social business. This is why the world is crying out for this new way of doing business.

When the social-business concept becomes well known and begins to spread through all the free-market economies of the world, the flood of creativity that this new business channel will unleash has the potential to transform our world.

Where Will Social Businesses Come From?

Because the concept of social business is still new and unfamiliar, it may seem difficult at first to imagine who will create such businesses and why. Everyone is familiar with traditional entrepreneurs, and whether or not we admire them, we feel that we understand their values and motivations. The same is not true for the founders of the social business.

I think, given the opportunity, every human being is a potential participant in a social business. The motivating forces behind social business are packed inside each human being, and we see bits and pieces of these forces every day. People care about their world, and they care about one another. Humans have an instinctive, natural desire to make life better for their fellow humans if they can; given the chance, people would prefer to live in a world without poverty, disease, ignorance, and needless suffering. These are the causes that lead people to donate billions of dollars to charity, to create foundations, to launch NGOs and nonprofit organizations, to volunteer countless hours to community service, and (in some cases) to devote their careers to relatively low-paid work in the social sector. These same drives will lead many to create social businesses, once this new path is widely recognized and understood.

To begin with, here are some of the specific sources from which the social businesses of the future might spring:

- Existing companies of all shapes and sizes will want to launch their own social businesses. Some will choose to devote part of their annual profit to social business as part of their existing "social responsibility" mandates. Others will create social businesses as a way of exploring new markets while helping the less fortunate. They may create social businesses on their own, with the help of other companies, or in partnership with specialized social-business entrepreneurs.

- Foundations may create social-business investment funds, operating parallel to but separate from their traditional philanthropic windows. The advantage of a social-business fund is that its money will not be exhausted even as it works to produce social benefits, continually replenishing the foundation's ability to support good works.

- Individual entrepreneurs who have experienced success in the realm of PMBs may choose to test their creativity, talent, and management skills by establishing and running social businesses. They may be driven by the desire to give something back to the communities that have enriched them, or simply by the urge to try something new. Those who enjoy success in their first experiments may become "serial social-business entrepreneurs," creating one social business after another.

- International and bilateral development donors, ranging from national aid programs to the World Bank and the regional development banks, may choose to create dedicated funds to support social-business initiatives in the recipient countries, or at international, or regional, or institutional levels. The World Bank and regional development banks can create subsidiaries to support social businesses.

- Governments may create social-business development funds to support and encourage social businesses.

- Retired persons with wealth to spare will find social businesses an attractive investment opportunity to pursue. Similarly, inheritors of wealth or recipients of windfall gains may be inspired to think of launching or investing in social businesses.
- Young people fresh out of college or business school may choose to launch social businesses rather than traditional PMBs, motivated by the idealism of youth and the excitement of having the opportunity to change the world.

Young people all around the world, particularly in rich countries, will find the concept of social business very appealing. Many young people today feel frustrated because they cannot recognize any worthy challenge that excites them within the present capitalist system. When you have grown up with ready access to the consumer goods of the world, earning a lot of money isn't a particularly inspiring goal. Social business can fill this void.

With so many potential sources, I predict that, within a few years, social businesses will be a familiar fixture on the world business scene.

Human Beings Are Multi-Dimensional

We might enrich the economists' narrow-minded view of society by assuming a world in which there are two kinds of people—one that wants to maximize profits and one that wants to create social benefits and do good things for people and the planet. But even with this new assumption, we still remain in a world of one-dimensional people—only two kinds of one-dimensional people, instead of the single kind imagined by classical economics.

In the real world, there are not two types of one-dimensional people. Instead, there is only one type of person: people with two, three, four, or *many* interests and goals, which they pursue with varying and ever-changing degrees of interest. For the sake of simplicity, we can divide these interests into two broad categories—profit and social benefit—which correspond to the two types of businesses we've described in this chapter: traditional PMBs and social businesses.

How will individuals, companies, and investors choose which of these two paths to follow? The beautiful thing is that people will not be faced with an absolute, either/or choice. In most cases, they will have the opportunity to participate in both PMBs and social businesses in varying proportions, depending on the goals and objectives they most value at a particular moment in time. For example:

- An individual with a nest egg to invest might choose to invest part in PMBs (with the goal, for example, of creating a retirement fund) and the rest in social businesses (in order to help society, humanity, and the planet).
- The board of directors of a PMB might decide to use part of one year's surplus to buy out another company in order to expand their business into a new market—and use the rest of the surplus to launch a social business or to invest in an existing one, as an alternative to traditional philanthropy or corporate charity.
- The trustees of a foundation might choose to use part of its endowment income to fund one or more social businesses whose objectives coincide with the goals specified by the foundation's donors.
- Even when it comes to making career or life choices, social businesses will only increase the possibilities we enjoy rather than foreclosing any of them. The same person might choose to work for part of his or her life for a PMB; another part for a traditional charity, foundation, or NGO; and still another part for a social business. The choice will depend on how the individual's career interests, goals, and social concerns vary and evolve over time.

There is no reason why we need to feel constrained, in either our investment choices or our life decisions, to follow a single, one-dimensional model of human behavior. We humans are multidimensional creatures, and the business models we recognize should be equally diverse. Recognizing and encouraging social business as an option will help make this possible.

TWO

The Grameen Experiment

3

The Microcredit
Revolution

The idea of social business did not arise in a vacuum. It grew out of my thirty-one years' experience on the front lines of the battle against poverty, first in Bangladesh and later in countries around the world.

Observing the failure of existing institutions to lift the terrible burdens of deprivation from the shoulders of the poor, I was moved, like many other people, to seek a better answer. And because I am a practical-minded person who initially had no experience in rural development or banking, I was relatively free of the preconceived ideas that tend to limit the thinking of most people in the field. I was able to experiment with new ideas and new methods based solely on my understanding of the needs of the poor and the dictates of common sense.

Thus began a lifelong involvement in efforts to alleviate social problems using innovative organizational structures—structures that, I hoped, might be more effective, flexible, and self-sustaining than the failed institutions of the past. Not all of my experiments have succeeded. But most of them worked better than I ever dreamed, and these have provided the basis for my evolving sense of what works and does not work when it comes to introducing large-scale, beneficial social changes.

Thus, to understand the origins of the social-business concept and to see how it builds on the learning experiences of the past thirty years, you need to understand its roots in the work of Grameen Bank and the network of sister organizations that has grown up around it.

The Birth of a
"Banker to the Poor"

I was born in 1940 in (East) Bengal, in what was then British India and which in 1947 became part of the newly-created country of Pakistan. In December 1971, after a nine-month-long War of Liberation, East Pakistan became a new nation—Bangladesh.

I originally became involved in the poverty issue not as a policymaker, scholar, or researcher, but because poverty was all around me, and I could not turn away from it.

The year was 1974. I had returned home, in June 1972, to Bangladesh after resigning my position as assistant professor at Middle Tennessee State University in the United States. My decision to return was stimulated by the battle for Bangladeshi independence, and I was eager to do my part to help build a free and prosperous new nation. I joined the Economics Department at Chittagong University and became chairman of the department. I enjoyed teaching, and I was looking forward to an academic career.

But something happened that made this impossible—the terrible Bangladesh famine of 1974–75.

As with most famines, this one had many causes: a devastating series of natural disasters in the early 1970s, including floods, droughts, cyclones, and monsoons; and the War of Liberation, which brought with it the destruction of much of Bangladesh's infrastructure, the collapse of the transportation system, and the creation of countless refugees. The response by our fledgling government was badly disorganized, and assistance from the international community was inadequate, made worse by dislocations in the foreign exchange markets after the 1973 oil crisis.

However we analyze the causes, the human consequences were unmistakable. Agricultural production and per-capita income plummeted. Millions of Bangladeshis could not afford food for their families. As the famine wore on, hundreds of thousands died, while the world looked on in seeming indifference.

This was not the Bangladesh which I'd hoped to play a role in building. I found it increasingly difficult to teach elegant theories of economics and the supposedly perfect workings of the free market in the university classroom while needless death was ravaging Bangladesh. Suddenly, I felt the emptiness of those theories in the face of crushing hunger and poverty. I wanted to do something immediate to help the people around me get through another day with a little more hope.

My first attempt to alleviate hunger involved a program to improve agricultural productivity through irrigation. I worked with the farmers of Jobra to create a farmers' association that operated a deep tubewell and a water distribution system. This project met with immediate success. The farmers were able to use the new irrigation system, together with supplies of fertilizer, seeds, and insecticides provided through the association, to create a new, third harvest during the normally unproductive dry season. The productivity of the fields around Jobra was significantly improved, and the landowners benefited.

But I was not satisfied. In working with the village people on the irrigation project, I soon discovered that the poorest of the poor received almost no benefit from the improved crop yield. These people owned no land. They tried to eke out a living as day laborers, craft workers, or beggars. Their homes—if they had any—were devoid of furniture and got muddy when it rained. Their children were badly malnourished and had to work or beg rather than attend school. In times of famine, these poorest of the poor were the first to die.

I realized that improving farm yields, while important, would not solve the problems of hunger or poverty. A solution that would go deeper into the roots of the problem was needed.

I spent as much time as possible among the people of Jobra, trying to learn what was holding them back. It was not lack of effort: Everywhere I went in the village, I saw people working hard to try to help themselves—growing crops in their tiny yards, making baskets, stools, and other craft items to sell, and offering their services for practically any kind of labor. Somehow all these efforts had failed to secure a path out of poverty for most of the villagers.

I eventually came face to face with poor people's helplessness in finding the tiniest amounts of money to support their efforts to eke out a living.

It was a village woman named Sufiya Begum who taught me the nature of this problem. Like many village women, Sufiya lived with her husband and small children in a crumbling mud hut with a leaky thatched roof. Her husband worked as a day laborer, earning the equivalent of a few pennies for a day's work—when any work at all was to be had. To provide food for her family, Sufiya worked all day in the muddy yard of her home making bamboo stools—beautiful and useful objects that she crafted with noticeable skill. Yet somehow her hard work was unable to lift her family out of poverty.

Through conversations with Sufiya, I learned why. Like many others in the village, Sufiya relied on the local moneylender for the cash she needed to buy the bamboo for her stools. But the moneylender would give her the money only if she agreed to sell him all she produced at a price he would decide. Between this unfair arrangement and the high interest rate on her loan, she was left with only two pennies a day as her income.

Once a woman like Sufiya borrowed any amount, no matter how small, on terms like these, it was virtually impossible for her to work her way out of poverty. This, to me, was not lending as we normally understand it. Rather, it was a way of recruiting slave labor.

I decided to make a list of the victims of this moneylending business in the village of Jobra. A student and I spent a week visiting families in the village to compile this list. When it was done, it had the names of forty-two victims who had borrowed a total amount of 856 taka—at the time less than $27 (U.S.).

What a lesson this was for an economics professor! Here I was, teaching my students about our country's Five-Year Development Plan with its impressive goal of investing billions of dollars to help the poor. The gap between the promised billions and the pitiful sum that a few starving people actually needed seemed incredible.

I offered the equivalent of those twenty-seven U.S. dollars from my own pocket to get these victims out of the clutches of those moneylenders. The excitement that was created among the people by this small action got me further involved in it. If I could make so many people so happy with such a tiny amount of money, why not do more of it?

That is what I have been trying to do ever since.

The first thing I did was to try to persuade the bank located on the university campus to lend money to the poor. But the bank said the poor were not credit-worthy. They had no credit histories and no collateral to offer, and because they were illiterate they couldn't even fill out the necessary paperwork. The idea of lending to such people flew in the face of every rule the bankers lived by.

The bankers' rules struck me as arbitrary and counterproductive. In effect, they meant that the bank would lend money only to people who already *had* money. But whenever I tried to point this out, the bankers would merely shrug and politely end the conversation.

After all my efforts, over several months, failed, I tried a new tack. I offered to become a guarantor for the loans to the poor. In effect, the bank would lend me the money, and I would turn around and give it to the poor villagers. The bank agreed to this plan. And when I started lending funds to the villagers, I was stunned by the result. The poor paid back their loans, on time, every time!

You might think that this positive record would cause the traditional bankers to change their minds about lending to the poor. But there was not the slightest change.

Individual bankers sometimes expressed sympathy with my cause, and a couple were even able to mobilize concrete support for it. For example, in 1977, Mr. A. M. Anisuzzaman, the managing director of one of the largest national banks in the country, the Bangladesh Krishi (Agriculture) Bank, became enthusiastic about my idea. He agreed to have a special bank branch created in Jobra to test the idea of lending to the poor. This was the first time that my students, who had been working as "bankers" on a volunteer basis, would have steady, formal employment. It was also the first time that the name Grameen (which means "village") was used in our work: We called our little project the Experimental Grameen Branch of the Agriculture Bank. It enjoyed the same kind of success as our earlier, informal efforts, including nearly perfect repayment rates.

But every time I urged the bankers to expand the program to cover an entire district or, better yet, the entire nation, they showed no interest. They had plenty of reasons to explain why the success we'd already enjoyed was sure to end. They could not accept the fact that the poor would actually pay back their loans.

"The people you are serving must not be really poor," some would say. "Otherwise, how can they afford to repay the loans?"

"Come and visit their homes with me," I would reply. "You'll see that they are definitely poor. They don't even own a stick of furniture! They repay the loans through nothing but hard work, every day."

The grounds for making excuses would then shift. "Well, your program must be successful because you and your students are so deeply involved with the clients. This isn't banking, it's babysitting! We could never expand such a program on a district-wide level."

It was certainly true that our staff were very dedicated and hardworking. But it struck me as unfair that we should be penalized for this! I believed that a program designed purely for the benefit of the poor could, and would, attract dedicated and caring young people interested in helping their fellow human beings. (And the subsequent expansion of Grameen Bank into over 2,500 branches staffed by some of the brightest and most hard-working young people of Bangladesh has proved that I was right.)

Still other excuses were offered. "Your bank is too unconventional. You don't have proper internal controls, financial benchmarks, or auditing procedures. Eventually your staff will begin cheating you. The problem is that you are a professor, not a banker."

Yes, I *was* a professor, not a banker—which is why I'd spent years trying to convince real bankers to take over my business! But this argument really cut two ways. If our banking program for the poor had been financially successful *without* proper skill—as everyone had to admit—then just imagine how successful it could be once it was run by people who knew what they were doing!

But all of my arguments were to no avail. The truth was that the "real bankers" wanted nothing to do with making tiny loans to the poor. It was easier and more lucrative for them to make fewer loans but for larger amounts, to people with lots of collateral to offer, even if they didn't pay back the loan. Seeing no prospect of changing the rules of the banks, I decided to create a separate bank for the poor, one that would give loans without collateral, without requiring a credit history, without any legal instruments. I kept on appealing to the government to allow us to convert our project into a special bank under a separate law. Finally, I succeeded. In 1983, the bank for the poor was born within the framework of a new law created especially for the purpose. We named it Grameen Bank.

A Shift in Thinking

Grameen Bank started very small and grew slowly. What was revolutionary about it was the shift in thinking it represented.

In the past, financial institutions always asked themselves, "Are the poor credit-worthy?" and always answered no. As a result, the poor were simply ignored and left out of the financial system, as if they didn't exist. I reversed the question: "Are the banks people-worthy?" When I discovered they were not, I realized it was time to create a new kind of bank.

None of us like the idea of apartheid. We object when we hear about such a system in any form, anywhere. We all understand that no one should suffer because he or she happened to be born in a certain race, class, or economic condition. But our financial institutions have created a worldwide system of apartheid without anyone being horrified by it. If you don't have collateral, you are not credit-worthy. To the banks, you are not acceptable on our side of the world.

Imagine if the global electronic communications system of the banking world suddenly collapsed and every financial institution in the world suddenly stopped functioning. Banks everywhere would shut their doors. ATM screens would go blank. Credit and debit cards would no longer work. And billions of families would be unable even to put groceries on the table. Well, this is exactly the situation that half of the world's population lives with every day—a non-stop horror story.

If the poor are to get the chance to lift themselves out of poverty, it's up to us to remove the institutional barriers we've created around them. We must remove the absurd rules and laws we have made that treat the poor as nonentities. And we must come up with new ways to recognize a person by his or her own worth, not by artificial measuring sticks imposed by a biased system.

The problem I discovered in Bangladesh—the exclusion of the poor from the benefits of the financial system—is not restricted only to the poorest countries of the world. It exists worldwide. Even in the richest country in the world, many people are not considered credit-worthy and are therefore ineligible to participate fully in the economic system.

In 1994, I received a letter from a young woman, Tami, in Hixon, Texas, a writer working for a newspaper. Tami wrote to me about her adventures in trying to do business with the American banking system:

> *When I was a child trying to open a simple savings account, I was put off by the bank's demand that I produce two pieces of photo identification. What would a child be doing with photo ID in the first place?*
>
> *My experiences as an adult have not been better.*
>
> *My mother just received a $500 money order refund from the U.S. government to pay her back for a money order the post office had lost. She took it to the bank we were using the day we went to close out our account. They refused to cash it for her because, as they said, "You no longer have an account here." She had to take it to one of the many check-cashing companies that have sprung up in the United States in recent years, and we were shocked when they took twenty percent—$100!—as the fee for cashing it.*
>
> *I started checking into these places and found that many people are forced to use them, mainly elderly people who live on social security checks and the working poor who cannot establish bank accounts because they cannot keep minimum balances, afford per-check charges and service charges, or show the bank that they already have good credit. Some people have trouble providing I.D. to banks to open accounts. It's hard enough to show them the I.D. they require to cash a check.*
>
> *At the newspaper where I worked, I received a paycheck every week. I always took it to the very bank it was drawn on and always to one of the same two tellers. Every week they insisted on seeing my driver's license and as if having a state-issued license with my photograph on it was not enough, demanded to see a credit card too. Presumably if I am in debt, I must be honest.*

Isn't it outrageous that low-income people who are struggling to make ends meet are the ones who have to pay *the most* for basic financial services—when they can get access to those services at all?

In the years since I heard from Tami, the problem has not improved. New ways to exploit the poor are always being invented. For example, if you are a member of the middle class, you may never have heard of payday loans, small, short-term loans, usually for less than $1,500, that are given to low-income Americans who don't have access to mainstream sources of credit. They use these loans to get from one payday and the next—to pay an unexpected doctor's bill or fix a car or a broken appliance when money runs short.

Middle- and upper-income individuals would use a credit card to cover such expenses. If the credit card bill is paid in full and on time, no finance charge would be assessed. If it takes a few months to pay the bill, an annualized interest rate in the neighborhood of 25 percent might be charged. But the working poor, who don't qualify for a conventional credit card, are forced to take payday loans instead. And the fees and interest charges for these loans can come to an annual rate of 250 percent, or even higher.

It is so tempting to blame the poor for the problems they face. But when we look at the institutions we have created and how they fail to serve the poor, we see that those institutions and the backward thinking they represent must bear much of the blame.

At Grameen Bank, we challenged the financial apartheid. We dared to give the poorest people bank credit. We included destitute women who had never in their lives even touched any money. We defied the rules. At each step along the way, everybody shouted at us, "You are wasting your money! The money you lend will never come back. Even if your system is working now, it will collapse in no time. It will explode and disappear."

But Grameen Bank neither exploded nor disappeared. Instead, it expanded and reached more and more people. Today, it gives loans to over seven million poor people, 97 percent of whom are women, in 78,000 villages in Bangladesh.

Since it opened, the bank has given out loans totaling the equivalent of $6 billion (U.S.). The repayment rate is currently 98.6 percent. Grameen Bank routinely makes a profit, just as any well-managed bank should do. Financially, it is self-reliant and has not taken donor money since 1995. Deposits and other resources of Grameen Bank today amount to 156 percent of all outstanding loans.

The bank has been profitable every year of its existence except 1983, 1991, and 1992. And most significant of all, according to Grameen Bank's internal survey, 64 percent of our borrowers who have been with the bank for five years or more have crossed the poverty line.

Grameen Bank was born as a tiny homegrown project run with the help of several of my students, all local girls and boys. Three of them are still with me in Grameen Bank, after all these years, as its leading executives.

More Economic Blind Spots

Simply being willing to extend credit to the poor was a revolutionary step in terms of conventional economic thinking. It meant ignoring the traditional belief that loans cannot be made without collateral. This assumption, which the vast majority of bankers hold without analyzing it, questioning it, or even thinking about it, in effect writes off half the human race as being unworthy to participate in the financial system.

Viewed more broadly, however, the Grameen Bank system also involves rethinking many other assumptions in mainstream economics. I have already discussed the fact that economic theory sketches a radically oversimplified image of human nature, assuming that all people are motivated purely by the desire to maximize profit. It only takes a few seconds of thought about the people we all know in the real world to realize that this is simply untrue. And this is only one of the many blind spots of conventional economic theory that Grameen Bank has had to overcome.

A second is the assumption that the solution to poverty lies in creating employment for all—that the only way to help the poor is by giving them jobs. This assumption shapes the kinds of development policies that economists recommend and that governments and aid agencies pursue. Donor money is poured into massive projects, mostly government run. Private capital is invested in big enterprises that are supposed to jump-start local and regional economies, employing thousands of people and turning the poor into affluent taxpayers. It is a nice theory—except that experience shows that it doesn't work because the necessary supportive conditions don't exist.

Economists are wedded to this approach to alleviating poverty because the only kind of employment that most economics textbooks recognize is wage employment. The textbook world is made up solely of "firms" and "farms" that hire different quantities of labor at various wage levels. There is no room in the economic literature for people making a living through self-employment, finding ways to develop goods or services that they sell directly to those who need them. But in the real world, that's what you see the poor doing everywhere.

An American friend recently visited Bangladesh for the first time. After traveling through one of the poorest areas in our country, he wrote me:

> *In the United States, I associate rural poverty with apparent absence of economic activity. I'm thinking of the scenes my wife and I have observed when driving through the depressed counties of upstate New York—deserted downtown areas, storefront windows with just a few tired old articles on display, shuttered offices and factories, and so on. You can drive all day through these communities, scarcely ever see a soul, and arrive at your destination utterly baffled as to how anyone there makes a living. (And of course fewer and fewer people in those counties can make a living these days, which is why many of them have moved to the city.)*
>
> *But the tiny slice of rural Bangladesh that I saw today, while far poorer (in monetary terms) than any place in New York, is an incredible bee hive of economic activity. Every village has its shopping street where dozens of tin-roofed sheds jostle one another, piled high with goods for sale (shoes, medicines, furniture, clothing, DVDs, foodstuffs—you name it) or offering services from barbering to tailoring. On the back roads, the villagers offer their wares spread out on mats—baskets, hats, rounds of bread, a few potatoes or vegetables. And in practically every house or yard you pass, you see people at work, making or fixing or preparing things for trade—tending milk cows, carving wooden furniture, soldering jewelry, gathering crops.*

The villagers my American friend observed do not have "jobs" that conventional economists would recognize. But they are working hard, producing income, feeding their families, and trying to lift themselves out of poverty. What they lack is the economic tools they need to make their work as productive as possible.

At Grameen Bank, I have tried to demonstrate that credit for the poor can create self-employment and generate income for them. By not recognizing the household as a production unit and self-employment as a natural way for people to make a living, the economic literature has missed out on an essential feature of economic reality. I am not arguing against creating jobs. Go full speed ahead on that. But don't assume that people must wait for jobs to materialize, and that self-employment is merely a temporary stopgap. People should have options to choose from, including both jobs and self-employment. Let people choose what suits them. Many people do both.

This mistake is linked to another blind spot in standard economic thinking: the assumption that "entrepreneurship" is a rare quality. According to the textbooks, only a handful of people have the talent to spot business opportunities and the courage to risk their resources in developing those opportunities.

On the contrary, my observations among the poorest people of the world suggest—and decades of experience by Grameen Bank and other institutions confirm—that entrepreneurial ability is practically universal. Almost everyone has the talent to recognize opportunities around them. And when they are given the tools to transform those opportunities into reality, almost everyone is eager to do so.

To me, the poor are like bonsai trees. When you plant the best seed of the tallest tree in a six-inch-deep flower pot, you get a perfect replica of the tallest tree, but it is only inches tall. There is nothing wrong with the seed you planted; only the soil-base you provided was inadequate.

Poor people are bonsai people. There is nothing wrong with their seeds. Only society never gave them a base to grow on. All that is required to get poor people out of poverty is for us to create an enabling environment for them. Once the poor are allowed unleash their energy and creativity, poverty will disappear very quickly.

Economic theory has other blind spots as well. Read most economic textbooks and you will never encounter any such thing as a "man," a "woman," or a "child." As far as economists are concerned, none of these things exist. The closest they come to acknowledging the existence of human beings is when they talk about "labor"—a collection of robot-like beings whose only mission in life is to work for factory owners, office owners, or farm owners. And since economic theory doesn't recognize that "labor" is made up of both men and women, its view of the world is male-dominated (treating "male" as the "default value" between male and female).

When challenged, economists defend this retreat into extreme abstraction by saying they do it for the sake of "simplicity." I understand that sometimes it is necessary to simplify in order to see things clearly. But when "simplification" means ignoring essentials, it goes too far. Albert Einstein has been quoted as saying, "Everything should be made as simple as possible, but not simpler than that." Mainstream economics makes everything "too simple," and therefore it misses reality.

At Grameen Bank, we quickly discovered that, in the real world, it is important to think about men, women, and children not as units of "labor" but as human beings with varying capacities and needs. Observing the actual behavior of the people we lent money to, we soon found that giving credit to poor women brings more benefits to a family than giving it to men. When men make money, they tend to spend it on themselves, but when women make money, they bring benefits to the whole family, particularly the children. Thus, lending to women creates a cascading effect that brings social benefits as well as economic benefits to the whole family and ultimately to the entire community. At Grameen Bank, we discovered the mother first. Then we discovered the children—not through any emotional or moral compulsion, but for sound economic reasons. If poverty is to be reduced or eliminated, the next generation must be our focus. We must prepare them to peel off all the signs and stigmas of poverty, and instill in them a sense of human dignity and hope for the future.

So any program addressed to children should not be looked upon as a "humanitarian" or "charitable" program. In reality, it is a prime development program—no less so (and much more so, I would argue) than building an airport, a factory, or highways.

And this leads to yet another major blind spot in conventional economics: the focus, in development strategy, on material accumulation and achievement. This focus needs to be shifted to human beings, their initiative and enterprise.

The first and foremost task of development is to turn on the engine of creativity inside each person. Any program that merely meets the physical needs of a poor person or even provides a job is not a true development program unless it leads to the unfolding of his or her creative energy.

This is why Grameen Bank offers the poor not handouts or grants but credit—loans they must repay, with interest, through their own productive work. This dynamic makes Grameen Bank sustainable. Loan repayments supply funds for future loans, to the same individuals or to new bank members, in an ever-expanding cycle of economic growth. It also helps the poor demonstrate to themselves that they can change their world for the better—and it gives them the tools to do just that, for themselves.

Critics often say that microcredit does not contribute significantly to economic development. Are they correct? I think the answer depends on how you define "economic development." Is it measured by income per capita? Consumption per capita? Or anything per capita?

To me, the essence of development is changing the quality of life of the bottom half of the population. And that quality is not to be defined just by the size of the consumption basket. It must also include the enabling environment that lets individuals explore their own creative potential. This is more important than any mere measure of income or consumption.

Microcredit turns on the economic engines among the rejected population of society. Once a large number of these tiny engines start working, the stage is set for big things.

The Evolution of
Grameen Bank

As Grameen Bank became more and more deeply rooted in the social conditions of the poor in Bangladesh, it uncovered additional areas of economic imbalance and opportunity. In response, its mandate evolved and broadened.

For example, in 1984, we began offering housing loans. Here, too, we ran into bureaucratic resistance. When we applied to the Central Bank of Bangladesh for the same kind of funding being offered to commercial banks for housing loans, our proposal was rejected on the grounds that the very small loans we were suggesting—5,000 taka, at the time about $125 (U.S.)—were too tiny to create anything that the government could recognize as "housing." This may have been true, but it didn't change the fact that the poor people we served were desperately eager to buy tin roofs to keep the rain off their heads. We tried rewriting our application several times, hoping to come up with appropriate words that the bureaucrats couldn't find fault with. But we didn't get the approval to offer housing loans until a friendly bank governor intervened at my request. He agreed to ignore the rules and allow Grameen Bank to help poor people improve their tumble-down huts.

Since we introduced them in 1984, housing loans have been used to construct 650,000 houses. The legal ownership of these houses belongs to the women members of Grameen Bank themselves—an important step in empowering the women of Bangladesh, who historically have been among the most powerless and oppressed groups in the country.

As we worked with the poor, we quickly realized that it was not enough for Grameen Bank to provide financial services. It was also important for us to promote a strong social agenda. The basic organization of the bank and its lending programs offers one example.

No one who borrows from Grameen Bank stands alone. Each belongs to a self-made group of five friends, no two of whom may be closely related. When one of the five friends wants to take out a loan, she needs approval from the remaining four. Although each borrower is responsible for her own loan, the group functions as a small social network that provides encouragement, psychological support, and at times practical assistance in bearing the unfamiliar burden of debt and steering the individual member through the unfamiliar world of "business." Neither does the group of five stand alone. Ten to twelve such groups come together for a weekly meeting in a center, which is a simple hut-like structure built by them in their own village. There are over 130,000 centers around the country, each serving fifty to sixty

Grameen Bank members. At the weekly meeting, loan repayments are collected by a local branch officer, applications for new loans are submitted, and various inspirational, instructional, and practical activities are undertaken, from discussions about new business ideas to presentations about health or financial topics to brief periods of group exercise. The center leadership is elected democratically.

There's no doubt that the community-oriented dynamic of Grameen Bank is an important reason for the success of our system. The positive social pressure created by the group and the center does a lot to encourage borrowers to remain faithful to their commitments. When Grameen members are surveyed about *why* they repay their loans, the most common answer is, "Because I would feel terrible to let down the other members of my group."

Some critics worry that this might seem coercive. But since no one is ever *forced* to join Grameen Bank—and since the only agenda of the bank is to help poor people lift themselves out of poverty—I think it's more appropriate to recognize it as an example of the power of community to encourage people to achieve things they might otherwise find impossible.

Another important way we support our social agenda is through the Sixteen Decisions. This is a set of social and personal commitments that have evolved over time, initially through ideas that surfaced at intensive sessions among Grameen Bank borrowers and staff during the early 1980s. Versions of the Sixteen Decisions were created at various bank branches and centers around the country. These were shared with other branches over time. By 1984, they were accumulated into what became known as the Sixteen Decisions. They have become an integral part of the Grameen program. Every new member of the bank is expected to learn the Sixteen Decisions and to pledge to follow them.

The Sixteen Decisions:

1. The four principles of Grameen Bank—Discipline, Unity, Courage, and Hard Work—we shall follow and advance in all walks of our lives.
2. We shall bring prosperity to our families.

3. We shall not live in dilapidated houses. We shall repair our houses and work towards constructing new houses as soon as possible.
4. We shall grow vegetables all the year round. We shall eat plenty of them and sell the surplus.
5. During the plantation season, we shall plant as many seedlings as possible.
6. We shall plan to keep our families small. We shall minimize our expenditures. We shall look after our health.
7. We shall educate our children and ensure that they can earn to pay for their education.
8. We shall always keep our children and the environment clean.
9. We shall build and use pit latrines.
10. We shall boil water before drinking or use alum to purify it. We shall use pitcher filters to remove arsenic.
11. We shall not take any dowry at our sons' weddings; neither shall we give any dowry in our daughters' weddings. We shall keep the center free from the curse of dowry. We shall not practice child marriage.
12. We shall not inflict any injustice on anyone; neither shall we allow anyone to do so.
13. For higher income we shall collectively undertake bigger investments.
14. We shall always be ready to help each other. If anyone is in difficulty, we shall all help.
15. If we come to know of any breach of discipline in any center, we shall all go there and help restore discipline.
16. We shall take part in all social activities collectively.

Because of the Sixteen Decisions, Grameen borrowers have taken great care to send their children to school. Virtually every Grameen family has all of its school-age children attending classes regularly— quite an achievement for borrowers who were mostly illiterate. The spread of education to an entire generation of rural Bangladeshis has been a dramatic historical breakthrough.

As the years passed, children from Grameen families went on to high school, and many performed at or near the top of their classes. To celebrate this achievement, we began giving scholarships to the best students. Today Grameen Bank awards the children of its borrowers over 30,000 scholarships each year.

Many of the children went on to higher education to become doctors, engineers, college teachers, and other professionals. We introduced student loans to make it easy for Grameen students to complete higher education. Now some of them have PhDs. At present, there are 18,000 students on student loans. Over 8,000 students are now added to this number annually.

As these examples illustrate, Grameen Bank is much more than a financial institution. We are creating a completely new generation that will be well equipped to take their families way out of the reach of poverty. We want to make a break in the historical continuation of poverty. Grameen Bank is a tool for doing so.

Notice, too, that the success of Grameen Bank has grown from our willingness to recognize and honor motivations and incentives that transcend the purely economic. Human beings are not just workers, consumers, or even entrepreneurs. They are also parents, children, friends, neighbors, and citizens. They worry about their families, care about the communities where they live, and think a lot about their reputations and their relationships with others. For traditional bankers, these human concerns don't exist. But they are at the heart of what makes up Grameen Bank. The credit we offer the poor is not just a matter of entries in a ledger book or even a handful of bills handed over to a person. It is a tool for reshaping lives, and neither the staff of Grameen Bank nor our borrowers ever lose sight of that reality.

The Evolving
Grameen System

Grameen Bank is both a business and an institution for the poor. And for both kinds of organizations, one of the greatest tests is how they survive a terrible economic and human catastrophe. Most institutions can thrive in good times, but only the most resilient can survive disasters.

In 1998, Bangladesh experienced the worst flood in its history. As I wrote at the time, this was "not just another flood: it is THE FLOOD, which all Bangladeshis will remember for generations to come." Starting in mid-July, two-thirds of the country was under water for eleven weeks, causing terrible suffering and economic dislocation. Thirty million people were driven from their homes, over a thousand people were killed, and two rice crops were badly damaged.

As you can imagine, the members and staff of Grameen Bank were not spared. One hundred and fifty-four members died in the flood; many more lost family members and the homes, farms, and farm animals of many were washed away. Over half of our borrowers, and more than 70 percent of our branches, were affected by the flood.

As economic activity came to a halt in vast regions of Bangladesh, many Grameen members lost all sources of income and were unable to continue their loan repayments. At the same time, their economic needs increased enormously. The bank responded with programs of emergency help. We declared 42 percent of our centers "disaster centers" and suspended the collection of loan installments for what proved to be a five-month period. We also provided large infusions of cash through emergency loan programs. Members who'd built homes through Grameen housing loans were given supplemental loans of 5,000 taka (at the time, $125 U.S.) to make repairs, and other members received 2,500-taka loans for the same purpose.

These measures helped alleviate the suffering of Grameen members and accelerated the rebuilding of communities destroyed by the flood. But they put tremendous economic pressure on the bank. By mid–1999, we were experiencing serious problems with large-scale loan defaults in certain regions of the country. This wasn't unexpected; it would have been unrealistic to think that a devastated economy could rebound quickly from so serious a blow. But when we studied the problems closely, we discovered a surprising pattern. Some of the bank centers experiencing the most serious default problems were directly alongside other centers that were performing well.

As we examined these discrepancies in search of an explanation, we realized that the great flood was only part of the problem. The bank centers where members were experiencing the greatest difficulties had actually been struggling for years. The stress created by the flood had simply exacerbated the problems and made them much more obvious.

Over the years, we occasionally tried adding new rules and amending specific features of the basic Grameen system without conducting any major overhaul of the entire program. As a result, the Grameen system remained a "one-size-fits-all" program that worked generally well but could not address any special needs that borrowers might have. After more than fifteen years of operation, Grameen was ripe for change—and the great flood of 1998 provided the opportunity for a major upgrade of the system.

Over the next two years, Grameen staff around the country participated in an extensive process of rethinking the bank's operations, looking for ways to strengthen its economic footing, make its products more relevant to the needs of members, and increase its flexibility for dealing with changing conditions and needs.

In particular, we focused on two areas of need. First, we wanted to greatly increase the amount of savings deposited with Grameen Bank. This would improve the bank's capital structure and create a reserve of funds that we could fall back on during times of economic stress—for example, the next time nature wreaks havoc on the people of Bangladesh. In 1995, we had decided that Grameen Bank would be completely self-sufficient. It would no longer accept money from bilateral or multilateral donor institutions, instead relying completely on its own financial resources. But when the flood hit, we needed additional funds. We did not go to the donors. We went to the central bank of Bangladesh to borrow money. Then we issued bonds to borrow money from commercial banks. We felt confident that the redesigned Grameen system would be strong enough to avoid having to borrow even in a time of disaster.

Second, we wanted to introduce greater flexibility into our loan products. We gave borrowers more options as to how and when they would repay their loans—making it easier for them to pay back more money at times when their business was at peak season, while paying less during the slack seasons.

We approached the challenge in the same spirit of open-ended experimentation that had driven the founding of Grameen Bank. Dozens of ideas surfaced, were debated, and experimented with. Those that worked best became part of the blueprint for a new Grameen system. By the end of 2001, the new system, which we dubbed Grameen II, had been fully defined. The various zones into which the bank as a whole is divided began to implement it, one by one, as their local circumstances and their ability to retrain bank employees dictated. By August 2002, Grameen II had been adopted throughout the country.

The differences between Grameen I and Grameen II are many and interesting. Those who want to know the full story of how Grameen II came to be and the details of its implementation are urged to read *The Poor Always Pay Back: The Grameen II Story*, which covers all these matters thoroughly.[1] The chart on the next page is adapted from that book and offers a handy summary of some of Grameen II's major innovations.

The chart illustrates how Grameen Bank, like any other business, has had to evolve and adapt over time in order to serve its customers and their needs most effectively. It's a lesson that founders of social businesses need to master: Just as PMBs must be nimble and flexible to meet the changing demands of an ever-evolving competitive environment, social businesses, too, must never stop developing and improving.

Grameen Bank offers four different loan products at four different interest rates. All are simple interest, unlike the compound interest charged by conventional banks. The amount collected from the borrower in interest can never exceed the principal amount. Even if a borrower takes twenty years to repay her loan, she won't pay a total of more than twice the sum she borrowed.

The basic income-generating loan—the classic product with which we started our program back in 1976—is offered at a rate of 20 percent. We charge 8 percent for housing loans. Under a program that we launched in the year 2000, we offer student loans at a rate of

From Grameen I to Grameen II:
A More Flexible, Responsive System

Grameen I	Grameen II	Reason for Change
No provision to save for pension.	Borrower deposits a fixed monthly amount in Grameen pension scheme.	To help borrowers build a nest egg for retirement.
Fixed, one-size-fits-all savings program.	Varied savings plans to fit members' individual needs.	To encourage saving for special needs and long-term economic benefit.
No initiative to collect savings from nonmembers.	Active campaigns to collect savings from nonmembers.	To enable the bank to self-fund future loans.
Mostly one-year loans with fixed installment amounts.	Loan duration and installment size may vary.	To allow borrowers to tailor loan products to individual needs and changing circumstances.
Common loan ceiling for an entire branch.	Individual loan ceilings based on savings and other measurements.	To reward and incentivize good borrowing and repayment practices by members.
Family responsible for loan of deceased borrower.	Special savings fund ensures that outstanding loans are paid off after death.	To alleviate borrowers' fears of leaving debt behind after death.
Borrower becomes defaulter if loan is not repaid in 52 weeks.	Borrower becomes defaulter if repayment schedule is not met within six months.	To create an early warning signal of potential borrower problems.
Funds for new bank branches borrowed from head office at 12 percent interest.	New branches are self-funding from Day 1, using savings from borrowers and non-borrowers.	To ensure that branches become self-sufficient quickly.

zero percent during the study period, 5 percent after finishing the degree. And in 2004 we introduced a program that offers credit to the very poorest—beggars, whom we refer to as "struggling members."

None of Grameen Bank's ordinary rules apply to the beggars. The loans—typically in an amount around $15—are interest-free, and the borrowers can pay whatever amount they wish, whenever they wish. The struggling members use the loan to carry small merchandise such as snacks, toys, or household items, when they travel from house to house begging. They soon figure out which houses are best for selling to, which for begging.

The idea works. There are now 100,000 struggling members in the program. Over 10,000 of them have already stopped begging and become full-time salespeople. Most of the rest are now part-time beggars. And, yes, the struggling members repay their loans. Of the total monies disbursed under this program—currently about 95 million taka—almost 63 million taka has already been repaid.

Other attractive innovations of the Grameen II program include a pension fund savings program, the flexi-loan program, and loan insurance.

A borrower opens a pension fund account by promising to deposit a fixed amount every week or every month. If she keeps her promise for ten years, she receives an amount equal to almost twice the sum of her deposits (a return equal to about 12 percent on her savings). Grameen members love this program and are excited to watch their savings grow, year by year. By mid–2007, total deposits from borrowers amounted to over $400 million (U.S.), of which pension fund deposits are about 53 percent.

If a borrower has difficulty in repaying a loan according to her original schedule, she can covert it to a flexi-loan, which permits her to pay in smaller installments over a longer time period. Loan insurance makes it possible to write off all outstanding debts when a borrower or her husband dies. These features of Grameen II help ensure that a microloan remains a source of help to a poor family rather than a burden in times of need.

Thanks to the changes implemented under Grameen II, the financial position of Grameen Bank is now stronger than ever, even as the services provided to the poor have expanded and become more flexible and useful. In 2006, the bank earned a profit of $20 million and distributed dividends for the first time (as previous government-imposed restrictions were lifted). Borrowers received these dividend payments as shareholders of the bank.

Microcredit around the World

In Bangladesh, 80 percent of poor families have already been reached with microcredit. (Millions have been served by Grameen Bank, many others by a number of microcredit NGOs, especially the Bangladesh Rural Advancement Committee, or BRAC, and ASA.) Today, we project that nearly 100 percent of poor families in Bangladesh will be reached by 2012, making our country the first in the world to bring financial services to every poor family.

The microcredit idea, which began in the village of Jobra in Bangladesh, has spread around the globe. There are now microcredit programs in almost every country in the world. Microcredit has made the greatest inroads in Asia. But it also has a foothold in countries of Africa, Latin America, and the Middle East. Microcredit has also begun to operate among the poor in many countries of the developed world, including the United States.

Many of these programs have closely modeled their operations on Grameen Bank, and some have sent their officers and staff to learn from us firsthand. So great is the demand for training in the Grameen methodology that we have established a separate organization, Grameen Trust, specifically devoted to that mission.

It should be understood that Grameen Bank itself operates only within Bangladesh; we do not have branches or divisions in any other country. Nor are we affiliated with or responsible for microcredit institutions operating anywhere else in the world, even those that may cite Grameen Bank or me as a source of inspiration and guidance. The sole exception is a handful of programs created under special agreement between donors and Grameen Trust and implemented by Grameen Bank personnel under a program we call the Build-Operate-Transfer (BOT) program.

One of the best forums for fruitful conversations among many types of microcredit practitioners from around the world is the Microcredit Summit Campaign. The story of this global organization offers a good way of tracing the development and growth of the microcredit movement.

In 1997, the first meeting of the Microcredit Summit was held in Washington, DC. It was attended by nearly 3,000 delegates from 137 countries who represented microcredit programs of many kinds and sizes. Together we adopted a goal of reaching 100 million of the world's poorest families with microcredit and other financial services, preferably through the women in those families, by the year 2005.

This was an audacious goal. At the time, the number of families reached with microcredit was only 7.6 million, of whom five million were in Bangladesh. One hundred million families seemed to many a distant dream. And if you have tracked the history of similar bold goals in the world of development economics, you know that they are rarely attained. Most often, the efforts fall far short, the goals are quietly abandoned, and no one ever speaks about them again.

In this case, the outcome was very different: We were able to announce at the third global Microcredit Summit in Halifax, Nova Scotia, that we had achieved our 100-million-family target by the end of 2006, just a year behind schedule.

It was a cause for celebration, and celebrate we did. But we also used the occasion to set new goals for the years to come. First, we agreed that, by 2015, we would expand our services so that 175 million families around the world would have access to microcredit. More important, we vowed to ensure that our efforts would have a large and measurable impact on world of poverty. Specifically, we committed ourselves to the goal of helping 100 million families lift themselves, through the use of microcredit and other financial services, out of poverty. Based on an estimate of approximately five people affected per family (a figure that experience in the developing world suggests is roughly accurate), this will mean that half a billion people will have become poverty-free during the next decade—just as projected under the Millennium Development Goals.

The Return of
the Moneylenders

Over the years, as more and more organizations have gotten involved in microcredit, some have found it convenient to ignore the original meaning of the term. Microcredit is supposed to describe loans offered with no collateral to support income-generating businesses aimed at lifting the poor out of poverty. Yet today there are many organizations that call themselves "microcredit" programs that offer loans to people who are not poor, that require regular collateral, and that are used primarily for consumption rather than income generation. There are even "microcredit" programs that generate enormous profits for investors by charging interest at rates as high as 100 percent or even higher!

Under the circumstances, we really don't know what we are talking about when we talk about microcredit. I think it is time we classify microcredit programs according to clear, consistent categories. Here are the categories I would propose:

TYPE 1: POVERTY-FOCUSED MICROCREDIT PROGRAMS
These are poverty-focused, collateral-free, low-interest microcredit programs. Grameen Bank was created to provide this type of microcredit. Type 1 programs charge interest rates that fit into one of two zones: the Green Zone, which equals the cost of funds at the market rate plus up to 10 percent, and the Yellow Zone, which equals the cost of funds at the market rate plus 10 to 15 percent.

TYPE 2: PROFIT-MAXIMIZING MICROCREDIT PROGRAMS
These are programs that charge an interest rate higher than the Yellow Zone. They operate in the Red Zone, which is moneylenders' territory. Because of the high interest they charge, these programs cannot be viewed as poverty-focused but rather are commercial enterprises whose main objective appears to be earning large profits for shareholders or other investors.

This classification may be adjusted for special situations, such as when high salary costs make operating expenses unusually heavy. And these principles will not apply where the microcredit organization is owned by the borrowers.

However, I think the secretariat for the Microcredit Summit Campaign, which maintains a database of all microcredit programs, should classify programs according to a system like the one I propose. What's more, I believe that the Microcredit Summit Campaign should include only Type 1 programs, since only these contribute to the campaign's goal of using microcredit to help eliminate global poverty.

I would like to see all the poor people of the world being reached by microcredit programs delivered through social businesses, while profit-maximizing (Type 2) programs should focus their operations on people belonging to the lower middle class and above.

There are those who contend that profit-maximizing microcredit programs are actually beneficial to the poor and to the world economy in general. They argue that charging higher rates of interest enables a microfinance institution (MFI) to become sustainable more quickly. They also claim that high rates of profit make MFIs attractive to capital market investors from the richest countries, allowing the MFIs to expand their services to the poor. Finally, they say that high interest rates enable bigger loans to create larger enterprises, which, in turn, can employ larger numbers of poor people.

The business model behind these arguments is a familiar one from the world of conventional finance, and I have no problem with it—so long as the customers are middle-class or wealthy people. But I have serious problems when people try to justify high interest rates (30 percent real interest and above) and even very high interest rates (over 70 percent) on loans given to the poor. I say, "Make all the profit you want from your middle-class customers! Feel free to take advantage of your financial position, if you can! But don't apply the same thinking to the poor. If you lend to the poor, do it without concern for profit, so that they can have the maximum help in climbing out of poverty. Once they've completed the climb, then treat them like every other customer—but not till then."

Microcredit was created to protect the people from moneylenders, not to create more moneylenders.

Like most of my fellow microcredit practitioners, I believe that there is room for many varying models of microcredit, and that experimentation across a wide range of options is likely to produce the greatest progress and the most valuable insights into what does and doesn't work. I've learned a lot from my meetings and discussions with other microcredit practitioners, and I think we can find many areas of common ground for cooperation, collaboration, and mutual support, provided we share a common goal—helping the poor get out poverty through their own efforts.

Problems with Funding Microcredit

The biggest problem we face in trying to expand the reach of microcredit is not the lack of capacity. Instead, it is the lack of availability of money to help microcredit programs get through their initial years until they reach the break-even level.

However, this doesn't mean that Type 1 microcredit organizations need external loans and foreign equity investment. It is very risky for MFIs in economies subject to sustained inflation—which applies to most of the developing world—to accept such foreign funds. When it's time to repay the international loans or pay dividends in hard currency, the MFI ends up paying a lot more in local currency than they had received. Thus, the effective interest rate on the external loan becomes several times higher than that agreed upon.

The fact is that there is plenty of money in any country to lend money to the poor. It is all a question of mobilizing it and making it available to the poor. Local banks cannot lend it to MFIs because MFIs cannot provide collateral. However, if an international or domestic organization steps forward to act as a guarantor, local banks are happy to provide the money. This is a market-based solution already being practiced by such organizations as Grameen Capital India and Grameen Jameel Pan-Arab Microfinance.

There are two other market-based solutions to the funding problem. The first is for MFIs to accept savings deposits—something that microcredit organizations run by NGOs are legally forbidden to do. It's a strange thing: Conventional banks that lend money to the well-to-do, and that often have repayment rates of 70 percent or even lower, are allowed to collect huge amounts of public deposits, while microcredit institutions with loan repayment rates of 98 percent or better are forbidden to do the same thing!

When we in the microcredit community protest this discrepancy, we are sometimes told, "Microcredit programs aren't covered by any law, which means it would be highly risky to allow them to take deposits from customers." This strikes me as a funny argument. If the problem is a lack of legal coverage, let's remedy that. Let's create a law to convert microcredit organizations into microcredit banks to bring their programs within the framework of law and create a regulatory body for microcredit organizations that is separate from, different from, but parallel to the regulatory body that already exists for conventional banks.

I've long urged that every country take this logical step, but progress has been frustratingly slow. After a long process of negotiation, the Bangladesh government has created an independent Microcredit Regulatory Authority, but it has not passed the law for creating microcredit banks. A draft of the law agreed on by the government and the practitioners is waiting to be passed by the parliament.

If the restriction on taking deposits were lifted, the expansion of microcredit outreach could be very rapid, as microcredit programs would be freed from dependence on donor money. This is the ideal and ultimate solution for bringing financial services to the poor. Everybody benefits from this arrangement. Depositors are happy to earn a good return on their money. The poor enjoy financial services without any limitation or uncertainty about the supply of funds. Deposits will go to the poor people in the community in the form of microcredit, helping to build up the local economy. And the microcredit banks will be financially self-reliant.

Grameen Bank operates exactly this way. When we select a location to start a new branch, we tell the manager, "Here is your location. Go there and open a branch. You'll get no money from us. Instead, mobilize deposits in your area, lend money to the poor, and try to reach the break-even point within twelve months—that is your task." Most of the new-branch managers achieve the goal. Some take slightly longer than twelve months, but no one has difficulty in mobilizing deposits to lend money. Using this system, we opened an average of one-and-a-half branches every day during 2006.

However, since the legal system does not allow MFIs to accept customer deposits, the present system for funding microcredit programs is not adequate. So they have to depend on donors.

International aid is at least a $50-billion-a-year activity. At present, support for microcredit constitutes less than 1 percent of this amount. If we are serious about bringing financial services to the poor, this sum should be raised to at least 5 percent of the annual foreign aid money—in other words, around $2.5 billion.

This money should be used to build local microcredit capacity through the creation of what are called wholesale funds, which channel donor funds to initiate and support microcredit programs.

Each country should have a number of independent, nongovernmental wholesale funds. In large countries, like China, India, Indonesia, Nigeria, and the Philippines, there should be wholesale microcredit funds in various regions of the country. In regions with a number of small countries, like Central America, one common microcredit fund can serve several countries simultaneously. There is also a role for regional and global wholesalers, although it will be limited to supporting national-level and local-level funds rather than going directly to the grass-roots organizations.

I'm personally familiar with the workings of two such wholesale funds: Grameen Trust (GT) and the Palli Karma-Sahayak Foundation (PKSF), both in Bangladesh.

Since 1991, GT has been providing funding and technical support to 140 microcredit programs in forty countries in Asia, Africa, Europe, and the Americas. The soft loans GT offers are denominated in local currency, so that GT bears the foreign exchange risk, not the MFI.

GT also provides a package of start-up support, training, and technical assistance from experienced microcredit practitioners, almost like the guidance that a new franchisee of a business might receive. GT's role is to be a catalyst, with a comparative advantage in starting programs that established funders can then support. With funds from donors, GT has helped establish many top-ranking microcredit programs around the world.

The Palli Karma-Sahayak Foundation (whose name, translated from Bengali, means Rural Employment Support Foundation), is a national-level wholesale fund to promote microcredit programs. It finances start-ups as well as scaling-up projects of all sizes. It was created in 1990 by the government of Bangladesh with its own funds. Later, PKSF borrowed twice from the World Bank: $105 million in 1996 and $151 million in 2001. It has disbursed $554 million to 186 microcredit organizations in Bangladesh.

In-country wholesale funds reduce overhead costs dramatically. A fund based in a Third World country can deliver a loan to a very poor woman in a village in that country at a fraction of the cost of providing such a loan from a donor headquartered in Europe or North America. Through the wholesale fund mechanism, more donor money can go into the hands of the poorest as loans rather than into the pockets of officials and consultants to pay for salaries, fees, and international travel.

Another advantage of wholesale funds is that they can provide continuous, uninterrupted funding for microcredit programs up to institutional viability and beyond. Donors frequently leave a program when funding ceases at the end of an arbitrary project period. Another problem is that donor funding often arrives late because of long approval procedures that are not designed with microcredit programs in mind. Many chief executives of microcredit programs tell me that they spend a great deal of their time mobilizing financial resources for the program rather than ensuring the quality of the loan program. Multiple reporting procedures to various donors take up a lot of time— a problem that can be solved with a wholesale fund serving as a single source of ongoing funding within a business framework with a standard reporting format.

Finally, wholesale funds can help microcredit programs in mobilizing local and international financing by offering guarantees and other financial intermediations—for example, by marketing bonds on their behalf. Thus, wholesale funds can lead microcredit programs toward sustainability, helping them to be transformed from grant- and donor-funded charities into true social businesses.

The G8 meeting held in Heiligendamm, Germany, in June 2007 decided to create a microfinance wholesale fund for Africa, the Africa

Microfinance Fund (AMF). This is a welcome decision. Its management structure will be critical in ensuring its success. I would hope to see AMF as an independent fund with the mission of providing funding to one or more microfinance funds within each country in Africa, as well as rigorous training to those who disburse and manage the funds. A well-run AMF can play an important role in jump-starting the establishment and growth of MFIs in Africa, the continent that is currently most in need of the economic energy microcredit can bring.

Mainstream Banks and Microcredit

Can conventional banks run microcredit programs? Of course they can, as long as they have trained people, a methodology, and a management structure that will do the job. My usual suggestion to them is to create a microcredit subsidiary, run on the social business principle, with a totally separate management, or at least a separate microcredit branch with dedicated staff.

In India, NABARD (National Bank for Agriculture and Rural Development) is encouraging commercial banks to lend money to the poor through Self-Help Group (SHG) methodology, under which a group of about twenty people, usually women, affiliates with a branch of a commercial bank. After saving for a minimum of six months, the SHG becomes eligible for a loan from the bank. The bank usually lends to the SHG at about 10 to 12 percent interest (the prime lending rate), and the SHG in turn lends to members at a higher rate, usually 25 to 30 percent.

NGOs provide support in forming SHGs, training the members to maintain books and manage their savings. When groups are formed with the help of government poverty programs, the loans may be subsidized by up to 50 percent.

As of March 2006, India has 2.2 million SHGs with a total membership of thirty-three million clients, roughly half of whom are poor. A total of $1.98 billion was disbursed under the program in 2006.

The SHG model allows commercial banks to get involved in microcredit without creating a microfinance subsidiary or hiring specially trained personnel.

Credit: The Vital Foundation

Everyone understands that money is important. The unique problem of the poor is that there is no institution to bring money to them. Microcredit solves that problem in a businesslike way. Now that the methodology is known, it should be given legal status and made an integral part of the mainstream financial system.

Some critics are eager to point out that microcredit alone cannot solve the problem of poverty. No one ever claimed that it could. But microcredit lays down a solid foundation on which all other anti-poverty programs can find firm grounding and achieve better results.

Poverty is a multi-dimensional phenomenon. It is about people's lives and their livelihoods. To free people from poverty, all aspects of their lives need to be addressed, from the personal level to the global level, and from the economic dimension to the political, social, technological, and psychological dimensions. These are not separate and disconnected elements but closely intertwined.

Our experience in building a successful microcredit program forced Grameen Bank to recognize the importance of all these other dimensions. In the next chapter, I'll describe some of the other kinds of ventures that I have gradually become involved in. They range from programs to promote health, education, information technology, and self-sufficiency among the poor to large, successful businesses, including the single biggest for-profit corporation in all of Bangladesh. In the development of these varied enterprises you can see the earliest seeds of the bigger concept that would later become known as social business.

Note
1 Asif Dowla and Dipal Barua, *The Poor Always Pay Back: The Grameen II Story* (Bloomfield, CT: Kumarian Press, 2006).

4

From Microcredit to Social Business

My first book was titled *Banker to the Poor*, and since its publication I have often been referred to as "the banker to the poor." I take pride in that designation. But not many people know that I became a banker to the poor quite by accident. I had no intention of becoming a banker of any kind. When I began my efforts to help the poor in the village of Jobra over thirty years ago, I was an economics professor, not a banker. I had little knowledge of banking and certainly no direct experience in the field. When I began lending to the poor in the village next door to the university campus, I had no idea what it would lead to.

In the years since then, I have come to see that my innocence about banking helped me a lot. The fact that I was not a trained banker and in fact had never even taken a course on bank operations meant that I was free to think about the processes of lending and borrowing without preconceptions. If I had been a banker, I would probably never have tried to explore how the banking system could serve the poor. And if I had, I would almost certainly have gone about it the wrong way. I would have started with the banking system as it existed and then tried to figure out how the poor could be fitted into that system. Any solution I might have devised would have been jerry-rigged and probably ineffective. Instead, as an outsider, I started by looking closely at the poor themselves—their problems, their skills, their needs, and their abilities. Then I built a lending system around them. One day I woke up and discovered, much to my surprise, that I had become a banker, though a very unconventional one.

In much the same way, my colleagues at Grameen Bank and I have found ourselves becoming "accidental entrepreneurs." We never planned to launch a series of companies. We were simply working closely with the poor in our role as bankers, striving to understand the social and economic conditions that had consigned them to poverty and trying to develop tools to help them free themselves from that fate. In the process, we began to stumble upon opportunities to launch new ventures that we thought might be helpful to the poor. In other cases, opportunities were dropped in our laps by people who believed we could make good use of them. Driven by circumstances, and lured by the possibility of transforming opportunities into tangible benefits for the poor, we began experimenting with new business ideas—first one, then another, then another. Some of the ideas took root and flourished, while others failed, at least for the time being.

Now, after almost twenty years of this experimentation, we find ourselves operating twenty-five organizations, often described collectively as "the Grameen family of companies." (See the table below for a complete list.)

The Grameen Family of Companies

Company Name	Founded	Purpose
Grameen Bank	1983	Financial services for the poor
Grameen Trust	1989	Training, technical assistance, and financial support for MFIs around the world
Grameen Krishi (Agriculture) Foundation	1991	Experimentation and training to improve agricultural practices and output
Grameen Uddog (Enterprise)	1994	Export of Grameen Check hand-loom fabrics
Grameen Fund	1994	Social venture capital funding for entrepreneurial start-ups
Grameen Motsho O Pashusampad (Fisheries and Livestock) Foundation	1994	Fish pond and livestock breeding programs
Grameen Telecom	1995	Telecommunications services for the poor

Company Name	Founded	Purpose
Grameen Shamogree (Products)	1996	Domestic sales of Grameen Check hand-loom fabrics, handicrafts, and products
Grameen Cybernet	1996	Internet service provider
Grameen Shakti (Energy)	1996	Renewable energy sources for rural Bangladesh
Grameen Phone	1996	Cell-phone service
Grameen Kalyan (Welfare)	1996	Health and welfare services for members and staff of Grameen Bank
Grameen Shikkha (Education)	1997	Scholarships and other assistance to students of poor families
Grameen Communications	1997	Internet service provider and data processing services
Grameen Knitwear	1997	Manufacture of knitted fabrics for export
Grameen Capital Mgmt.	1998	Investment management
Grameen Solutions	1999	Development of IT solutions for businesses
Grameen IT Park	2001	Development of high-tech office facilities in Dhaka
Grameen Byabosa Bikash (Business Promotion)	2001	Provision of small business loan guarantees
Grameen Information Highway Ltd.	2001	Data connectivity and Internet access provider
Grameen Star Education	2002	Information technology training
Grameen Bitek	2002	Manufacture of electronics products
Grameen Healthcare Trust	2006	Funding for Grameen Health Care Services
Grameen Health Care Services	2006	Health care services for the poor
Grameen Danone	2006	Affordable, nutritious foods for the poor

These companies are engaged in a remarkable array of activities. Grameen Phone is now the largest company in Bangladesh. The Village Phone Project, operated with support from Grameen Phone, has helped almost 300,000 women become "telephone ladies," providing cell-phone service to villagers all over Bangladesh (although the business of the telephone ladies has begun to decline since 2005). Grameen Telecom and Grameen Communications are installing Internet kiosks in rural areas, bringing the benefits of the World Wide Web to some of the most remote regions of Bangladesh. Grameen fisheries and textile companies are creating jobs and bringing newfound prosperity to hundreds of villages through simple, self-sustaining, appropriate technologies. More than thirty Grameen Energy centers are promoting solar home and biofuel systems, and engaging and training local women to produce solar energy-related electronic accessories.

Is there any common thread that links all these varied enterprises? Just one. They all share the same goal: to improve life for the people of Bangladesh, especially the poor.

The Grameen companies fall into two categories for legal purposes. Most are registered under the Companies Act as nonprofit companies, which means that they issue no stock and have no "owners," but they are subject to taxation. And a few are registered as for-profit businesses, owned by shareholders and, of course, subject to tax.

We certainly had no master plan in mind as we created our network of companies, piece by piece, over two decades. Instead, we simply selected an organizational structure for each company at the time we launched it, based on what seemed to be the most practical approach to helping the poor. The result is what now looks like an unrelated patchwork of companies. But what matters is that each of the pieces should work well in support of the larger mission.

Looking back, I can see a common pattern in the founding of the various Grameen companies. Some initiatives were taken because we saw a sustained common problem among the poor, such as the lack of health care. Research studies told us that one major reason for borrowers not being able to overcome poverty is chronic diseases in the family. Some families spend most of their income treating the sick. We saw how ineffective or nonfunctional the government-run healthcare system was. As a result, the poor spent a significant part of their income on village healers and quacks whose treatments were not only worthless, but actually harmful to the patients.

First we tried to address this problem within our existing framework. We created awareness campaigns—for example, encouraging the growing of vegetables to fight vitamin A deficiency and the related disease of night blindness among children—as part of the Sixteen Decisions. We took many piecemeal initiatives before we created health centers through Grameen Kalyan. Even now we have several programs running simultaneously, trying to find which format works better. It's a good example of how we work through experimentation.

We work out the details of each project through continuous discussion with field-level staff and the intended beneficiaries. We start with a tentative structure and work procedure, then gradually adjust them as we go along. Sometimes we abandon the whole structure if we see that it is not working. We design a new structure and try again.

The process of exploring ideas and transforming them into viable businesses is an ongoing one that is continuing to this day. For example, in recent months, our world-famous telephone lady business has declined very quickly. This was expected, but we did not expect it to happen so fast. Competition among cell phone operators in Bangladesh is so intense that the prices have come down greatly. Now there are 32 million cell phone subscribers in the county, one for every five people. This means that not many people need to go to the telephone lady any more to make a phone call. So we are trying out new business models for the telephone ladies. We are helping them to get into the pre-paid service market by making them agents of Grameen Phone to accept pre-payments for airtime. We are also getting them involved in providing Internet access and other services.

In September 2007, we signed a memorandum of understanding between Intel and Grameen Solutions to set up a WiMax infrastructure in Bangladesh, to introduce classmate PCs to high schools in Bangladesh and to bring advanced information technology to education and health services. This may lead us into a variety of businesses, particularly benefiting the poor.

A sense of constant ferment and creativity is one of the exciting things about working in the Grameen environment.

However, for the purposes of this book, the most important thing to note about the Grameen family of companies is the fact that they represent a historic stepping stone toward the concept of social business. As we look at the story behind each of these companies, we can see the gradual emergence of the social-business concept: a self-sustaining company that sells goods or services and repays its owners for the money they invest, but whose primary purpose is to serve society and improve the lot of the poor. Many of them have the legal shape of nonprofit organizations, but we have gradually tried to steer them toward operating as business enterprises, adopting business principles, rather than operating as typical nonprofit enterprises. This has brought them closer and closer to the concept of social business, encouraging us to move into the business world with social objectives.

I won't walk you through the stories of all the Grameen businesses, but just a few that illustrate the range of activities in which we are currently involved.

Spreading the Word about Microcredit: Grameen Trust

By the late 1980s, Grameen Bank had successfully demonstrated the viability of microcredit as a business proposition and, more importantly, as a means of improving the lives of the poor. As a result, many people in the development community around the world wanted to emulate Grameen Bank by launching microcredit programs of their own. A steady stream of visitors began to appear on our doorstep in Bangladesh, asking for advice, guidance, and help.

Because we believe so strongly in the power of microcredit as a tool for helping the poor, we were glad to offer our time to others interested in promoting the concept. But eventually the amount of energy demanded became a serious distraction from our primary mission, which is to serve the poor people of Bangladesh. So in 1989 we founded Grameen Trust, a nonprofit organization whose mission is to promote microcredit around the world.

Grameen Trust provides many kinds of assistance of microfinance institutions (MFIs) that seek our help. We've developed training programs for staff and managers of MFIs, workshops that facilitate the sharing of ideas and experiences among MFI leaders from around the world, and dialogue programs for institutions and individuals eager to learn how microcredit works. Grameen Trust experts also provide consulting, evaluation, monitoring, and other forms of technical assistance to MFIs.

In the early 1990s, Grameen Trust moved into a different area by becoming a wholesaler of donor funds to MFIs that are too small to arrange their own funding. It was a concept I'd been considering for quite some time, having recognized the fact that many worthy microcredit institutions were withering on the vine for lack of funding. But Grameen Trust didn't have the money to provide this kind of support, until a fortuitous encounter at a lecture in Chicago led to a generous grant from the MacArthur Foundation, one of the world's most innovative donor organizations. Encouraged by the support from MacArthur, additional grants were soon forthcoming from the World Bank, the Rockefeller Foundation, USAID, and several other government and international agencies.

Many microfinance institutions around the world owe their start to seed money from Grameen Trust. Today the Trust works with 138 MFI projects in thirty-seven countries, providing funding, training, and many other kinds of support. Over the years, the Trust has provided funding totaling $21.82 million.

The greatest degree of Grameen Trust involvement takes place with what we call our Build-Operate-Transfer (BOT) program. When a sponsor feels the need for rapid implementation of a microcredit program in an area where many poor people are in dire immediate need, or when many doubts are being expressed about whether microcredit can work in a particular country or location, Grameen Trust will move in with its own team from Bangladesh to launch the project. Grameen Trust sets up the microfinance program right in the target country, manages it to the point of sustainability, and trains local people to take over control of the program. It's a kind of "turnkey system" for creating a ready-to-operate Grameen-style program. Once the program is up and running, and reaches the sustainable level, which usually takes around three to five years, Grameen Trust either leaves or retains ownership of the program, depending on the wishes of the donor.

Grameen Trust has implemented or is in the process of implementing BOT projects in Myanmar, Turkey, Zambia, Kosovo, Costa
Rica, Guatemala, and Indonesia. They vary greatly in size, from
94,000 members in Myanmar, where we started the program in
1997, to just 1,000 in our Indonesia project, started in 2006. Many
more are in the development stage.

Revitalizing an Age-Old Craft:
Grameen Uddog and Grameen Shamogree

Bangladesh has a long history of creating beautiful textiles. For centuries, hand-woven fabrics from Bangladesh were much in demand
around the world. But once the industrial revolution launched a
mechanized textile industry in England, the market for fabrics from
South Asia gradually disappeared. Making matters worse, the British
government actually forbade the local manufacture of textiles in
the Indian subcontinent, even enforcing the ban by chopping off the
thumbs of weavers who dared to violate it. You probably recall the
famous pictures of Mahatma Gandhi sitting at a spinning wheel during his campaign for Indian independence: For Gandhi, local self-
sufficiency was both an economic necessity and a symbol of the
proud cultural heritage of the people of the region.

Today, the Bangladeshi textile industry faces some basic challenges. We have millions of small local weavers who use hand looms
to create beautiful fabrics, especially all-cotton textiles in a variety of
colors and patterns. But marketing such materials is difficult, especially when large clothing manufacturers are interested in purchasing
thousands of yards of fabric made to uniform specifications. So in
1993, we created Grameen Uddog (Grameen Enterprise), to help the
local weavers bring to the international markets a new, uniform line
of fabrics. We gave it a brand name: Grameen Check. Three years
later, we founded a sister company, Grameen Shamogree (Grameen
Products), to focus on local sales of Grameen Check garments.

When we launched the Grameen Check businesses, our initial
hope was both to promote the hand-loom industry and to reduce imports of fabric from our neighbor India, where mechanized weaving
in vast quantities is the norm. We've succeeded at the former objec-

tive—the hand-loom weavers of Bangladesh now have a much bigger market than before. But we've been less successful at the latter, since Indian fabrics are generally cheaper than the hand-loomed goods. Bangladeshi weavers must import most of their raw materials, including cotton thread and dyes, from India, which naturally makes Bangladeshi production costs higher.

Today, the export of Grameen Check products is almost dormant, but Grameen Shamogree is doing very well in the domestic market. Young Bangladeshis take great pride in wearing shirts, saris, and other garments made in traditional patterns with cloth produced by local hand-loom weavers. I have turned myself into a full-time fashion model for Grameen Check, wearing tunics of the fabric all the time, as you'll notice when an appearance or meeting in which I participate is covered in the press: The newspaper photos typically show me as the only person in a colorful checked garment amid a sea of gray or navy blue suits. (I can certify that Grameen Check garments are very comfortable!) Because of the new attention, the local hand-loom industry is doing well, and a number of competitors to Grameen Check have emerged, each producing and marketing their own lines of attractive Bangladeshi-made clothing. The street in Dhaka where Grameen Bank's head office is located is lined with shops and boutiques displaying various competing brands of colorful Bangladeshi cotton garments.

Promoting Entrepreneurship: Grameen Fund and Grameen Byabosa Bikash

In a sense, Grameen Bank is a giant seedbed for entrepreneurship. The vast majority of the loans we make go to support small businesses of every imaginable kind in the villages and farmlands of Bangladesh. One of the significant social impacts of the microcredit movement has been the realization that the key to alleviating poverty is often *not* the creation of "jobs"—that is, salaried work for large corporate employers—but rather the encouragement of self-employment for all individuals, particularly women, who create goods and services and market them on a local level. Millions of such small-scale entrepreneurs are now active throughout Bangladesh, lifting themselves, their families, and their communities out of poverty—and many owe their start to Grameen Bank.

Grameen Fund takes the same philosophy to a higher level. A venture capital fund, it exists to invest in start-ups and business experimentation of various kinds, both within the Grameen family of businesses and by outside individuals and organizations with innovative, entrepreneurial ideas.

The program originated in the late 1980s as a donor-funded initiative within Grameen Bank that was dubbed SIDE (Study, Innovation, Development, Experimentation). In a few years, SIDE had grown so big that it was spun off as a separate venture capital fund, especially designed to focus on projects that bring new technology that encourages economic development in Bangladesh.

Today, Grameen Fund provides several kinds of financial assistance to new business ventures, many of which are themselves members of the Grameen family of companies. These include loan financing, bridge and mezzanine financing, management buyouts of promising but troubled companies, and corporate guarantees for borrowing by growth-oriented enterprises. However, the most common type of financing provided by Grameen Fund is equity financing, in which the Fund generally prefers to take on 51 percent of the total equity in the company. This gives us a degree of control that allows the Fund to ensure that the financed company is well managed, efficient, and faithful to its original business concept and plan.

Among the companies financed by Grameen Fund are Grameen Knitwear, which produces knitted fabrics and garments for export; Grameen Bitek, a company that was originally launched by a young physics professor that made backup power equipment and surge protectors and now markets many kinds of technological products, including elevators; and Gram Bangla Autovan, which manufactures three-wheel vehicles with highly efficient four-stroke engines of the kind that are popularly used for taxis on the streets of Dhaka and throughout Bangladesh.

Another company that helps to encourage entrepreneurship in Bangladesh is Grameen Byabosa Bikash (GBB, Grameen Business Promotion Company), whose role is to provide loan guarantees for enterprises larger than those served by the typical small Grameen Bank loan. Whereas normal Grameen Bank loans are in amounts like $100 to $300, these loans may range as high as $10,000 or more. A borrower seeking a large loan from Grameen is referred to GBB. Once GBB approves the application, the Grameen branch manager will be willing to extend the loan. (Otherwise he would probably be unable to take on such a large risk, since a default could endanger the overall strength of the branch's loan portfolio.)

Thus, GBB has a role somewhat similar to the one played by the Small Business Administration in the United States, which also provides loan guarantees for small-scale entrepreneurs. GBB also provides some technical and training assistance, especially for rural entrepreneurs who need guidance on modernizing their poultry and dairy businesses.

As you can see, these Grameen organizations are designed to provide part of the business infrastructure that is needed to let people grow out of poverty. Out of these experiments grew the concept of social business—an idea that can help foster hundreds of individual companies that will promote economic growth while directly benefiting those who are most in need.

Improving Rural Livelihoods: Grameen Fisheries and Livestock

One of the very first ventures outside of microcredit in which Grameen Bank became involved was the management of fish farms, mostly in northern and western districts of Bangladesh. These farms had a curious history. Originally dug for the kings of the Pal dynasty over a thousand years ago and now owned by the government, the ponds, almost a thousand in number, had remained unutilized until 1977, when they came under a development project funded by a British aid agency.

The concept was a good one: Fish is a popular food in Bangladeshi culture, and well-managed local fish ponds could provide an excellent source of protein for Bangladeshi villagers. But the economic results were poor, largely due to corruption: Officials collaborating with local politicians, it seemed, had managed to siphon off most of the benefits from the ponds while neglecting their upkeep, using pond development as an excuse for personal gain. Despite big investments, many of the ponds had remained silted over, production did not get off the ground, and, in disgust, the British funders were threatening to cut off their assistance.

To avoid such an outcome, in 1986 the permanent secretary of the government fisheries ministry, called on Grameen Bank for help. Although we had no experience with managing fish ponds, he offered to turn them over to us. Despite our initial hesitation, he persuaded us to accept the offer, hoping we could find a way to turn the ponds into economic assets for their communities.

It took time for us to work out the problems with the fish ponds. Serious flooding in 1987 hampered our work, some of the local people resisted our efforts to establish management of the fisheries, and some of our offices were even burned down by vested interests that identified themselves as ultra-left-wing political groups.

Gradually, however, we reached an understanding with the local people. Today, we've organized over 3,000 poor people into groups who raise fish and work to maintain the ponds. These members receive a share of the gross income, and many have seen their family incomes increase significantly. Fresh-water shrimp have been added to the ponds, and the Joysagor fish farm has been expanded to include plant nurseries, which produce a large variety of saplings for planting and reforestation efforts around the region. Now we are expanding our fisheries program by developing new fish ponds in the Jamuna Borrow-Pits area. These new ponds are expected to help support about a thousand poor women.

Five years ago, a livestock program was added, which provides training, vaccination, veterinary care, and other support services to help poor women become dairy farmers and assist others to improve and expand existing dairy operations. They have become suppliers of milk to the Grameen Danone yogurt plant. Today, both programs are administered by a not-for-profit organization called the Grameen Motsho O Pashusampad (Fisheries and Livestock) Foundation.

Our experience with the fisheries and livestock programs has helped us to formulate the social-business concept in a very direct fashion. They illustrate how companies that produce useful goods for sale at market prices can be run by local people for the benefit of the communities in which they live.

Opening Opportunities for
Young Minds: Grameen Shikkha

Supporting education has always been part of the Grameen social philosophy. It began on the most basic level—with the fact that the vast majority of the women borrowers who become Grameen members are illiterate. Lacking the ability to read and write is just one of the many barriers that help keep the poor powerless and unable to help themselves. So we at Grameen Bank decided to try to do something about it, starting with something very simple: encouraging all our borrowers to learn to sign their names.

This goal is not as modest as it might sound. Many adults who have lived all their lives without knowing how to read or write shy away from trying to overcome their illiteracy. They find the effort and the help they must receive embarrassing, even humiliating. Helping would-be borrowers to get over this hurdle calls for enormous tact, sympathy, and compassion on the part of Grameen staff members. They often must spend hours working patiently with a single client, slowly teaching her the rudiments of holding a pen and making those magical marks that symbolize her unique identity.

But this painstaking process has proven to be tremendously valuable to our borrowers. It often represents the first step on a journey to full literacy, which brings with it the ability to interact with the world in a far richer way than she could ever do before. It also creates a precious sense of closeness between the borrower and the staff member who is her teacher, which makes it easier for the new Grameen member to turn to the staff member when economic, social, or family problems arise.

Most important, learning to write her name—a name that she formerly may not even have known precisely—also produces an enormous sense of pride in the newly empowered borrower. She has overcome a hurdle that she once considered insurmountable. And her presence and impact on the world are multiplied in a remarkable way. When she scribbles a pattern of lines on a piece of paper and somebody looks at it and says, "Hamida, how are you?" she gets the thrill of her life. "They know me from my signature!" She cannot get over her amazement. A new world has been opened up for her, and she is ready to take other great leaps into self-sufficiency.

Grameen Shikkha (Grameen Education), a separate enterprise, was created to build on this initial effort. It started with simple educational services for the children of our borrowers. This began at the grass roots, with individual branch and center managers who noted that many of their borrowers had small children in tow when they arrived for their weekly meeting. Soon someone suggested, "Let's invite the young ones to gather in the center house once a week, just the way their mothers do. We can give them some activities that will help them prepare for regular schooling. We'll teach them to read the alphabet, to count, and to learn a few rhymes." They invited a young girl from the village to help the children with these simple lessons. The idea spread from one center to another, and soon it became part of the Grameen system.

It's wonderful to see the impact that this simple step has on the psychology of children. Participating in these preschool activities helps them develop the self-confidence and courage that will enable them to go to school willingly, happily, and without embarrassment. Many a Grameen child who was nervous about his or her first day of classes has ended up saying, "Oh, I know how to read those letters and sing those songs! I even know more than the other kids! I'm going to *like* going to school!"

Today, Grameen Shikkha is focusing on an idea it originated in 2003, which is called the Scholarship Management Program, to help poor families in Bangladesh overcome the difficult economic barriers that prevent many young children from attending school.

The effects of poverty can be very insidious. Public schools in Bangladesh are available even in the countryside, tuition is not charged, and books are free. But this doesn't mean that money is not a barrier to education. Paper, pens, pencils, and other supplies cost money. So does a school uniform. Even more important, sending a child off to school for several hours a day has a hidden cost in the income-generating potential that must be forgone. A small child can help make money for the family in many ways—fetching water from the local stream or well, carting supplies around the farm. When even a few cents makes a meaningful difference in the income of a family, a mother and father must think carefully before making the sacrifice of committing a child to continued education.

Grameen Shikkha's Scholarship Management Program combats this problem through an ingenious revolving fund. Here's how it works: A donor interested in supporting the program makes a contribution, with the minimum amount being 50,000 taka, about $750 (U.S.). The money is invested in a time deposit, and a guaranteed 6 percent annual income from that money goes to the child as a scholarship to fund her upkeep while she is in school. This gives the schoolchild financial value to the family and ensures that they are not tempted to withdraw her to work. A contribution of $1,000 produces a $60 annual scholarship, which is enough to keep a child in primary school; it takes $2,000 to support a child in secondary school or $3,000 for a student in college. Depending on instructions from the sponsor, the same student may keep receiving the scholarship until she finishes her education, at which time a new student may be chosen to begin the cycle again.

The donor can specify what kind of recipient is targeted: a boy or girl, an orphan, a child from one of the poorest families or from a particular district or village. The scholarship can even be dedicated in the name of a particular person or cause: For example, the sponsor can name it after a beloved friend or relative. The sponsor receives a report each year on the progress of his or her child. The sponsor also has a choice to terminate his scholarship, if he wants to, and withdraw his money, or allow it to continue perpetually, year after year.

By mid-2007, the Scholarship Management Program was assisting 1,200 students through help from 130 sponsors. Grameen Shikkha is working hard to expand the program, with a target of financing 10,000 scholarships each year by 2012, requiring a deposit of $10 million. So far, Grameen Shikkha has mobilized $1.2 million—a little less than $9 million to go.

Linking Every Village to the World:
Grameen Telecom and Grameen Phone

As everyone knows, new forms of information technology (IT) are quickly changing the world, creating a distanceless, borderless world of instantaneous communications. As time passes, the new IT is becoming less and less costly, creating enormous opportunities to put it to work on behalf of the poor. If the remote villages of Bangladesh can be linked electronically to the marketplaces of the world, the new economic opportunities created for the poor will be tremendous.

In 1996, we took a first step toward bringing the new IT to the poor of Bangladesh. In partnership with three outside companies—Telenor of Norway, Marubeni of Japan, and New York-based Gonofone Development Company—we created a mobile phone company to extend telephone service all over Bangladesh. We called this new enterprise Grameen Phone. At the time of its founding, 35 percent of Grameen Phone was owned by Grameen Telecom of Bangladesh, a nonprofit company we created specifically for this purpose. Today, ownership of Grameen Phone resides with just two companies: Telenor (62 percent) and Grameen Telecom (38 percent).

Back in 1996, Grameen Phone was one of four companies licensed by the government to provide cell phone service in Bangladesh. Initially, the experts were dubious about the potential market. Telenor, in fact, hired a business consultant based in the United Kingdom to estimate the size of the mobile phone market in Bangladesh. Using the historic growth rate in sales of color televisions as a benchmark, the consultant predicted that there would be 250,000 cell phones in use in Bangladesh by 2005.

I am no expert on technology trends, but even I knew that number was far too low. Just from living in Bangladesh I knew how desperate people were to have access to one another and to the outside world. At the time, our country had the lowest rate of telephone service penetration in the world, with only 400,000 phones for 120 million people. With no land-line service in most of the 80,000 villages of Bangladesh, cell-phone technology was made to order to bring the country into the age of electronic communication. I told Telenor to disregard the consultant's prediction and prepare for massive demand. (As it turned out, the number of cell phones in Bangladesh in 2005 was eight million, thirty-two times the consultant's prediction.) By the middle of 2007, Grameen Phone had become the largest tax-generating company in Bangladesh, with over sixteen million subscribers.

Most important from my perspective, cell-phone technology became an incredible tool of empowerment for Grameen borrowers and for the poor of Bangladesh in general. Seeing the potential synergy between microcredit and the new IT, we set up a program through Grameen Telecom that provided loans from Grameen Bank to poor women who wanted to buy mobile phones. Here was a new growth industry for Bangladesh: the spread of "telephone ladies" who represented their villages' sole lifeline to the outside world. Armed with a simple cell phone, the telephone lady could sell phone service, a few minutes at a time, to anyone in the village who needed to make a connection with a friend, family member, or business associate.

As mentioned earlier, the business of the telephone ladies has declined sharply since 2005. We are trying to build alternative businesses, such as providing Internet services through cell phones. A new business that is emerging for the telephone ladies is to accept payment from subscribers of Grameen Phone for pre-paid phone service. They earn commissions for this service.

Most people in the developed world have long taken telephone service for granted. Thus, it may be difficult for them to fully appreciate the revolutionary impact of cell-phone service on the typical Bangladeshi villager.

Imagine being a farmer in a remote village. Before the advent of the cell phone, you had no way of knowing what price was being paid for crops on the market in Dhaka or any other big city. There was no way to talk with suppliers of tools or equipment, such as a new irrigation pump, to compare prices or negotiate a delivery date. Your only choice was to walk or ride to the nearest marketplace, which might be miles away, and accept whatever price you were offered there, with no questions asked.

Today, the farmer with access to a cell phone can comparison shop and check fluctuating market prices with a few quick calls, putting himself in a far better position to demand a fair deal from the local merchant or middleman. Information is power, and the cell-phone revolution is finally putting a little of that power in the hands of the rural poor.

From the very start, my intention was to convert Grameen Phone into a social business by giving the poor the majority of shares in the company. Grameen Telecom was created to manage the shares of the poor people. But now I face a hurdle: Telenor refuses to sell the shares. Even as we were enjoying the festivities of the Nobel Peace Prize events, the Norwegian press was abuzz with reports about a conflict between Telenor and Grameen Telecom regarding a memorandum they'd signed when forming Grameen Phone. A commitment was made in that memorandum, and also in the shareholders' agreement, that six years after the company came into existence, Telenor would reduce its share below 35 percent, selling its shares to Grameen Telecom to make it majority shareholder of the company. Now Telenor is refusing to honor the signed agreement, saying it is legally unenforceable. Grameen Telecom's position is that Telenor should live up to its agreement.

I was very happy to see that the press and the people of Norway were overwhelmingly sympathetic to Grameen's position. Today negotiations to resolve the conflict are continuing. I hope that someday soon our dream of making Grameen Phone a social business will come true.

Renewable Energy for Rural Bangladesh: Grameen Shakti

If access to modern information technology is crucial to economic empowerment, so is access to energy—especially electrical power. But this is something that the majority of Bangladeshis don't have. Seventy percent of the population of Bangladesh is off the grid, and even in places where electrical service exists, it is very unreliable. Here is an area that is crying out for effective action to bring the benefits of modern technology to all the people.

We thought long and hard about what we could do to make affordable power accessible to the people of Bangladesh. Extending the national grid to all of the remote villages of the country would be a gigantic job and very expensive. Furthermore, such a solution would not be particularly green. In a world where supplies of fossil fuels are dwindling and where climate change caused by carbon emissions is a growing threat, we wanted to find an energy source that would serve the economic needs of our people without creating worse problems than it solves. After experimenting with wind turbines and other technologies, we decided that solar power was an option that worked well.

Grameen Shakti (Grameen Energy), founded in 1996, is working to bring this technology to the people of Bangladesh. One of the world's largest market-based suppliers of solar technology, Grameen

Shakti has installed 100,000 solar panel systems in homes throughout the country, with another 3,500 systems being added every month. It has an ambitious plan to install one million solar home systems by 2012.

Grameen Shakti's solar home systems are available to all villagers, rich or poor. Customers like the company's easy payment system— they can pay in easy monthly installments over two to three years. Shakti's staff members visit every month to collect the installment and do maintenance work on the solar unit. The size of the system varies depending on the resources of the homeowner. A simple fifty-watt unit consisting of a small roof panel and a converter unit will typically produce enough energy to power four light bulbs for four hours a night—enough to enable the children to do their homework and permit the parents to catch up with the world news via radio or television. Some ingenious rural people will buy a single solar unit then string wires from their home to neighboring houses or shops, so that the power generated can be shared. In this way, a small income is generated for the owner of the unit, and the benefits of electricity are spread to several families.

Grameen Shakti is reaching out to the poor by creating business and work opportunities for them. Solar-powered, fee-charging community TV kiosks and mobile-phone units have sprung up as income-generating enterprises. Women engineers are teaching rural women how to maintain and service solar energy equipment through twenty Grameen Technology Centers around the country. These Grameen Shakti Certified Technicians sign up clients to provide maintenance services after the Grameen Shakti maintenance contract expires. They are also hired by Grameen Shakti Technology Centers to work at the solar accessory production units.

Solar energy isn't the only field in which Grameen Shakti is active. Another is biogas technology—a renewable form of energy that takes advantage of such ubiquitous sources as cow dung, poultry droppings, and other common waste products. Grameen Shakti uses a simple bio-gas plant design that converts these wastes into methane gas that can be used as a fuel for cooking and even, with the right equipment, turned into electricity. By mid–2007, over 1,300 of these plants have already been installed, with another 150 going into operation every month.

Grameen Shakti's newest program sells improved, highly efficient cooking stoves through Shakti-trained rural youths.

Bringing Health Care to the Poor: Grameen Kalyan and Grameen Health Care Services

The mission of Grameen Kalyan (Grameen Welfare) is to provide good-quality, affordable health care for Grameen Bank members and other villagers. Experience has shown than the single greatest problem facing the poor of Bangladesh—and often anchoring them in poverty, despite their best efforts—is the exorbitant cost of health care, especially when serious illness strikes. Grameen Kalyan is our effort to remedy this problem.

The government-run health-care system in Bangladesh is far less effective than it should be. Theoretically, government health care is universal, but the reality is quite different. The government spends enormous sums in the health sector, but services hardly ever reach the people, particularly poor people. Many villagers rely on traditional healers with little or no education and storefront druggists selling self-prescribed medicines that may be inappropriate or even harmful.

In practice only the rich have access to health care, which they buy from expensive private clinics and hospitals. Private health insurance of the kind that many Americans rely on does not exist in Bangladesh. Most government agencies and private employers will provide their workers with small lump-sum benefits intended to cover most normal medical expenses. Private health services, which are very expensive, are growing in popularity. Many in the middle and upper classes travel to India, Thailand, or Singapore for health care. (So will the lower middle class, if they are desperate enough; some have been known to sell everything they own to pay for a trip to Kolkata, Chennai, or Mumbai in search of a cure for some serious illness.) In fact, a significant percentage of Bangladeshi travelers to India are the sick and their family members. So when we founded Grameen Kalyan in 1996, we knew we would have an uphill battle.

In the years since then, our progress has been slow but steady. Grameen Kalyan now operates thirty-three health clinics, each affiliated with a local Grameen Bank branch. Grameen Bank families within the coverage area of the clinic are entitled to health coverage for the equivalent of around $2 per family per year. Non-Grameen families are served at a cost of around $2.50 per year, while beggars receive health care absolutely free. In total, around half a million people are covered under the insurance program, and currently over a quarter million patient consultations take place every year. Another 1.5 million women receive home-care services from female health assistants employed by Grameen Kalyan.

The service provided by the clinics is basic but quite reliable. Each clinic has a doctor on staff and a team of paramedics and assistants who can answer routine questions, perform simple tests, and conduct health education programs in the community. The clinics have labs where basic tests can be run, and specialized physicians visit on a rotating schedule to take care of more serious problems; for example, a cataract expert visits the clinics periodically to perform eyesight-restoring surgery. In most cases, life-threatening, unusual, or complex medical problems will be referred to the nearest government-run hospital.

Our greatest challenge in maintaining and expanding the services of Grameen Kalyan is attracting and retaining enough doctors. Grameen Kalyan offers a good salary to doctors by Bangladeshi standards, but still it cannot retain them. A more serious issue than salary is the relative isolation of village life. Many young medical graduates would rather live and work in a big city than in rural Bangladesh, where life is slow and where economic, social, and cultural opportunities are scanty. The physicians who gravitate to Grameen Kalyan tend to be idealistic, high-energy people or young doctors waiting for their turn to get jobs with the government.

It's possible that one day Grameen Kalyan will have to open its own medical school to supply its staffing needs. In the meantime, we are planning to invest part of the Nobel Prize money won by Grameen Bank in Nobel Scholarships for medical students. In return for this educational support, we will ask the Nobel Scholars to commit to spending a certain number of years working for Grameen Kalyan.

One of my central interests in the health-care field is pregnancy care. Maternal and infant mortality in Bangladesh, though greatly improved in recent years, still remains high. Ninety-six percent of babies are born at home to mothers who usually received little or no prenatal care. Lack of access to a physician is part of the problem, but cultural factors also play a role. In our conservative society, pregnancy is not discussed openly. Sometimes it is not even acknowledged—a woman will just suddenly have a baby, as if out of the blue! (Without the modest, multi-layered clothing that Bangladeshi women wear, this would scarcely be possible.)

Furthermore, driven by the same innate conservatism, many women simply refuse to talk about private matters with a male doctor—in fact, some openly say they would rather die. For this reason, too, many women avoid seeking medical care, even when they are pregnant. It would help matters if we could staff our clinics with plenty of female physicians. Unfortunately, women doctors are even harder to recruit than males. Bangladesh produces fewer female medical graduates than males, and many women have a cultural bias toward jobs that keep them in the cities, close to their relatives. For them, life in a remote village would mean separation from their families.

In place of obstetricians, many of the villages are served by informal midwives—really just local women with little or no training, who have assisted at a number of births and therefore are considered knowledgeable by the other villagers. The government has provided these midwives with some formal training, but their skill level is still too low. As a result of all these factors, pregnancy care is generally inadequate. Complications are often not spotted early, and needless deaths are the result.

In an effort to alleviate this problem, Grameen Kalyan's staffers came up with the idea of building specialized childbirth kiosks alongside the health clinics. Prenatal and postnatal exams and checkups can be conducted in these kiosks, and women in labor can also be cared for throughout their delivery. Some of these kiosks are already in place, staffed by the same professionals as the clinics themselves. Our hope is that the existence of the kiosks will raise the visibility of childbirth at a time when medical care is essential, as well as providing modest women with a woman-oriented place where they will feel safe.

Given the extremely low cost of health care at the Grameen Kalyan clinics, you might assume that the operation is being run on a purely charitable basis. Not so. Our goal is to make Grameen Kalyan completely self-sufficient and, ultimately, able to finance its own expansion. Although the clinics vary considerably in the level of income their generate, the program as a whole is quite strong financially. Grameen Kalyan currently recovers about 90 percent of its costs, and we believe that the hundred-percent level will be within reach in a couple of years.

The two latest additions to the list of Grameen companies are Grameen Healthcare Trust and Grameen Health Care Services, Ltd. Grameen Healthcare Trust (GHT) is a not-for-profit company. It receives donor funds and invests primarily in social businesses. Grameen Health Care Services, Ltd. (GHS) has been created as a social business. One of its first programs is to set up eyecare hospitals, each capable of 10,000 cataract operations per year, for both poor and non-poor patients. The first eyecare hospital is under construction and will be opened during 2007. Doctors and support staff are under training in Aravind Eye Hospital in Madurai, India, a world-famous eye hospital set up by the late Dr. Govindappa Venkataswamy, popularly know as Dr. V.

This first eyecare hospital, named the Grameen Green Children Eye Hospital, is wholly owned by GHT. As a social business, GHT will recover its investment money from the hospital, but will not receive any dividend.

In the future, more eyecare hospitals will be set up at different locations in rural Bangladesh for cataract operations, alleviating a health problem that afflicts hundreds of thousands of people in Bangladesh. Investors are already in place for three more hospitals.

The business plan for these hospitals has been carefully worked out. Pricing will be done on the "Robin Hood" principle. Regular patients will pay the market fees, while the poor will pay only a token fee. If our calculations are right—and if we're able to provide first-class eyecare and thereby attract enough paying patients—the hospitals should be self-supporting and able to expand their service offerings indefinitely.

I'm quite excited about the potential for Grameen Health Care Services, and eager to see the results of this experiment in social business. It's an important program to watch because of the immense need for better and more affordable health care all around the world.

Of course, developing countries like Bangladesh, in regions through-out Asia, Africa, and Latin America, have a desperate need for med-ical care for the poor. But some nations of the developed world, including the United States, have health-care problems that are al-most equally serious.

For example, the forty-seven million people in the United States who are not currently covered by health insurance could be a fertile market to be served by well-designed, innovative social businesses. One could even argue that *only* social business has the potential to solve the entrenched problems of health care in the United States, since this is the only organizational structure that eliminates the enor-mous economic drain represented by corporate profit-taking while re-taining the beneficial personal and business incentives created by competition in the marketplace. Freed from the pressure to compete for funding on Wall Street, a social business that offered health insur-ance to the poor would not feel driven to drop the sick or elderly from its rolls, or to deny coverage for costly medical treatments, in order to boost its profit margins. Instead, its mission would be to focus on formerly unreached customers while generating sufficient income simply to cover its expenses.

Social Business:
A New Economic Frontier

This is not a complete roster of all the Grameen companies—just some of the highlights from a large and still-growing list. Some of the companies have already been remarkably successful in achieving their social goals; others are still working toward achieving their goals. Some have proven to be financially successful; others are still searching for the path to financial self-sufficiency. Some are highly active and rapidly expanding their operations; some (such as Gra-meen Information Highway Ltd. and Grameen Star Education) are largely dormant. In this sense, the Grameen family of companies is much like many other corporate networks. Even for top companies, not every venture is equally successful.

However, every company we've started has been a success in one way: Each has provided a learning experience that has helped to shape the concept of social business. When we've faltered, it has usually been because we misgauged the market or failed to structure the business so it could be self-sufficient. When we've succeeded, it has been because we created a business design that met genuine market needs. These are crucial considerations in shaping the designs of the social businesses of the future.

What I think is special about the Grameen family of companies is the spirit of innovation and experimentation that animates it. We are constantly looking for new ideas for businesses that can benefit the world, especially the poor, and we aren't afraid to try something that no one has ever tried before. (Grameen Bank itself is probably the best example of this spirit.) If our initial business plan succeeds, that's wonderful. If not, we make changes and try again. We have faith that, eventually, we will find a formula that will work.

The Grameen companies represent a first, evolving sketch of the world of social business, and a model for what I hope will be many thousands of companies serving diverse social needs the world over.

Social business is the missing piece of the capitalist system. Introduction of it into the system may save the system by empowering it to address the overwhelming global concerns that now remain outside of mainstream business thinking. Thus, generating ideas for social business is the most important immediate challenge for today's business thinkers. Once the ideas are circulating, it is only a matter of time before the best of them are translated into concrete actions for the betterment of humankind.

5

The Battle against Poverty:
Bangladesh and Beyond

Three decades back, I began with a small problem in a small village. I was shocked by the harshness of the problem of moneylending, but I was excited by the simplicity of the solution. My solution worked. It led me to the attempt to open the door of the banks for the poor. Since I could not do it, I came up with another kind of banking. It helped millions of women. But that was only through credit—microcredit. There are many other areas where the poor needed help. I tried to formulate many new institutions and new strategies to help the poor—through information technology, in education, health, agriculture, livestock, textile, renewable energy, marketing, and other activities. I saw how the concept of business could be reformulated simply by disconnecting the investors from the expectation of financially gaining from their investment. This is how the concept of social business was born.

I believe that social business has the potential to lift the struggle to eliminate poverty to a new level. Social business can be a very powerful format for the private sector, public sector, philanthropists, donors, NGOs, faith groups, or anybody else. How can the idea of social business be effective in the struggle against poverty, in overcoming the digital divide, in solving the crisis of climate change? These questions form an important part of the context in which the idea of social business should be considered.

Ever since its founding, Bangladesh has been known as one of the world's poorest countries. In the early 1970s, Henry Kissinger, at the time head of the National Security Council under President Richard Nixon, dismissed Bangladesh as an "international basket case." In the decades since then, our history has been an ongoing battle against some of the world's most challenging living conditions— extreme overcrowding, annual floods, deforestation, erosion, and soil depletion—often exacerbated by unpredictable natural calamities, including cyclones, tornadoes, and tidal surges.

Today, a new concern has been added to the litany: the danger of widespread inundation of our low-lying lands caused by the rising sea levels associated with global warming. No wonder so many people around the world think of Bangladesh—on the rare occasions when they do at all—as a country of disasters.

What's wrong with Bangladesh? Is the country cursed to remain always just one step away from utter destruction, each new disaster wiping out whatever resources our people have accumulated since the last cataclysm?

I don't think we can blame fate, nature, or God for our troubles. The real problem in Bangladesh is not the natural disasters. It is the widespread poverty, which is a man-made phenomenon. Cyclones, floods, and tidal surges occur in other countries. In most, they do not cause human misery of the magnitude we see in Bangladesh. The reason is that, in these countries, the people are rich enough to build protective systems and strong embankments. (Rivers in Canada, England, and France have tidal surges similar to those in Bangladesh, but dredging and causeway construction have minimized their effects and the threat to human life.) Furthermore, poverty and overcrowding have pushed the countless poor in Bangladesh to seek their livelihoods in more and more unsafe areas of the country, though they lack the capacity to organize even minimal safety measures for themselves.

Thus, poverty doesn't only condemn humans to lives of difficulty and unhappiness; it can expose them to life-threatening dangers. Because poverty denies people any semblance of control over their destiny, it is the ultimate denial of human rights. When freedom of speech or religion is violated in this country or that, global protests are often mobilized in response. Yet when poverty violates the human rights of half the world's population, most of us turn our heads away and get on with our lives.

For the same reason, poverty is perhaps the most serious threat to world peace, even more dangerous than terrorism, religious fundamentalism, ethnic hatred, political rivalries, or any of the other forces that are often cited as promoting violence and war. Poverty leads to hopelessness, which provokes people to desperate acts. Those with practically nothing have no good reason to refrain from violence, since even acts with only a small chance of improving their conditions seem better than doing nothing and accepting their fate with passivity. Poverty also creates economic refugees, leading to clashes between populations. It leads to bitter conflicts between peoples, clans, and nations over scarce resources—water, arable land, energy supplies, and any saleable commodity. Prosperous nations that trade with one another and devote their energies to economic growth rarely go to war with one another; nations whose people are brutalized by poverty find it easy to resort to war.

This is why it was appropriate that the Nobel committee in 2006 chose to award Grameen Bank, not the Nobel Prize for Economics, but the Nobel Prize for Peace. By lifting people out of poverty, microcredit is a long-term force for peace. And Bangladesh is a vivid example of what it can do.

Bangladesh today is a living laboratory—one of the world's poorest countries that is gradually being transformed by innovative social and business thinking. Over the past two decades, conditions among the poor people of Bangladesh have steadily improved. Statistics tell part of the story:*

- The poverty rate (as measured by international aid organizations such as the World Bank) has fallen from an estimated 74 percent in 1973–74 to 57 percent in 1991–92, to 49 percent in 2000, and then to 40 percent in 2005. Though still too high, it continues to fall by around 1 percent a year, with each percentage point representing a meaningful improvement in the lives of hundreds of thousands of Bangladeshis. The country is on track to

---

* Most of the figures that follow are drawn from statistical studies conducted by the World Bank and the Asian Development Bank.

achieve the Millennium Development Goal of reducing poverty by half by 2015.

- Even more remarkably, Bangladesh's rapid economic growth has been accompanied by little increase in inequality. The commonly used Gini index of inequality has changed only from 0.30 in 1995 to 0.31 in 2005. It's also noteworthy that, since 2000, the real per-capita income of the bottom 10 percent of the population has grown at the same annual rate as that of the top 10 percent (2.8 percent).

- The sharp drop in poverty is reflected in changes in economic growth, employment patterns, and the structure of the economy. Growth of the Bangladeshi economy—at $71 billion the third largest in South Asia, after India and Pakistan—has averaged 5.5 percent since 2000 and reached 6.7 percent in 2006, compared with just 4 percent in the 1980s, while per-capita growth has increased from 1 percent in the 1980s to 3.5 percent currently. Reliance on subsistence agriculture is gradually declining: In 2005, non-farm labor surpassed agriculture as the main source of income in rural areas, and fully 50 percent of the nation's GDP is now derived from the services sector.

- Population growth—a major problem in Bangladesh, one of the most densely populated countries on earth—has fallen sharply, from an annual average of 3 percent in the 1970s to 1.5 percent in 2000—close to India's 1.4 percent and much lower than Pakistan's 2.5 percent. This slowdown means that more families have the resources to care for their children and provide them with decent opportunities for education. It also means the liberation of millions of women from an endless cycle of child-bearing and child-rearing, giving them the chance to help their families improve their standard of living through productive work.

- The decline in population growth has been driven, in large part, by improvements in health care. (When more children survive, parents feel more confident about using birth control; they no longer believe they need to bear five or six children in hopes of raising two.) During the 1990s, the percentage of Bangladeshi mothers receiving prenatal health care doubled. Partly as a result, infant mortality rates in Bangladesh fell by more than half (from 100 to 41 per 1,000 children) between 1990 and 2006, while the mortality rate for children under five is 52 per 1,000 in Bangladesh compared with 87 in India and 98 in Pakistan. In 2005, the percentage of one-year-old children—among the poorest 20 percent of households who had been fully immunized—stood at 50 percent in Bangladesh compared with 21 percent in India and 23 percent in Pakistan. Around 81 percent of children had been vaccinated against measles, compared with 58 percent in India. And while child malnutrition remains a serious problem, the percentage of children whose growth is stunted has declined from almost 70 percent in 1985–86 to 43 percent in 2004.

- Statistics for life expectancy at birth, which were static at around 56 years through the early 1990s, have begun to climb. By 2006, life expectancy was estimated at 65.4 years, and the unusual situation in which women's life expectancy was lower than men's has finally been reversed, with women now at 65.9 years and men at 64.7 years.

- Educational opportunities for children have also improved. The percentage of children completing the fifth grade has increased from 49 percent in 1990 to 74 percent in 2004. National literacy rates have increased from only 26 percent in 1981 to 34 percent in 1990 and 41 percent in 2002. The 1990s witnessed a tripling in the number of children attending secondary school. More girls now attend secondary schools than boys, a feat unmatched in South Asia and a remarkable achievement given the fact that, in the Bangladesh of the early 1990s, there were three times as many boys as girls in secondary schools.

- The quality of shelter and access to basic sanitation and telecommunication services have all improved significantly in recent years. In 2000, eighteen percent of households lived under straw roofs; by 2005, the percentage had fallen to 7 percent. A sanitation campaign has resulted in increased access to safe latrines from 54 percent in 2000 to 71 percent in 2005. The mobile-phone revolution has boosted the fraction of the population with access to telephone services from 1.8 percent in 2000 to 14.2 percent currently.

- Bangladesh's capacity to withstand natural disaster shocks has improved significantly. Following the massive floods of 1998, per-capita GDP fell sharply, but a flood of similar scale in 2004 had a negligible impact on growth. This resilience is attributable to a more diversified economy and improved emergency response capabilities, including early warning systems and cyclone shelters, throughout the country.

- Between 1980 and 2004, the Human Development Index (a widely used measurement of key standard-of-living indicators for developing nations) increased by 45 percent in Bangladesh compared to 39 percent in India and 16 percent in Sri Lanka—despite the fact that, as of 2004, per-capita GDP in India was 68 percent higher than in Bangladesh, and in Sri Lanka over 200 percent higher.

As these numbers suggest, the problems of poverty in Bangladesh, though improved, are far from being solved. Bangladesh is still one of the poorest countries in the world, with tens of millions of people living at a level barely above subsistence. But the social and economic trends are moving in the right direction.

Many Bangladeshis are feeling hopeful about the future for the first time. Now we are ready to launch ourselves on a path to achieve several crucial goals: to surpass an annual per-capita income of $1,000 (U.S.); to exceed an 8 percent growth rate in GDP (as compared to a healthy 6.7 percent currently); and to reduce the poverty level to under 25 percent. I believe that all of these goals are reachable within the next decade, provided we take the right steps.

The challenges and opportunities facing Bangladesh illustrate some important themes that many of the world's developing countries share:

- The need to think strategically about development, analyzing a country's potential role in its region and the world in search of opportunities for growth;
- The need to get past myths, stereotypes, and assumptions about poor countries and their relations to their neighbors;
- The need to find fresh, positive approaches to development that emphasize the potential strengths of a country and its people, not just their problems; and
- The need to think about how social business can address social and economic problems that are usually left to be resolved by governments.

These ideas offer hope for alleviating the worst effects of poverty both in Bangladesh and in many other poor countries around the world.

Poverty Programs That Work

For too long, people in the developed nations have taken a fatalistic attitude toward global poverty. The problem seems so big, so complicated, and so intractable that many are tempted to shrug their shoulders and give up. The truth is that there are many things that can be done, provided we are willing to entertain fresh thinking about poverty and its remedies.

Traditionally, the poor have been looked upon as a social liability. Policies and institutions have grown up with this assumption in mind. As a result, the capacity of the poor to make productive contributions on their own behalf and to benefit the entire society has rarely been recognized. Once we recognize this capacity, we can create programs that will both support and make use of the creative gifts of the poor.

Social business will play an important role in this effort. But there will also be a continuing place for anti-poverty programs sponsored by governments and NGOs. It often takes time for the self-sufficiency of a community or a nation to be developed. During this time of transition, programs that bring outside resources to help poor people are often essential, especially when dire needs such as hunger, homelessness, disease, and the effects of natural disasters are waiting to be addressed.

But not all anti-poverty programs are equal. As we all know from observation and experience, some are very effective, while others merely squander energy and money. What are some of the characteristics of effective programs to alleviate the problems of poverty?

First of all, effective anti-poverty programs must start with a clear operational definition of poverty. In order to recognize those whom the program is designed to help, they must be defined by clear decision rules that will exclude the non-poor and keep them from siphoning off resources that the poor desperately need.

Every country and every region will probably have its own definition of poverty. The poor in Bangladesh live a very different life from the poor in the United States. (Most poor people in America own a television set, for example; very few of the poor in Bangladesh even have electricity.) Some students of global development complain about the inconsistency of definitions of poverty from one place to another. But I think this is a natural result of the variations in economic level, cultural habits, and living conditions from one country to the next. Consistency may be inconvenient for scholars trying to make international comparisons, but what's most important is coming up with definitions that are of practical use for aid workers on the ground.

At Grameen Bank, we had to develop our own definition of poverty so that we would be able to measure our success in helping people rise out of poverty through microcredit. We could have used a benchmark based on money income—for example, the equivalent of one U.S. dollar or two a day. These are both commonly used markers of poverty in the international development community.

However, we felt that this system would not be practical for day-to-day decision making. Instead, we developed a ten-point system that describes specific living conditions. Once a family has succeeded in clearing all ten of these hurdles, then we at Grameen Bank consider them to have escaped from poverty. The ten points are:

1. The bank member and her family live in a tin-roofed house or in a house worth at least 25,000 taka (roughly equivalent to $370). The family members sleep on cots or a bedstead rather than the floor.
2. The member and her family drink pure water from tube-wells, boiled water, or arsenic-free water purified by the use of alum, purifying tablets, or pitcher filters.
3. All of the member's children who are physically and mentally fit and above the age of six either attend or have finished primary school.
4. The member's minimum weekly loan repayment installment is 200 taka (around $3).
5. All family members use a hygienic and sanitary latrine.
6. All family members have sufficient clothing to meet daily needs, including winter clothes, blankets, and mosquito netting.
7. The family has additional sources of income, such as a vegetable garden or fruit-bearing trees, to fall back on in times of need.
8. The member maintains an average annual balance of 5,000 taka (around $75) in her savings account.
9. The member has the ability to feed her family three square meals a day throughout the year.
10. All family members are conscious about their health, can take immediate action for proper treatment, and can pay medical expenses in the event of illness.

Our ten indicators, obviously, were designed to define an individual and a family who are *not* in poverty any longer. But absence of the very same indicators can be used to define those who *are* in poverty. With appropriate modifications, the same system of indicators might work well in some other developing countries. In other cases, a unique definition tailored to local conditions is needed. The important point is that poverty must be clearly defined so that an anti-poverty program can have a clear target clientele and one or more clear objectives to attain.

Prioritization of those in need is also important. Not only should the non-poor be excluded from an anti-poverty program, but the poorest and the very poor should have higher priority than the less poor. One of the ways many aid programs fail is by allowing resources to be diverted to unintended people. What's more, the most effective anti-poverty programs are purpose-built programs specifically tailored to the needs of the poor, not general projects for serving society, providing worthwhile social services, or stimulating the economy. Programs to build infrastructure, provide health care, or offer job training may be fine things. But experience shows that, unless they specifically target the poor, the non-poor will eventually receive the lion's share of the benefits, leaving the poor as badly off as ever, or perhaps more so. Experience also teaches that it's important to specifically include women among the targeted recipients; otherwise it's likely that they will remain totally unreached even by an otherwise well-designed program.

In many cases, this means that new programs to help the poor must be created, rather than trying to adapt existing programs. When current arrangements, institutions, and policies have failed to respond sensitively to the needs of the poor, it's usually futile to tinker with them in hopes of making them effective. It's generally better to start from scratch, building and staffing new programs from the ground up.

Finally, a long-term commitment on the part of program sponsors is essential. Self-reliance isn't achieved over night, especially when a large number of people have been stuck in poverty for decades or even generations. Even a well-designed program will encounter periods of difficulty that will tempt sponsors to abandon the effort. These hard times must be overcome with determination, flexibility, and intelligence if a satisfactory outcome is to be reached.

Many anti-poverty efforts are funded by well-intentioned people in the developed countries, either through NGOs, government grants, or international aid agencies. It's sad to see much of this money being invested in ways that are wasteful. In many cases, money that is supposed to help the poor ends up creating business for companies and organizations in the developed world—training firms, suppliers of equipment and materials, consultants, advisers, and the like. In other cases, it finds its way into the hands of corrupt local governments or elite social groups.

When this happens, people who are concerned about poverty and eager to help those in need become bitter and cynical. Eventually once-idealistic people become hardened to the plight of the poor and shut down the aid pipeline. It's a needless tragedy.

Those in the developed world who want to reach out to the poor should make a political commitment to build solidarity with the bottom half of the population in the developing countries, especially the women among them. Taxpayers in donor countries should make it plain to their aid officials and legislative representatives that they want their money to go directly toward the reduction of poverty through the support of the productive capacities of poor people themselves. Insisting on criteria like the ones I've just outlined would be a good place to start.

Credit Comes First

We've listed some of the most important criteria to be met by any effective anti-poverty program. But where should such programs begin? Does education come first? What about infrastructure? Health care? Technology for information and communications? Sanitation? Housing? The needs are almost endless and hard to prioritize.

All of these are important. If it were possible, the best thing would be to start them all simultaneously. But at Grameen Bank, we concentrated on credit—literally handing out cash to poor people as the very first step in helping them work their way out of poverty. It was an unconventional strategy that deserves a word of explanation, especially since most anti-poverty programs start elsewhere.

I firmly believe that all human beings have an innate but generally unrecognized skill—the survival skill. The very fact that the poor are *alive* is a clear proof that they possess this ability. They do not need us to teach them how to survive—they already know! So rather than waste our time teaching them new skills, my efforts have focused on trying to help them make the most of their existing skills. Giving the poor access to credit lets them immediately put into practice the skills they already have—to weave, to husk rice paddy, to raise cows, or to pedal a rickshaw. The cash they raise through these efforts then becomes a tool, a key with which they can unlock their other abilities.

This is not to say that the poor always recognize the skills they possess. When we first went to poor women in the villages to offer them credit, they were afraid to take any money and said they would have no idea how to put it to use. These women had many skills, but they had accumulated so much fear and insecurity through years of exposure to repressive social attitudes that they didn't even know it. By offering a lot of encouragement and by holding up a few successful examples before them, we were able to gradually peel off those layers of fear. Soon the women realized that they had enough skill to use money to make money.

Government decision-makers, international consultants, and many NGOs usually start from the opposite assumption—that people are poor because they lack skills. Based on this assumption, they start anti-poverty efforts built around elaborate training programs. This seems logical, based on the underlying assumption—and it also perpetuates the interests of the anti-poverty experts. It creates plenty of jobs supported by large budgets at the same time as it relieves them of any responsibility to produce concrete results. After all, they can always point to so-and-so many thousands of people who have experienced training—regardless of whether or not those people and their families have managed to escape poverty—and claim "success" on the basis of those numbers.

To be fair, most anti-poverty experts are well-intentioned. They opt for training because that is what their flawed assumptions dictate. But if you spend enough time living among the poor, you discover that their poverty arises from the fact that they cannot retain the genuine results of their labor. And the reason for this is clear: They have no control over capital. The poor work for the benefit of someone else who controls the capital. It may be moneylenders like those who exploited the poor people of Jobra, where I began my work. It may be landlords, factory owners, or agents who recruit poor people for work under conditions of near-slavery. What they all have in common is the ability to steal the productive labor of the poor for their own benefit.

And why is this the case? Because the poor do not inherit any capital, nor does anyone in the conventional system provide them with access to capital or to credit. The world has been made to believe that the poor are not credit-worthy. I've become convinced that changing this assumption is the necessary first step to relieving the poverty problem.

And what about job training? There is nothing bad about training *per se*. It can be extremely important in helping people overcome their economic difficulties. But training can be provided only to a limited number of people. To address the needs of the vast numbers of the poor, the best strategy is to let people's natural abilities blossom before we introduce new skills to them. Giving the poor credit and letting them enjoy the fruits of their labor—often for the first time in their lives—helps to create a situation in which they may start feeling the need for training, begin looking for it, and are even willing to pay for it (though often no more than a token amount). These are conditions in which training can be truly meaningful and effective.

Charity Is Not Always the Answer

The importance of charity cannot be denied. It is appropriate in disaster situations and when helping those who are so seriously disabled they can do nothing to help themselves. But sometimes we tend to overdo our reliance on charity.

In general, I am opposed to giveaways and handouts. They take away initiative and responsibility from people. If people know that things can be received "free," they tend to spend their energy and skill chasing the "free" things rather than using the same energy and skill to accomplish things on their own. Handouts encourage dependence rather than self-help and self-confidence.

Even in disaster situations, Grameen Bank encourages borrowers to create their own disaster funds rather than rely on donations. When we were distributing free wheat to Grameen Bank borrowers during the 1998 flood, we encouraged them to agree to make small weekly savings in a disaster fund. After normalcy returned and they started earning money, that would eventually add up to the value of the wheat they'd received. This new savings pool will be a community fund to help them cope with the next disaster.

Handouts also encourage corruption. When aid monies are donated to help the poor, the officials who are in charge of distributing the free goods and services often turn themselves and their favored friends into the first beneficiaries of the program.

Finally, charity creates a one-sided power relationship. The beneficiaries of charity are favor-seekers rather than claimants of something they deserve. As a result, they have no voice, and accountability and transparency disappear. All such one-way relationships are inequitable and only make the poor more vulnerable to exploitation and manipulation.

To strengthen the capacity of the poor to create, expand, and improve their own communities, I would emphasize the creation of democratic institutions for local self-government. The smaller the area over which local government has its jurisdiction, the more chance the poor have to let their voices be heard. The poor must have a chance to participate in decision-making that affects their lives. Paternalism, however well-intentioned, leads only to a dead end. When the poor have the ability to control their own destinies, they can achieve a lot more, a lot faster.

Bangladesh and the Developed World

Bangladesh can continue to grow economically if the global context is favorable. Three things are required: large amounts of foreign direct investment, duty-free access for its products to the U.S. market, and continued access to overseas job markets.

Foreign direct investment (FDI) can help Bangladesh achieve high growth and build a strong economy, as we see from the rapid development of countries that have attracted large amounts of FDI. For example, it is estimated that FDI is contributing 14 percent to the GDP of Vietnam, providing about $1 billion per year to the national budget, directly generating 800,000 jobs and indirectly supporting two million others. This is because Vietnam has attracted $18 billion in new FDI over the last five years—$10 billion in 2006 alone—while Bangladesh, with twice the population, attracted only $700 million in 2005. There is no reason why Bangladesh could not achieve gains through FDI similar to those enjoyed by Vietnam.

Of course, all FDIs are not necessarily beneficial. One priority area should be to attract investors in production units for manufacturing global products. Creating and maintaining special manufacturing zones, providing infrastructure, and ensuring a transparent regulatory regime are essential to attracting these kinds of investments.

A second crucial element in supporting future growth for Bangladesh will be free access to U.S. markets. Bangladesh is among the unfortunate half a dozen least developed countries in Asia that face high tariff barriers on most of their exports to the United States. Bangladesh is actually subject to the fourth-highest average tariff rates among all U.S. trading partners. On $3.3 billion in exports to the U.S. in 2006, Bangladesh paid half a billion dollars in duties—the same amount paid by the United Kingdom on exports of $54 billion.

Annual garment exports from Bangladesh reached $9 billion in 2006—80 percent of our total exports. At current growth rates, Bangladesh will soon overtake giant India as a garment exporter. The positive effects of duty-free access to U.S. markets will go beyond the purely economic. I've explained how microcredit has contributed to the empowerment of women in Bangladesh over the last two decades. A second major factor in this social change has been the growth of our garment industry.

Today, two million Bangladeshi girls work in garment factories. This is silent testimony to the degree to which religious sensitivities about girls working in factories have been overcome. Many poor girls are choosing to work, earn money, and save for a decent life rather than getting married at an early age or, far worse, becoming victims of abuses like the international trafficking of women. Children of these working mothers will have a far better upbringing and a more hopeful future than the children of girls who get married at an early age.

What's more, this new generation of working women is adopting liberal, modern attitudes that promise to transform our traditional culture. Poverty and powerlessness are breeding grounds for terrorism. The families of these women will not provide such breeding grounds anymore.

If Bangladesh is allowed duty-free access to U.S. markets, I believe that, within five years, export volumes will double, wages will rise, and the growth rate of the Bangladeshi economy will increase—along with exports of cotton and other goods from the U.S. to Bangladesh. And because Bangladesh's garment industry is focused on the low-end market that American firms have long abandoned, few U.S. apparel firms will suffer as a result. Everyone will win.

The Millennium Development Goals of 2000 included a commitment to give the least-developed countries duty-free access to world markets. Honoring that commitment will help Bangladesh enormously.

Finally, Bangladesh also needs continued access to international labor markets.

In my world travels, I meet many young people from Bangladesh—not just in major cities like New York but also in villages in Spain, on islands in Italy, and in towns in Argentina, Chile, and Colombia. Most are doing well, having mastered the local language and made friends among the local people. But when I ask them how they got there, they tell me stories of perseverance, tenacity, and high-risk adventure, often involving travels through many countries and experiments with different kinds of work. The tales also include episodes of abuse: cheating by manpower agents, mistreatment by airport officials, and harassment, extortion, and neglect by government officials.

Yet these young people are making a big contribution to Bangladesh's economy. In 2006, Bangladesh received $6.0 billion in remittances from overseas citizens—one third of the country's total foreign exchange—compared to $21.7 billion received by India and $21.3 billion by China. It's a remarkable figure, considering that India's population is more than seven times that of Bangladesh and China's is almost nine times as great.

Furthermore, remittances go directly into poverty reduction. The World Bank Global Economic Prospects Report says the remittance inflow has helped cut poverty in Bangladesh by 6 percent. It's a fascinating example of how low-income people make direct strategic contributions to the nation's economic and social goals, as well as the initiative they take in changing their own lives.

Bangladesh needs to do more to support its young emigrants and to reduce the risks they take in venturing into unknown territories. We need to reform the practices of our government agencies to reduce the stress, humiliation, and anxiety they suffer as they deal with the emigration bureaucracy.

Given the demographic and economic reality of the world, one can easily project that more and more workers from Bangladesh and the countries around it will be required to work in other countries, even in China. The need for airplane seats will expand greatly. This will be a good time to think about building a global air-travel hub in Bangladesh to facilitate the transportation of larger number of workers from the region, as well as the growing numbers of regional and international business travelers.

Toward Regional
Peace and Prosperity

As with many countries in the developing world, the future of Bangladesh is closely linked with the peace and prosperity of its entire region. No matter what their political past, the countries of South Asia—Afghanistan, Bangladesh, Bhutan, India, Maldives, Nepal, Pakistan, and Sri Lanka—can achieve rapid economic and social transformation only if they band together strongly and irrevocably. There's no reason that South Asia can't achieve the same kind of economic miracle the members of the European Union have enjoyed, but with an even greater positive impact on millions of lives.

For precisely this reason, the South Asian Association for Regional Cooperation (SAARC) was formed in 1985. But in twenty-two years, the spirit of SAARC has never gotten a chance to blossom. The periodic SAARC summit meetings have become more a forum for political one-upmanship than part of a genuine quest for ways to build trust and cooperation among our peoples.

As a result, South Asia is the least integrated region in the world. Intraregional trade is less than 2 percent of GDP, compared to more than 20 percent for East Asia. Annual trade between India and Pakistan is currently estimated at $1 billion, but could be as great as

$9 billion. The costs of cross-border trade in the region are far higher than necessary. Crossings between India and Bangladesh are so congested that queues on the Indian side often exceed 1,000 trucks, and a trip that should take twenty-one hours may run ninety-nine hours or more. Partly because of this lack of integration, South Asia is the hub of world poverty, home to nearly 40 percent of the world's poor.

Several lagging parts of South Asia are border economies that suffer from the disabilities typical of land-locked or isolated countries. Examples include northeast India, northwest Pakistan, northern Bangladesh, and parts of Nepal and Afghanistan. Regional cooperation, especially in transport and trade facilitation, could transform these regions. Northern Bangladesh can become a vibrant, dynamic region once trade with Nepal and India is in full swing.

The SAARC nations recognize the potential value of trade integration to the region. This is why they negotiated an agreement, signed in January 2004, to create the South Asia Free Trade Area (SAFTA). If the plans embodied in this agreement are implemented, by the year 2015 virtually all products will be traded without tariff or other duties among all eight South Asian countries.

SAFTA is a good agreement in many respects, although it has specific problems that need to be addressed. Trade in services as well as manufacturing and agricultural products should be covered by SAFTA, and the potential loss of customs and VAT revenues as a result of trade liberalization will create problems, particularly for the smaller SAARC countries. In addition, the practical application of SAFTA rules will need to be monitored to ensure that small countries benefit and inefficient producers do not crowd out non-SAFTA competitors. For instance, better quality products from competing countries (China, South Korea, Malaysia, Thailand) will not be able to compete with Indian or Pakistani products simply because these products are tariff-free. As a result, consumers will lose out.

Of course, we'll have initial problems. Countries joining in a free trade association can be expected to go through transitional problems. Nonetheless, SAFTA is a big step in the right direction for South Asia. It can mobilize the private sector to begin stripping away the layers of mutual distrust that have divided our region for so many years. As regional trade expands, it will defuse the risks of armed conflict between long-time regional rivals such as India and Pakistan.

Governments, civil society, and the business community can do a lot to encourage closer ties among the nations of our region. For example, I've proposed that every university in the SAARC countries offer at least one scholarship to a student from a different South Asian country. A similar exchange program for faculty members should also be created. Many people have urged that the regular SAARC summit meetings among government ministers should be supplemented by simultaneous regional conferences involving business leaders, journalists, writers, NGO leaders, and students, along with cultural festivals and educational programs. SAARC should be about people, not just governments; it should help to unite the peoples of the region.

Travel restrictions among the SAARC nations should also be gradually lifted. Currently only Nepal has been far-sighted enough to provide automatic visas to all SAARC nationals. This has resulted in a sharp boost in travel to Nepal from other SAARC countries. The other nations in the region should follow suit.

I have always pleaded that SAARC nations should issue SAARC passports to important citizens of the region. Each year, an agreed-upon list of eminent persons may be announced recognizing their contributions in political, social, cultural, economic fields of the region. They will be given SAARC passports or SAARC ID cards in addition to their regular passports. The process could start with the selection of, say, 5,000 distinguished citizens from all eight SAARC nations. These notable men and women would be able to travel throughout the region without visas, spreading ideas and promoting goodwill. Their number could be augmented annually until free travel through South Asia would become the norm rather than the exception.

I've heard some people say that administering a SAARC passport would be a technological nightmare. I don't see why. With modern information technology, keeping a central data base for these passport holders should not be a difficulty at all. One can add all biometric information for the passport holders. I have no doubt that this initiative will contribute enormously in melting the ice of distrust.

As with other seemingly intractable social problems, social business can play a crucial role in changing the economic, social, and political environment in the region. This initiative can begin by creating a SAARC Social Business Fund, launched by businessmen and businesswomen of the region. It will start by funding at least one social business in each country—relating to poverty, healthcare for the poor, woman and child trafficking, clean water, mothercare, and other key issues. The fund can start with a small amount and launch small programs in each country to create confidence and trust that we can join hands to solve our common problems. The advantage of such a fund is that nobody will see it as a way for businesses in one country to profit from their financial or technological superiority over others, since social businesses, by their nature, are not profit-disbursing enterprises.

Among other projects, these SAARC social businesses could be about building infrastructure, like bridges over common rivers or building roads connecting two countries. This infrastructure may be owned by the local poor from both sides of the border. They can be owned by social investors from the region. They will be symbols of friendship as well as practical tools for improving the lives of the poor by stimulating the local economies, encouraging trade, and facilitating communications.

The long-term success of SAARC and SAFTA will depend particularly on the attitudes and actions of India, the largest and most powerful nation in the region. India borders almost all of the other SAARC countries. It is not unusual that neighboring countries will have political difficulties with each other. But there is one problem between two SAARC countries that seriously impacts on the entire region. India and Pakistan's attitude and actions are vastly influenced by this problem. Kashmir remains the biggest problem for India, Pakistan, and the region. India and Pakistan have fought three full-scale wars with each other, driven by rival claims for the Kashmir region. Because of this festering dispute, both countries have raised huge armies equipped with the most advanced weapon systems, including nuclear capabilities that pose a grave threat to regional peace.

Can the Kashmir problem be solved? Of course it can. All human conflicts can be solved because they originate in the human mind, which is the real battlefield we should be focusing on. When all the countries of the region are ready to move forward enthusiastically to form a true political and economic union, it will be much easier to find a just solution to the Kashmir dilemma.

Bangladesh and
Its Giant Neighbors

Bangladesh is a lucky country. It can easily create a dynamic economy by exploiting its attractive geographical location, flanked by two giant, rapidly growing neighbors, India and China. India has already achieved an 8 percent GDP growth rate while China has surpassed 11 percent; and both have reduced their poverty rate to less than 25 percent. They are becoming such political and economic powerhouses that the whole world is paying serious attention to them.

With our giant neighbors bringing the whole business world to their doorsteps, Bangladesh can benefit simply from being in the neighborhood. Growing neighbors are convenient sources of technology, experience, skills, and contacts. Bangladesh, in turn, can be an attractive venue for both countries for all kinds of outsourcing. If even a small portion of the business flowing into India or China comes to our shores, we will be a fast-moving economy.

Some Bangladeshis worry that our smaller country will be overwhelmed by its giant Indian neighbor if we open our borders for free trade. India, they say, will flood our markets with goods—taking advantage of the free trade zone—and stifle the potential for nascent industries in Bangladesh.

But India already "floods" the Bangladeshi market with goods, only through unofficial channels that generate no government revenues (other than bribes to border personnel and customs officials). According to figures from Bangladesh Bank, officially recognized imports from India exceeded U.S. $1.8 billion in 2005–6, and estimates are that unofficial trade may be as much as 50 percent higher. Free trade rules will legalize this unrecognized flow of goods and capture revenues for the government in the process. If reasonable provisions for adjustments by businesses and communities are made, and if safeguards are put in place to prevent exploitation of the weak by the powerful, small countries can benefit just as much from free trade as large ones. Bilateral free-trade agreements are already in effect between some of the SAARC countries—for example, India and Sri Lanka. If tiny Sri Lanka, with a population under twenty million, can benefit from open borders with India, why not Bangladesh?

There are many reasons why Bangladesh should have an excellent relationship with India, but tensions between the two countries remain needlessly high. Although Bangladesh remains grateful to India for its military help during our liberation war, a pervasive feeling of fear about India persists in Bangladeshi minds. Perhaps this is understandable: India is seven times bigger than Bangladesh, surrounds Bangladesh almost completely, has the third largest army in the world, and is predominantly Hindu rather than Muslim (although India, in fact, has a larger Muslim population than Bangladesh). Some Bangladeshi politicians exploit Bangladeshi anxieties by blaming India for anything that goes wrong in Bangladesh and promising to "protect" Bangladesh from the unnamed threats supposedly posed by India.

For its part, India complains about illegal immigration by poor Bangladeshis looking for work in India. (In this respect, India and Bangladesh have a relationship comparable to that between the United States and Mexico, where border crossings by poor people in search of economic opportunities have also caused international tension.) India also complains that Bangladesh harbors and supports armed guerrilla leaders from Eastern India. Bangladeshi leaders continue to deny this allegation, but it does not seem to disappear.

In an atmosphere of general distrust, it is easy to stoke people's fears—in this case, the fear of domination by a giant neighbor. But in today's world, countries generally don't dominate one another through military might but rather through economic power. If Bangladesh remains a poor country, everybody will dominate her, not just India. Moving up the economic ladder as quickly as possible is the best protection against every form of foreign domination.

Bangladesh's Strategic Location

Bangladesh's strategic location can be the key factor in shaping our country's future. Located at a regional crossroads, Bangladesh can be a converging point for international trade for all its neighbors. All that it has to do is provide shipping facilities for all these countries: landlocked Nepal and Bhutan, virtually landlocked eastern India, western China, and northern Myanmar. These areas have a total population of over 300 million and fast-growing economies with per-capita annual incomes rising steadily beyond the $1,000 mark.

Bangladesh has to prepare itself to take on a big development venture—to create world-class port facilities for the growing economies of Bangladesh as well as her neighbors, and to build a network of superhighways to connect these countries with the port facilities. This deep-sea mega-port may be built near Cox's Bazar, a city ninety miles south of Chittagong near the Myanmar border. This mega-port could serve this entire region and bring significant greater prosperity to millions of people.

Under current conditions, Bangladeshi goods are at a great disadvantage compared to those of other nations. It takes several times longer to process products manufactured in Bangladesh for export than in Singapore, and the average cost for exporters in Bangladesh is almost double that in Indonesia. A mega-port at Cox's Bazar, equipped to accommodate the vast new vessels now being used in global trade and the new ships with even deeper draft that will be built in the coming years, will solve these problems. The port should be equipped with the latest cargo-handling technology and linked to neighboring regions and countries by a network of super highways that will support a continuous flow of vehicles carrying modern containers.

Singapore became one of the most prosperous countries in the world because of its location as a strategic port. There is no reason why Cox's Bazar can't play a similar role in the future development of Bangladesh. (Myanmar is already building a port in Akyab, a fact that doesn't diminish the need for a mega-port in Bangladesh. In fact, Akyab would benefit from serving as a feeder port for Cox's Bazar, just as the mega-port in Hong Kong is supported by the smaller facility in nearby Guangdong.)

The Mega-Port Can Be a Social Business

An important way to ensure that infrastructure projects benefit the poor is to give them actual ownership of the infrastructure. We can apply this idea to the Cox's Bazar mega-port.

Here's how it might work. Social investors can raise the money with the explicit understanding that, once the investment money has been recovered from the port's initial profits, the investors will sell the company at a negotiated price to a trust created especially for the purpose. The trust will be owned by poor people, at least 50 percent of them women, and it will pay for the port on a deferred basis out of further profits from operations.

Where will the investment money to build the port come from? Social investors can organize themselves to come up with the money to build the mega-port with the explicit understanding that when the investment money is wholly or partly recovered from the profit of the port, investors will sell the company to a trust. The trust will own the company on behalf of the poor people. Since the investors will not take more money than they have invested, and they may have already taken a part of it, they can sell it for whatever the outstanding amount is left to be recovered. The mega-port may be handed over to the trust on a deferred payment basis. The trust will hire a professional port management company to manage the port.

Alternatively, a donor country, or a consortium of donor countries, can provide the investment funds for building the mega-port and follow a procedure almost similar to an existing procedure, but with an important difference. The existing procedure comes from Japan's official aid to Bangladesh. A Japanese aid agency provided the loan to build Chittagong airport. The money was used to buy equipment and hire engineering and construction firms that were mainly Japanese, so that most of the funds flowed back into the Japanese economy. After a time, according to the existing unwritten procedure, Japan will quietly cancel the loan, transforming the loan into a grant. As a result, Bangladesh got a modern airport free of cost. In this case, the ownership of the airport would remain with the government of Bangladesh.

The alternative scenario that I am proposing for creating a social business around the mega-port will be the following: Under an agreement with the donors, the government of Bangladesh will establish a nonprofit mega-port trust and a mega-port company that will be the owned by the trust. It will be a for-profit company. The ownership of the mega-port will be handed over by the government of Bangladesh to this trust. The board of the trust will be made up primarily of eminent persons who have demonstrated their commitment toward improving the quality of lives of the poor people. Other members may represent the government of Bangladesh, the city of Cox's Bazar, and the poor people who will benefit from the mega-port.

The "shadow shares" of this company will be sold by the trust to the poor people. Fifty percent of the shadow shares will be reserved for the local poor. Of the total shadow shares sold, at least fifty percent will go to poor women. A shadow share will not give any legal ownership of the mega-port company to the shareholder, but it will create an entitlement to a dividend of the company as determined by the board of the company. Shadow shares cannot be traded outside. A shareholder can sell his share only to the trust. A shadow share can be sold on credit—the shareholder can pay the price of the share from the dividend of the company.

The trust may hire a professional port management company to manage the mega-port, or assign the task to the mega-port company if it has the required capability to manage it.

The same scenario can be repeated for any other infrastructure. There may be many variations in the ownership. Whatever the configuration of the ownership, I would like to see that such an infrastructure belongs to social business in either of the two ways: (1) as a non-loss non-dividend company, or (2) as a company where majority shares are owned by the poor—half of whom being poor women, through an ownership trust.

The mega-port would be a mega-size social business, and a daunting economic and financial challenge. In order to gather experience in designing and operating social businesses for infrastructure ownership and operation, we might want to start with smaller infrastructure projects—bridges, roads, tunnels, and the like. This is just a small step from the present system in Bangladesh, where the right to collect tolls on bridges is auctioned off to the highest bidder. Now instead of the highest bidder we can give it to a well-designed trust dedicated to bringing benefits to the poor. As confidence in the system grows, bigger and bigger projects can be converted into social businesses.

Of course, infrastructure is only one of the elements that needs to be put in place if Bangladesh is to become a thriving crossroads of South Asia. There are other problems that need to be addressed. First on the list is the need to establish good governance and drastically reduce the level of corruption at all levels of government. Other areas that need improvement are the provision of reliable and easily available electric power and state-of-the-art information and communication technology. Some of these challenges may be addressed in the same spirit I've proposed for the mega-port project—by looking for opportunities to create social businesses focused on long-term benefits for the national economy and especially for the poor.

I am convinced that, in the foreseeable future, say by 2030, Bangladesh can escape from poverty completely. When we achieve this goal, as I believe we will, it will represent a breakthrough of global importance. Because if Bangladesh, not so long ago described as an "international basket case," can lift itself out of poverty, there's no reason to doubt that every country in the world can do the same.

6

God Is in the Details

We now come to the story of how the idea of social business took a giant, and this time very international, step into reality.

At the beginning of this book, I told how the head of a large corporation and I had lunch at a fashionable Paris restaurant and agreed to work together. We were more than excited. Franck Riboud made a big decision that day. He wanted to participate in a business that would not produce any profit for Danone, and in the process we were going to take a small but significant step toward bringing better health to the malnourished children of poor families in one corner of Bangladesh.

Within a few weeks of that October 2005 Paris lunch where I first met Franck Riboud, the head of Groupe Danone, the notion of a Grameen Danone partnership was already beginning to take concrete form. The process started in high spirits with a visit by Emmanuel Faber and his Danone team to Bangladesh.

Emmanuel, Danone's executive vice president for Asia Pacific operations, turned out to be an enthusiastic leader for the Grameen Danone project. He visited Dhaka, the Bangladeshi capital, in November 2005, bringing with him a large team that included experts from his offices in Shanghai and Jakarta and others from Danone's head office in Paris.

Emmanuel was especially suitable as the principal actor in making our concept successful. He told me that he'd been following the story of Grameen Bank since 1987, when a group of his best friends, shortly after graduating from French universities, had traveled to

Santiago, Chile. Among the projects they'd participated in had been the creation of Contigo, a Grameen-style credit operation inspired by their visit to Bangladesh that has since grown into one of Chile's leading microcredit organizations.

Emmanuel himself had done volunteer work among the poor in Majnu ka Tila, a shantytown north of Delhi in India, where he witnessed what he called "the very practical approach to coping with tough living conditions by extremely poor people." Poor people, he'd discovered—as I'd learned many years before—have tremendous survival abilities, honed in the most demanding school on earth: the school of poverty. With this background, Emmanuel was totally committed to making Grameen Danone successful, and in that mission he had the vital backing of Franck Riboud and Groupe Danone's board of directors.

From our end, we designated Imamus Sultan, an experienced Grameen manager, to lead the project. He had no experience in working to develop a consumer products company, but he knew the poor people of Bangladesh intimately. I knew he would be a fast learner and would have sound instincts for figuring out what would and wouldn't work in designing a business to serve and work with the poor. I had total confidence in Sultan and knew that I could rely on him to build up our relationship with Danone and supervise the project. He was already responsible for overseeing the implementation of another social business—the series of eyecare hospitals to serve the poor of Bangladesh that I've already described.

The First Planning Meeting

Emmanuel Faber's first order of business was to understand in very specific terms what I'd had in mind when I'd told Franck Riboud that we should create Grameen Danone in Bangladesh—and make it a social business. Emmanuel and his team wanted two solid days with me to go through all the details that I could give. But our discussions quickly turned into a two-way conversation. I had a very clear idea what I meant by "social business," but I had no concrete design in mind when I proposed Grameen Danone to Franck. Turning the broad idea into a specific plan would be very much a joint venture.

My general idea was a joint venture with Danone to produce some kind of food to improve the nutrition of the children of Bangladesh. The food item that I was thinking about was a "weaning food," to help babies to get proper nutrition after passing the breast-feeding stage. The concept had been in my mind for a long time because of what I'd seen happening to babies in the villages of Bangladesh. From mother's milk they often move straight to rice, which does not give them the nutrition they need at that stage of life. Several years back, Grameen Bank had undertaken an experimental project to develop a local weaning food to compete with imported baby food in the market. We named it Cerevit and trial-marketed it at a much lower price than that of imported products. But we did not succeed, probably because we lacked the right kind of partners to make it happen.

Now I thought that Grameen Danone would be the ideal vehicle to do the job.

Emmanuel and his team raised all the key questions related to our concept: "What kind of product do you want to produce? What kind of market information do you have? What studies have been conducted regarding malnutrition in Bangladesh? What baby foods are already on the market? How are they priced? Who produces, markets, and sells these competing foods?" The questions went on and on.

At first, I thought the Danone team were being too academic in their analysis and too focused on getting precise statistics. Their scientific approach made us feel rather pressured. We thought, "We know what there is to know about the nutritional needs of Bangladesh, even if we can not express it in numbers." But after hours of discussion, it became clear why all the information that our Danone partners were seeking was so necessary. As more information became available, we began discarding old ideas and developing new ones, new business plans, and a whole new framework for our business.

Fortunately, Emmanuel came totally prepared for the situation. He didn't wait for us to give all the answers. Assisted by some of my Grameen colleagues, his team members were soon running around Dhaka, visiting grocery shops, shopping malls, supermarkets, and local street bazaars. They interviewed shop owners and customers, purchased samples of all kinds of food products (biscuits [cookies and crackers], milk drinks, yogurts, candy, and so on), and gathered information on brand names, prices, package types, and many other vital details. They met with scientists from nutrition research institutions, high government officials in the Bangladeshi health ministry, and experts from UN agencies. They visited large milk-processing plants and biscuit-making plants and tiny yogurt- and biscuit-making plants, and factories that produce bottled water and other packaged drinks.

The time, energy, and resources that Danone dedicated to research and development for our new social business were truly impressive. They showed what can be accomplished when experts from the corporate world turn their attention to solving the social problems facing our poorest citizens.

Fortified Yogurt for Children

It was soon clear that Grameen Danone would not start in the baby food business. For Danone, without any experience in Bangladesh, it was too risky at this stage. Babies are very vulnerable to disease, and baby food therefore requires a very strict standard of hygiene. We decided to keep this item in mind for future production.

We agreed that reaching small children was crucially important. And the more we talked, the more we felt that yogurt was the best choice for an initial product. There were several reasons. As a dairy product, yogurt contains many healthful nutrients. The active cultures in yogurt are also beneficial because they promote good intestinal health and help reduce the effects of diarrhea, a deadly scourge in the developing world. Additional micronutrients could be added to yogurt in the form of supplements. And of course Danone was the world's foremost yogurt maker.

What's more, yogurt was likely to be a popular food among Bangladeshi children and their parents. It's creamy and slightly sweet—the kind of food that children the world over appreciate. And there is a local tradition of eating and enjoying yogurt. Under the name of *mishti doi* (sweet yogurt), it is a popular snack and dessert food, sold in clay pots at local shops or roadside stalls all over the country. However, mishti doi is usually sold for around 20 taka (30 cents), which is beyond the reach of most poor people. If we could produce a fortified Danone yogurt that would appeal to Bangladeshi children—and sell it at a price the poor could afford on a regular basis—we might have a winning product.

So the decision was made: Grameen Danone would be launched with a fortified yogurt product. Later, perhaps, other products could be added. But for now, we would stake our business on yogurt.

Now we had a whole new range of questions to explore. Where would our yogurt factory be located? How big would it be? How could we ensure adequate milk supplies? What marketing channels would we use? What would be the right price for our product?

In one of our first conversations, I made it clear that I was in favor of making the plant as small as technically possible and economically feasible. Emmanuel liked this idea. It coincided with what he called the "proximity business model," bringing food production, retailing, and consumption as close to one another as possible. He thought this would reduce the cost of the product, too, because strictly local production would mean we could skip the so-called cold chain of distribution that Danone employs in most parts of the world. Daily yogurt products could be sold in the neighborhood within forty-eight hours of its manufacture, eliminating the need for long-distance shipping, refrigerated warehouses and trucks, and other costly distribution measures.

Guy Gavelle, Industrial Director of Danone's Asia Pacific operation and an expert on safe methods of food production and distribution, was listening intently as Emmanuel and I spoke. Guy had designed facilities in many countries, including China, where he had worked for Danone for eighteen years, and Brazil and Indonesia. Several weeks later, in recollecting his impression about this first meeting, Guy told me that he had been alarmed by the direction of the discussion. He did not like the idea of a small plant. But he said nothing at the time, knowing we would return to this topic for full discussion at a later date.

Next, we discussed the practical implementation of our concept of social business. What would be our governance structure and business model? What kind of people would be needed to operate the business?

I explained that a social business is just like any other business in its governance structure and in its recruitment policies. "It's just the same as running a profit-maximizing company. You want to get the best person for the job, and pay the market salary. You define the qualities needed to determine the best person in the context of your business objective. Then you ask: Does he understand your objective? And will he commit himself to the objective? Once you've found the person who fits these criteria, you've got the right person for the job."

In the case of Grameen Danone, our objective is to reach malnourished children with fortified yogurt. We have to make the product tasty and attractive for the children so that they enjoy eating it and want more of it, rather than thinking of it as a medicine. The price must be low enough so that poor parents can afford it, and our marketing methods should be such that our yogurt will be sold mainly to the poor, rural families who need it most.

At the same time, we realized that some supplies of our product might end up in the hands of relatively wealthy, urban families. Because of the prestige value of the Danone brand name, our yogurt would be attractive to rich families who are willing to pay a higher price for their foodstuffs. Under the circumstances, distributors of the product would want to sell it to urban shops for a higher price, and even some entrepreneurial poor people might buy it and resell it for urban consumption.

Of course, sale of Grameen Danone yogurt to well-off families is not the purpose of our social business. But it would only subvert that purpose if supplies of the yogurt were insufficient. Solution: to increase production and sell the yogurt to everybody. We've even talked about marketing a higher-priced yogurt for more affluent consumers. Profits from these sales could help subsidize expansion of the business to benefit the poor.

After all our preliminary research—rushing around the city, collecting a fascinating basket of food samples from local bazaars—and after intensive discussions, we understood each other better and had a clearer picture of the new company and its objectives. A plan of action was prepared and approved. It was decided that the Danone team would prepare a draft business plan on the basis of the discussions we'd held as well as information to be collected during future visits to Bangladesh by other Danone teams. It was also agreed that we should finalize the text of our joint venture agreement for signature by March 2006. Franck Riboud was eager to come to Dhaka to sign the agreement in a public event.

Many important decisions were made in these early intensive meetings with Danone. I was very impressed by the level of their interest in this tiny project. They assembled virtually all the big guns in the company in Dhaka to give their highest attention to this project where their financial stake was so insignificant. Emmanuel Faber later explained to me that Danone's financial involvement was not what excited and inspired the company, but rather the philosophical and emotional stakes.

I'd never heard such a statement from a top executive of a huge multinational company before. I wondered whether to take him seriously or regard his words as some kind of promotional talk. I realized that I had a lot to learn about how the business world works.

In Search of Answers

After our first meeting, we had many more visits by groups of Danone officials. They were piling up all the necessary information and making contacts with Bangladeshi officials, regulators, designers, architects, contractors, and consumers. They commissioned surveys and conducted opinion polls and taste tests using samples of yogurt produced in Spain and Indonesia according to formulas they wanted to try out in Bangladesh. Grameen staff members, their families, and Grameen borrowers—particularly the children—were asked to eat cup after cup of yogurt and fill out forms indicating their preferences in regard to taste, texture, sweetness, color, flavor, and other qualities.

Ashvin Subramanyam, Danone's marketing director based in Indonesia and originally from India, made several trips to Bangladesh to investigate how our country was similar to and different from other areas in South Asia. He and his team learned a great deal about consumer preferences and behaviors in Bangladesh. They noted, for example, the lack of diversity in the diet of rural householders; the fondness of Bangladeshi people for salty, spicy, and especially sweet foods; and the widespread and well-founded popular concern about the safety of drinking water. Most significant, they recognized the importance of keeping the price point for any snack-food purchase aimed at the poorest Bangladeshis at ten taka or less (about fifteen cents).

The Danone team spread around the country to ask about the eating habits of Bangladeshi villagers: What were their favorite foods? What ingredients did they favor or dislike? How many meals a day did they eat, and when and where did they eat them?

They wanted to know about the nutritional needs of our children: What deficiencies had been identified that a Grameen Danone product might help to alleviate? What did our children eat in school? Were there programs of midday meals for children in the schools, and, if so, could our yogurt be included on the menu?

Danone experts explored the business conditions in which Grameen Danone would be competing: how local food and beverage companies operated in Bangladesh; the kinds of processing, packaging, and distribution systems that were available; the varieties of marketing, advertising, promotion, and sales tools already in use in the country; and the attitudes, interests, needs, and preferences of Bangladeshi consumers. They were especially interested in the consumption patterns of our specific target audience—rural villagers and their children who fall into income categories of people who live in households that subsist on roughly two dollars or less a day.

A full-blown market study was commissioned, a research team was assembled under the supervision of Ashvin, and an international consulting company was engaged to undertake a product sample survey.

Simultaneously with the efforts at sharpening the details of fortified yogurt making, Danone teams were also following up on two other areas of interest: baby food and water. Water experts from Paris came to explore the possibility of producing bottled water for low-income groups. Another visit was made by a baby food expert—André Carrier, director of Bledina, a Danone-affiliated company based in France that specializes in foods for young children. We arranged for André to meet with a team of local nutritionists led by Dr. David A. Sack, director of the International Centre for Diarrheal Diseases Research in Bangladesh (ICDDRB), which had become world famous for developing the oral saline to cure diarrhea, thereby saving the lives of millions of children.

Studies already undertaken in the country had documented that people in Bangladesh had serious nutritional deficiencies that were crying out for help. Millions of Bangladeshi children suffer from calorie deficits as well as serious shortfalls in their intake of iron, vitamin A, calcium, iodine, and other important nutrients. As a result, over 40 percent of children from newborn to fifty-nine months in rural Bangladesh are stunted in their growth.

Our decision to produce a fortified yogurt for children was validated by our nutrition experts in February 2006. In a conference that month, Dr. Sack and his team of physicians reported that the best way for Grameen Danone to help improve the nutritional status of children in Bangladesh would be by providing a healthful food, well supplied with nutrients, that could serve as a more nourishing alternative to the rice gruel that most mothers gave to their toddlers. They also said that a product that could encourage "self-feeding" by children (rather than feeding on a fixed schedule by parents) would be especially beneficial in creating healthy eating habits. A sweet, creamy yogurt in a small, easy-to-handle package could work well on all these counts.

A New Venture Takes Shape

Many of the early conversations between the Danone and Grameen team members focused on broad questions about the business model and its governance structure. As the world's first consciously designed multinational social business, we wanted its design to be right, and as the first experiment in social business, we wanted it thoughtfully planned and executed. The proper combination of incentives, rewards, and risks had to be developed, a workable revenue and profit plan created, and the mutual interests of Grameen and Danone analyzed accurately, so that our partnership could survive any bumps along the way. If the first social business was a success in terms of both economic sustainability and benefit to human beings, it might stimulate others to follow in our path. But if it failed, it would be a blow to the cause of social business.

A social business must be *at least* as well-managed as any PMB. In fact, if you are thinking of starting a social business, I urge you to make sure it is even *better* managed than competing PMBs. Especially in these early years of experimentation with the new model, we must be certain that every social business is an example of the right way to do it, so that we create sustainable businesses that can serve as guide-posts for later followers.

Nearly fifty years ago, the German-American architect Ludwig Mies van der Rohe said, "God is in the details." If you think about it, it's as true of any complex organization, such as a social business, as it is of architecture. Get all the ground-level details right, and the big picture will usually fall into place.

By February 2006, Grameen Bank and Groupe Danone had reached an understanding about the structure and objectives of our project. This would become the basis of a memorandum of under-standing (MOU) between our two organizations, specifying that we'd agreed to enter into a fifty-fifty joint venture to form a company called "Grameen Danone Foods—A Social Business Enterprise." Half of the start-up capital would be provided by the Danone Group, the other half by the Grameen companies. (This is above and beyond the large investment Danone had already made in the planning, re-search, and development effort, bringing some of the world's leading experts on producing and marketing nutritious foods to analyze the needs of the children of Bangladesh.)

We would run the business in such a way as to incur no losses and to generate a small surplus. Out of this surplus, the initial invest-ments of the two parties would be repaid as early as possible. After that, the joint venture would pay the investors a 1 percent annual div-idend on their original investment.

Why a dividend? As I've explained, I define a social business as a non-loss, non-dividend company. Danone was totally agreeable to that proposition, but at the last minute, we added to the MOU the provision for a token 1 percent dividend as a way of publicly recog-nizing the ownership of this company and to make it possible for Danone to show a figure in the appropriate line of its balance sheet. (Now, in hindsight and with further thought, I am in favor of remov-ing the dividend clause, making the company dividend free. If Danone agrees, we'll do that, to make it match with the definition of social business as I have formulated it—a non-loss, non-dividend business.)

New Ways of Thinking:
In Production and Distribution

The decision to focus on fortified yogurt as our first Grameen Danone product led to the next logical question: Where and how would we manufacture the yogurt?

Danone's normal procedure, like that of most multinational food companies, would be to build a big factory that could serve a large geographic area. For example, Danone operates a single factory in Indonesia, feeding a market of over 200 million. In Bangladesh, however, I had been urging that we build the smallest plant technically possible, located in a rural area, surrounded by the village people it would serve.

"Remember, this is to be a social business," I said. "Our goal is not only financial efficiency, but also maximum social benefit. Grameen Danone will make tasty, nutritious food. But it should also serve the community in other ways. The milk we use to make our yogurt should come from local suppliers. Many villagers in rural Bangladesh keep milk cows. In fact, many of them buy their first cow with a small loan from Grameen Bank. These people should be our suppliers as well as our customers. If the factory is small and produces food that is sold immediately to the people who live nearby, they will think of it as *their* factory."

Emmanuel Faber liked my idea, and we agreed to start with one mini-factory. If it was successful, we would expand as rapidly as possible. Ultimately, up to fifty small factories could be located throughout the country.

For our first location, we decided to try to find a plot in the industrial zones developed by the Bangladesh government's Small and Cottage Industries Agency. A team of five graduate students, led by a professor of anthropology from a Bangladeshi university, was sent to survey four possible locations. They visited both rural and urban homes, made notes about economic and demographic conditions, and administered questionnaires, gathering information about people's eating habits, preferences, and beliefs. The interview questions were detailed and probing.

Ultimately we selected a location just outside the town of Bogra, 140 miles northwest of Dhaka, for our first plant. Bogra is near the center of the North Bengal region and is connected with the rest of the area by properly constructed and well-maintained roads. The immediate vicinity contains a large population of three million potential customers. There was also a plot of land available of the right size and shape for our factory. The area had not been polluted by any previous industrial occupant. Roads, water supply, and a source of compressed natural gas to run an electricity generator were all accessible. Because electrical service to rural Bangladesh is spotty at best, it was important that our factory have its own source of reliable power. It was also important that the factory be located in an area that is not flood-prone.

Bogra was a good choice for one final, somewhat coincidental reason. It so happens that Bogra is well known in Bangladesh for the yogurt it produces—a sweet, thick mixture usually taken as a dessert. Bangladeshi people are familiar with the *mishti doi* (sweet yogurt) made in Bogra and they are fond of it, so the idea of introducing our new product here made good marketing sense.

The idea of building many small plants rather than one large one came as a surprise to Danone's industrial design department. This was Guy Gavelle's first experience working in Bangladesh, and it was the first time he had been asked to make a *tiny* plant rather than a large one.

Guy started spending more time in Bangladesh than in Indonesia, where he is normally based. One day he came to me excited and with a huge smile. "Professor, I want to report some very happy news. I have designed the plant that you wanted—a very small plant. But it is not only small. It is very cute and very efficient, equipped with a full range of state-of-the-art technology. In fact, it is more advanced than the huge plants I have designed in Brazil, Indonesia, China, and India. I am very happy today."

Guy went on to confess that, at first, he had been alarmed about my insistence on setting up a series of small plants. He thought it would make the yogurt production costly and inefficient. But the process of drawing up the designs had convinced him otherwise. Small could be just as efficient as big, despite his years of assuming the opposite.

Actually, the shift in thinking that our small Bogra plant demanded was even more drastic than this. In the rest of the world, Danone yogurt is produced in huge quantities. Large shipments of the product are then delivered in refrigerated trucks to special air-

The early days of Grameen Bank (Tangail, 1979). I am disbursing a loan to a borrower. At that time, Grameen Bank had more male borrowers than female borrowers. Today, nearly all of our borrowers are women.

Grameen Bank today. Members arrive at the local center for their weekly meeting.

The headquarters of Grameen Bank in Dhaka, the capital of Bangladesh.

In a center meeting, chatting with some borrowers.

A cow-fattening business launched with the help of a Grameen Bank loan.

A village resident takes advantage of the cell-phone service provided by the local Grameen "phone lady."

A Grameen family poses around their Grameen-financed power tiller.

A basket-maker displays some of her beautiful handi work.

This local weaver is creating a bolt of Grameen Check, the beautiful cotton fabric native to Bangladesh.

Grameen members share their stories with me as they work on weaving baskets from bamboo leaves.

This row of village shops would be without electricity if not for the solar panel (top left) provided by Grameen Shakti, our renewable energy company that provides electricity to villages off the national grid.

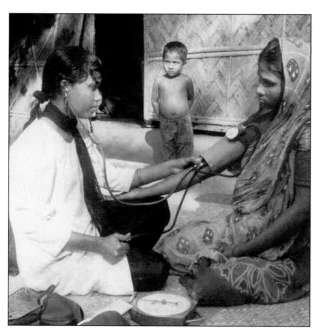

A paramedic from Grameen Kalyan consults with a villager who might otherwise have little opportunity to receive health care.

A borrower from a Grameen-style microcredit program in China.

Some of the thousands of recent recipients of higher education loans provided by Grameen Bank.

Launching a dream: CEO of Danone Franck Riboud and soccer star Zinedine Zidane arrive in Bangladesh to celebrate the creation of Grameen Danone, our multinational social business.

A supply of yogurt departs the factory on its way to a village market.

A Grameen lady arrives in the village with a bag full of Shokti Doi, with an eager crowd of children following her.

The nutrients in Shokti Doi should help youngsters like this one avoid malnutrition, diarrhea, and other complaints that commonly afflict children in Bangladesh.

With Senator Hillary Clinton, who has been a supporter of Grameen Bank and microcredit since her days as the First Lady of the state of Arkansas.

With my two daughters, Monica and Deena, in 2005.

An artist's rendering of Grameen Green Children Eye Care Hospital, a social business now under development.

With members of the Grameen Bank board who represented the bank at the Nobel Prize ceremonies in Oslo, Norway in December 2006.

We have accomplished so much—yet so much remains to be done to eliminate the disease of poverty from every corner of the world.

conditioned warehouses, from which the yogurt is finally taken to supermarkets and grocery stores in various cities and towns. At every step in the process, refrigeration is used to keep the product cool and maintain the live cultures in the yogurt in a dormant state (the "cold chain" system). This ensures that there is absolutely no variation in the acidity or flavor of Danone yogurt.

In Bangladesh, maintaining the same kind of refrigeration regime from factory to consumer would be impossible. Most rural Bangladeshis are off the utility grid, and many shops and stores in village markets don't have electric power. Refrigerators are few and far between.

This reality does not necessarily pose a health risk to yogurt consumers. Bangladeshis eat plenty of locally made *mishti doi* served in clay pots and stored in the open, right on shop counters, with no ill effects. But it did require some flexibility on the part of Danone's management and some creative thinking by our entire team. We realized that our distribution system would have to emphasize a quick turnaround from factory to consumer, with yogurt leaving the production line in the morning and ending up in children's stomachs within no more than forty-eight hours. This would be the only way to ensure that the flavor, texture, and acid content of our yogurt would be consistent.

We began making plans with these unusual requirements in mind. The distribution system we developed employs the "Grameen ladies" who are the borrowers of Grameen Bank, living in the villages we serve. These women would become the key to the sales program for our yogurt. And their help would ensure that the yogurt remained tasty and healthful throughout the distribution and selling process, with or without refrigeration.

Finding the Winning Formula

A social business must be prepared to compete with traditional PMBs. It must provide customers with high-quality goods and services, provide excellent value for the prices it charges, and offer the same level of convenience and ease of use as any other company—if not more so. A social business can't expect to win customers just because it is run by nice people with good intentions. It must attract consumers and retain their loyalty by being the best. Only in this way will it thrive financially and be able to provide the social benefit for which it was created.

With today's consumer products, marketing is a key element for business. This is especially true when children are a major part of the target audience. Parents usually choose and buy the foods they give their young ones, but if the children don't like the products, sales will dry up and the business will fail.

For this reason, we knew we had to develop a marketing plan that would make our yogurt popular with the children of Bangladesh. Danone's enormous experience in marketing dairy products around the world, including Asia, would play a significant role. But Grameen's intimate knowledge of Bangladeshi culture, and our economic and social ties to village communities throughout the country, would also be crucially important.

Launching a successful food product begins with product formulation. Danone's nutrition experts figured out the nutrients that should go into our yogurt. The yogurt, they'd decided, would be made from pure, full-cream milk, containing an average of 3.5 percent fat. It would be fortified with vitamin A (beneficial for the eyes), iron, calcium, zinc, protein, and iodine (to help maintain thyroid function). The active cultures in the yogurt are also very good for children; they help to minimize the incidence and seriousness of diarrhea. These specifications ensured that our yogurt would serve the social goal of improving the health of village children—provided we could convince them to eat it.

To achieve that, Danone had to make sure that the taste would appeal to children and to their mothers. Danone developed a trial recipe and began conducting taste tests. They chose representative members of our target audience—mothers and children from the Bogra district who we hoped would become enthusiastic customers for our yogurt—and sent teams of researchers into their homes during the spring of 2006 to sample their reactions.

The initial results were not positive. The yogurt had a noticeably "off" taste from the fortifying ingredients, and so the Danone flavor experts set to work to modify the formula. Imamus Sultan suggested sweetening the product with molasses made from dates from palm trees, a favorite flavor enhancement in Bangladeshi desserts. In most of the world, Danone yogurts are sold in unsweetened formulas that appeal to the global palate. But Bangladeshis have a notable sweet tooth, and in particular we are accustomed to eating yogurt that is quite sweet. The Grameen Danone team experimented with different recipes, looking for a level of sweetness that would delight village children while still being healthful.

We also tested the product concept and the packaging. Based on its global experience in marketing healthful foods to youngsters, Danone had suggested that a friendly animal would be an attractive symbol to use in promoting our yogurt.

On the advice of the Danone experts, Grameen conducted a survey on the popularity of various animals among children. Somewhat to our surprise, the monkey came out on top. But we had been thinking of naming our yogurt Shokti Doi, which means "Yogurt for Power." It was a good name, which captured the benefits of the nutrients that fortify the yogurt. But we did not think that the monkey was a good symbol for power.

The next most popular animals were the tiger and the lion. The former is very popular in Bangladesh, land of the Royal Bengal Tiger, one of the most beautiful (and rare) feline species in the world. But since the tiger is already used in Bangladesh as a symbol for products, we chose the lion.

So when we sent our researchers into the villages to test the marketing concept, they brought with them sample plastic cups bearing the picture of a lion and the brand-new Grameen Danone logo. This image, in which the well-known blue lettering of Danone is surrounded by the red-and-green house-shaped Grameen symbol, is the first time that the Danone logo has appeared *inside* another logo anywhere in the world.

The researchers explained in detail the contents of the product, mentioning both the sweet, creamy taste of the yogurt and its many health benefits. Both mothers and children seemed attracted by this concept. They liked the idea of an affordable, tasty yogurt snack that would improve their nutrition. The positive response encouraged us to believe that we were on the right track.

The Official Launch

In March 2006, Franck Riboud came to Dhaka to sign and publicize the memorandum of understanding (MOU) that officially launched the Grameen Danone joint venture.

The MOU specified that the initial funding for the project (a total of 75 million taka, about $1.1 million) would be provided on a fifty-fifty basis—half by Danone and half by a group of four Grameen companies: Grameen Byabosa Bikash (Grameen Business Promotion), Grameen Kalyan (Grameen Welfare), Grameen Shakti (Grameen Energy), and Grameen Telecom, a nonprofit company that owns a large block of Grameen Phone, the biggest mobile-phone company in Bangladesh.

The MOU also laid out the purpose for which Danone and Grameen had joined forces:

Purpose:
Mission: Reduce poverty by a unique proximity business model which brings daily healthy nutrition to the poor.

The JV [joint venture] will be designed and operated as a social business enterprise and will aim at sharing the benefits with its community of stakeholders.

Specific objectives:
Daily healthy nutrition to the poor:
Allow lower income consumers of Bangladesh to have access (in terms of affordability and availability) to a range of tasty and nutritious foods and beverages on a daily basis, in order to improve their nutritional status.

More specifically, help children of Bangladesh grow strong, thanks to tasty, nutritious food and beverage products they can consume every day, so that they can have a better future.

A unique proximity business model:
Design a manufacturing and distribution model that involves local communities.

Reduce poverty:
Improve the economic conditions of the local bottom class population by:

- Upstream: involving local suppliers (farmers) and helping them to improve their practices;
- Production: involve local population via a low cost/labor intensive manufacturing model;
- Downstream: contributing to the creation of jobs through the distribution model.

The MOU left no doubt that Grameen Danone would be a social business, one designed to maximize social benefit rather than financial profit. It also specified very clearly *how* we intended to help the poor: by providing healthful food to improve their nutrition; by creating jobs in and around our factory; and by stimulating the local economy through the use of community people as suppliers and distributors of the product. Emmanuel used his phrase "unique proximity business model" to sum up our strategy.

This MOU, like some other features of our joint venture, is unusual. It combines social aspirations (nourishing the poor, reducing poverty) with practical business details in a way that captures the special power of social business. And because it spells out the unique commitment to reinvest virtually all of the profits in expanding and improving the business (rather than rewarding shareholders), the MOU also makes it clear that Grameen Danone is not a "corporate social responsibility" project of Danone—that is, a project of a profit-maximizing business with a charitable veneer—but rather an example of social business, something quite new in the corporate world.

I hope these features of our MOU will be useful guides for those designing future social businesses.

Franck was impatient to make progress. After the signing ceremony, he asked his Danone colleagues, "When do you plan to open the first factory?"

"Within one year," Guy answered.

Franck shook his head disapprovingly. "No, do it *this* year!" he insisted. "I want to come back in November for a ribbon-cutting ceremony!"

I loved what Franck said. It's how I act, too. Once I am sure about a business concept, I want to get moving on it. If it is successful, it can be quickly expanded; if it is not, it can be revised and re-launched using a new and better plan.

After Franck set the opening date, everybody got busy. By June, our plans were well advanced, but a hundred details still had to be nailed down. Emmanuel wrote me with a list of the urgent remaining issues.

One issue was the purchase of the land where our factory would be located, which was still not confirmed. Negotiations had stalled, with price being one sticking point: Apparently the landowner, realizing that a major multi-national corporation was involved in the purchase, had decided to hold out for the maximum possible price. The construction plans were all finalized and ready to go, so building could move ahead swiftly once the deed was obtained. But with such a short time frame in which to begin and finish the building project, we needed to take formal ownership of the land as soon as possible.

Another challenge was to develop detailed plans for local distribution of our products. With the help of a team of students from HEC, the renowned French business school, a sales and marketing manager would need to map the area within a radius of fifteen miles in terms of local consumption markets (villages), select about 100 depot locations for delivery of yogurt supplies, select shops for yogurt sales, and prepare the recruitment of the "Grameen Danone ladies" we were planning to involve in distribution of the product door to door. This was a full agenda that needed to begin as soon as possible.

We also needed to move quickly to take advantage of a new opportunity. The Global Alliance for Improved Nutrition (GAIN) is an organization based in Geneva that has done much to bring better food to poor people around the world. In February, Danone had become a business supporter of GAIN, and Franck Riboud had become a GAIN board member. Learning from Franck about Grameen Danone in Bangladesh, GAIN had expressed its readiness to support Grameen Danone.

GAIN would offer its expertise in a number of areas. It would help us define the nutritional benefit message to the consumers so as to be accurate, easily understandable, and appealing; it would help design the "nutritional marketing" tools to be used (such as leaflets and posters); and it would support and assist in the training of the Grameen ladies to distribute the product. Perhaps most important, GAIN's experts would conduct detailed follow-up efficacy studies according to the best scientific protocols to measure the health benefits enjoyed by consumers of Shokti Doi.

All of these would be invaluable in achieving our social goals. But these benefits wouldn't happen unless we quickly developed protocols for working with GAIN. If Grameen Danone had been a long-established company, we could have simply handed the task over to a staff member. But we were operating on the fly, developing ways to manage tasks as they arose, literally inventing the business day by day.

As spring turned into summer, we had just six months to get everything done.

7

One Cup of
Yogurt at a Time

One afternoon in early February 2007, Guy Gavelle of Danone and Imamus Sultan of Grameen met with sixty sari-clad women from the Bogra district. The meeting place, on the grounds of a local school, was a small tin-roofed clubhouse, a kind of cultural center. On one of its walls hangs a portrait of Rabindranath Tagore, the Nobel Prize–winning (1913) poet who is a proud symbol of our national heritage. The ceiling was made of traditional woven bamboo-leaf mats. Light was provided by two bare bulbs dangling from cords. The women, a few with small children on their laps, sat on rows of molded plastic chairs, while Guy and Sultan faced them from behind a plain wooden table on which a microphone had been placed. Colorful blue silk-screened posters about six feet tall, bearing the grinning face of a heavily muscled cartoon lion decorated the walls. The lion is the symbol of Shokti Doi—the "Yogurt for Power" that is the first product of the Grameen Danone joint venture.

This workshop was an important component of our new social-business company. These women, the Grameen ladies, would form the first distribution network for Grameen Danone. They would sell cups of yogurt either door to door, among their friends and neighbors, or across the counter of small grocery and sundry shops like those that serve the inhabitants of thousands of villages all across Bangladesh. Most significant, they were typical Bangladeshi mothers, very much like the target customers for the product. If they were convinced of the nutritional value and sales potential of Shokti Doi, they would be effective salespeople for the product, and the business would get off to a good start.

For an hour or more, Imamus Sultan, interim president of the company, and Guy Gavelle, Industrial Director of Danone Dairy, Asia Pacific, spoke. They spelled out the reasons that Shokti Doi ought to become a part of the staple diet of everyone in Bangladesh—especially children.

"This is a very good healthful food," Guy explained. "It is fortified with protein, iron, vitamin A, and other ingredients that children need to grow strong. And it is a living food. Yogurt contains good bacteria that fight the bad bacteria in your stomach. It will help prevent diarrhea in your children—or if they do get sick, it will be less serious and pass away more quickly." As Guy made each of his points in French-accented English, Sultan translated into Bengali. The women listened intently, many leaning forward, some nodding or offering quiet comments as Sultan spoke.

Guy also offered advice about selling Shokti Doi for this, the first group of Grameen Danone salespeople. "You need to know a little about how this product is made. We put the yogurt culture into the milk at thirty-eight degrees, the same temperature as your body, and leave it for about eight hours. This is what turns the milk into yogurt. We check the level of acidity during the process. As soon as this level is just right, we rapidly cool the yogurt to just four degrees to stop the process.

"This means that you need to keep the yogurt cool after you pick up your supply. Put it in the fridge, if you have one. Otherwise, store it in some other cool place. When you go to sell it door to door, carry your supply in the insulated blue bag we'll give you. This way, the yogurt will stay the same as when it leaves the factory. If the temperature goes up too high—if it reaches twenty degrees or more—the bacteria will start to multiply again. This means the acidity will rise, and children won't like the taste. We don't want that to happen! Do you understand?"

Heads nodded all around the room.

"Let me talk about the taste for a moment," Guy went on. "We make Danone yogurt in fifty countries around the world. In very few of them do we put sugar in the yogurt. But here in Bangladesh, we are putting a small amount of sugar into the product. Why? Because our taste tests show that this is what you and your children prefer. You are accustomed to a sweet yogurt. So we are making the yogurt to fit your taste. But it is not *too* sweet. We are putting only a little sugar in each cup—less than in the *mishti doi* that is sold in the local market. This is better for your children. Please don't add more sugar to the yogurt when you serve it! It's more healthy for children to learn to eat foods that aren't so sweet.

"And a word about selling the yogurt. In the beginning, when you go out to sell, don't carry too much yogurt with you. Suppose you take fifty cups in your case. It may happen that you only sell twenty cups. The other thirty will gradually get warm, turn more acidic, and lose the good flavor. Then, if you sell them a day or two later, people will eat them and say, 'This yogurt tastes bad.' Then they will never buy again.

"Instead, just carry twenty with you, and sell all twenty. If more people want to buy, tell them you will come back with more yogurt the next day. It's better to make the customer wait an extra day or two for the product than to sell a bad product. If the customer waits, she will appreciate the good yogurt more. But if you sell a yogurt that is spoiled, you may lose a customer forever, and even kill your own job!" The ladies around the room were nodding.

It was time for a few final words of encouragement.

"Remember," Guy said, "When you sell a cup of Shokti Doi, you are doing many good things. You are earning some money for yourself and your family. You are providing good nutrition for children. You are making jobs for farmers who sell us the milk. You are making jobs for workers in our factory. And you are helping to develop the business. If we are successful here in Bogra, we will build another factory somewhere else in Bangladesh. Then another, and another."

Then Imamus Sultan rose from his chair. He is a mild-mannered, bespectacled man with a shy demeanor. But he is an experienced Grameen hand, and from his years of working at Grameen Bank he understood intimately the conditions in which the Grameen ladies would be marketing our new product.

Sultan spoke in Bengali for several minutes, painting a vivid picture for the Grameen ladies of the benefits of this new social business. He recapitulated the health benefits of Shokti Doi. He reminded the women of the comments they'd heard earlier in the day from a physician who had spoken to them about the nutritional advantages of yogurt. He talked about the network of local suppliers who would gain income from the Grameen Danone venture—including many of the Grameen ladies themselves, who operated small dairy farms that would sell milk to the factory. And he discussed the business potential of yogurt sales: a commission of one-half taka per cup sold, which could increase a family's income by a few score or even a few hundred taka every month.

The Grameen ladies looked very interested.

Did anyone have questions? Many did. One by one, women around the room rose to throw out challenges or queries. Guy and Sultan answered them one by one.

A small debate erupted about the use of spoons to eat yogurt. Some of the village ladies were concerned about the lack of availability of spoons, especially when eating away from home. Would their customers have to scoop up the yogurt with their fingers? Sultan pointed out that the yogurt was soft enough to drink, straight from the cup. After some further discussion, it was agreed that Grameen Danone could make small plastic spoons available at the factory for half a taka each—the minimum possible price. The Grameen ladies could take a supply of these to carry with them on their rounds, so any customer who wanted to eat the yogurt on the spot could buy a spoon.

Finally, one of the ladies rose to offer a personal endorsement. "We've all had a chance to taste this yogurt," she said. "We like it. It's a little sweet, but not too sweet—a nice flavor. And I took some of the samples you gave us last week into the village. I gave them to my friends. They all said it was good—except for one child who said it wasn't sweet enough. But then the next day he asked if he could have some more!" Laughter burst out around the room. "This is going to be a popular product," she concluded, and sat down.

A Sports Super-Hero
Kick-Starts the Business

By the time of our February 2007 workshop with the Grameen ladies, the new Grameen Danone joint venture was almost ready to swing into full operation. It was all fairly amazing, especially considering how many important details had remained uncertain just six months earlier. Looking back, it is hard to believe that we accomplished so much in such a short time.

In early June 2006, we'd been bogged down in negotiations to buy a plot of land for our factory. Dreaming of a huge profit from a sale to a multinational corporation, one landowner had been holding out for an exorbitant price. We'd finally broken the logjam by discovering an alternative site on the outskirts of Bogra. It was almost four and a half acres, quite a bit larger than we needed for our factory. But we decided to purchase the whole thing for just under 15 million taka, a little over $200,000.

Actually, only half an acre was paid for by the Grameen Danone joint venture. The rest was purchased by the Grameen Group. We are planning to use the extra land as a site for one of our social businesses: a hospital that will provide eyesight-saving cataract operations to the poor at a fraction of the usual cost, while well-off people will pay full market fee.

Once we identified this alternative site, we were able to move quickly to conclude the purchase—fast enough, in fact, to hold a ceremonial ground-breaking on July 14th and have the major construction on the factory site completed by November.

We'd also needed a plan for working with GAIN, the Swiss-based nutrition organization that would help us develop, test, and validate our program for ensuring that the poor people of Bangladesh enjoyed meaningful health benefits from our new product. This, too, had fallen into place. In June and July, Ms. Berangere Magarinos, manager of GAIN's Investments and Partnerships Programs, had led a team of experts to Bangladesh, where they had worked closely with us on our nutritional program. Among other things, they worked with us on conducting more consumer research to understand what would encourage or discourage buying Shokti Doi. They also evaluated and helped us improve the training materials we'd developed for teaching our Grameen ladies about the health benefits of yogurt and the best ways to ensure that young children enjoyed those benefits to the fullest.

We were now confident that we'd developed an effective plan for getting the benefits of yogurt into the stomachs of the kids around

Bogra. What's more, GAIN had agreed to conduct a nutritional impact study during the first year after our product reached the market.

This is important. We need to be able to document in concrete, scientific terms the health benefits—if any—that local children enjoy as a result of the Grameen Danone intervention. A social business must be diligent about accurately measuring and reporting the social benefits it creates. This will tell the company whether all the hard work and the investment of time, money, and other resources by the company and its partners have paid off. Depending on the results, the managers can decide whether to expand their efforts or redesign the business for better outcomes in the future.

Franck Riboud, the Danone CEO, had made his second visit to Bangladesh in November for the official inauguration of our brand-new Grameen Danone yogurt-making plant. A spring and summer of intense planning, inspired improvisation, and hard work had turned Guy Gavelle's vision of a "cute" but highly efficient factory into a reality.

Occupying just 7,500 square feet, the Bogra plant features gleaming state-of-the-art equipment: stainless-steel intake pipes for milk; spotless tanks for heating and chilling the yogurt; a conveyor line where rows of tiny cups are molded, filled with yogurt, and labeled; and a cold room for storing the prepared product. Many features make the factory genuinely green. There is equipment for incoming and outgoing water treatment, to ensure that all the water we use as well as all the water we return to the environment is clean and safe, and also solar panels to generate renewable energy.

Guy Gavelle says that designing and building the Bogra plant has been one of the richest learning experiences of his decades-long career at Danone. In fact, he has learned so much that he predicts we will be able to build our second and third yogurt factories in other areas of Bangladesh, with greater capabilities, at a cost about 20 to 30 percent *lower* than the modest sum we spent in Bogra.

During his visit in March, Franck had asked me, "Is there any celebrity from France that everyone in Bangladesh is sure to know—someone who could visit Bangladesh to help publicize our new venture?"

Bangladeshi villagers don't know much about France. I was thinking of film stars, fashion models, and political leaders but could not come up with a name that I felt satisfied with. Seeing me hesitate, Franck asked, "How about someone from the world of sports? Do the Bangladeshis like football?" (He was speaking, of course, of the game that Americans call soccer.)

"Absolutely!" I replied. "They are crazy about it. You should visit Dhaka when the World Cup Football matches are taking place. Everybody in Bangladesh has a favorite team. When you look at the Dhaka skyline, you see thousands of national flags on the rooftops— Brazil, Argentina, Germany, France, Italy, Spain. And in the rural areas, every village has its own favorite team. They don't know where in the world the country of their favorite team is located, but they know the name of every single player."

"By any chance, is Zinédine Zidane a popular football player in Bangladesh?" Franck asked.

"What? Zinédine Zidane?!" I exclaimed. "He is a super-hero to all Bangladeshis, even to people living in the remotest villages. If he came to Bangladesh, the entire police force would have to be deployed to protect him from his fans."

Franck was smiling broadly. "Zizou is a friend of mine. I'll ask him to come. And he *will* come!" Franck said, total confidence in his voice.

I could scarcely believe my ears. Zizou coming to Bangladesh to launch Grameen Danone? The whole country would go wild!

The Grameen Danone team was electrified by the news. Newspapers carried the story in bold headlines: "Zizou is coming to Bangladesh!"

(During the World Cup finals, in July 2006, Zizou, the man considered the greatest soccer player of his generation, became even more famous when, responding to insults from an opposing player, he head-butted him and was thrown out of the game. The controversy did nothing to dim Zizou's popularity among soccer fans in Bangladesh, or anywhere else, for that matter.)

Zizou arrived in November, trailing Franck, his business colleagues, and an entourage of curious French journalists. Their visit caused a sensation.

Zizou visited the village of Bashan Gazipur to meet the borrowers of the Grameen Bank branch located in that village, so that he could learn about microcredit. The road from Dhaka to Bashan was lined with hundreds of thousands of people. As the caravan of cars accompanying Zizou rolled down the road, all one could hear was the thunderous sound of thousands chanting, "Zi-zou! Zi-zou! Zi-zou!"

Zizou excited the villagers by playing football with a group of local schoolchildren. I am sure those youngsters and the villagers who watched the game will never forget the experience. Later, in a packed stadium in Dhaka, Zizou joined two teams made up of boys under age sixteen and showed off some of his signature moves. The crowd went wild, cheering and chanting his name.

Zizou capped off his visit by signing his autograph on a marble slab. This would become the foundation stone of the Grameen Danone plant in Bogra. It was the kind of spectacular brand launch that could only be pulled off by one of the greatest companies in the world.

When Zidane met the president of Bangladesh at the end of his visit, he promised to come back with his children to let them meet the Bangladeshi children who had made such a deep impression on him.

A Win for the Company, a Win for the Poor

Soon after Zizou's visit, we enjoyed tasting the first test batches of fortified yogurt—quite delicious, with a unique sweetness that comes from molasses made from the juice of date palm trees, a popular rural drink here in Bangladesh. In January 2007, the first commercial batches of Shokti Doi rolled off the line. They were packaged in attractive plastic cups decorated with a picture of a cartoon lion, showing off his muscles (to indicate that the yogurt is fortified). An eighty-gram cup costs just five taka—the equivalent, at current exchange rates, of about seven cents. If you bring your own cup to the factory, you will get ninety grams for the same five-taka price.

Better nutrition for children is the central social mission of our Grameen Danone initiative, and through GAIN's research we'll keep on monitoring how far we are succeeding in our mission. But nutrition isn't the only social benefit for which we are striving. Our business plan was developed with several other benefits to the community in mind.

Those benefits can be seen on the downstream side of the business, with our locally based sales and marketing network. Think of a

Danone dairy factory and you might imagine gleaming steel trucks delivering large supplies of products to storage facilities and supermarkets around the country. That is not how our Bogra system will work. Our distributors are local villagers—women who are borrowers of Grameen Bank and have already used microloans to start family enterprises. Now they have added the distributorship of Grameen Danone yogurt to their daily work.

When I initially proposed this arrangement in an email to Danone back in the spring of 2006, I wrote:

> *By employing the Grameen ladies, we'll enjoy a number of business and social benefits.*
>
> *We can make use of a disciplined community of entrepreneurs that already exist and are waiting for more opportunities.*
>
> *Young children of Grameen families who are literate can get involved in this new business.*
>
> *Grameen can provide all the financing to the Grameen families for this purpose. To that extent, the project will need less cash and be exposed to less risk.*
>
> *If there is a need for two-stage distribution, involving both wholesalers and retailers, Grameen borrowers can get involved in both stages.*

Emmanuel and the rest of the Danone team agreed with my reasoning, and we are now following very much the plan I proposed. That is what led to the workshop for Grameen ladies that I described at the start of this chapter.

A similar approach is being taken on the upstream side of the supply chain, where we are using local people as suppliers. The milk for our factory comes from village farmers who own one or a few cows. The other ingredients—mainly sugar and molasses—also come from rural Bangladesh. The employees of the factory, some twenty in number, are also local people. (We had Danone advisers on hand during the construction phase, but now that the factory is up and running, it is purely a Bangladeshi operation.) So our business will directly support the local and national economies.

Organizing the milk supply for the Grameen Danone plant represents a challenge in itself, since 90 percent of the Bangladeshi milk

market operates on an informal basis. To avoid coming into competition with other milk purchasers, Grameen Danone has chosen to develop a series of microfarms. These will be financed in part through
microcredit arranged by Grameen Bank.

The villagers who own these microfarms will use the money they
borrow to buy more cows. They will sell the milk they produce to
Grameen Danone. In return, the company will guarantee them a
fixed price throughout the year. Other Grameen companies are also
getting involved. The Grameen Agricultural Foundation is organizing
and improving milk production in the Bogra district in collaboration
with Danone experts. We are using a comprehensive design for farm
improvement that involves cattle development, milk-quality enhancement, organic fertilizer, and bio-gas production. Grameen's renewable
energy company, Grameen Shakti, will also be involved. They will be
installing bio-digesters for producing organic fertilizer and bio-gas for
cooking and lighting, thereby helping the small dairy farmers who
will be the main suppliers of Grameen Danone to become even more
self-sustaining.

These efforts to work with the local community—especially the
existing pool of Grameen Bank borrowers—are an important aspect
of what makes Grameen Danone a social business. The existence of
the yogurt plant will benefit the local economy both directly and in-
directly, having a positive multiplier effect for many families. This explains the way we describe the mission of Grameen Danone: "To
reduce poverty by a unique proximity business model which will
bring daily nutrition to the poor."

The Grameen Danone factory is not some distant corporate be-
hemoth. It is a friend of the community and an integral and natural
part of its social eco-system.

Our community-supplier and community-distributor programs
are also sound business from a financial point of view. For example, it's
hard to imagine a group of marketers and salespeople who could be
more effective at promoting and publicizing our new product than the
Grameen ladies. They are themselves part of the target customer base
(village families, especially parents of small children); they are known
members of the community; they know potential customers and what
is likely to appeal to them; and they are already in daily touch with

customers for their other businesses, whether these involve poultry or dairy farming, craft production, services, food sales, or whatever.

As for the local dairy farmers who will supply our milk, this too is a good business strategy as well as a sound piece of social improvement. A major factor in the cost structure of Grameen Danone is the price of milk. When we first set the tentative price of a cup of yogurt in the fall of 2006, the wholesale market price of a liter of milk in Bangladesh was between 14 and 16 taka (equivalent to between 20 and 25 cents). By the time Grameen Danone opened for business, because of an increase in demand, the price had risen to 20 to 22 taka (30 to 35 cents). This is a large enough difference that it would make an appreciable dent in our slim profit margin.

It became obvious that the future management of Grameen Danone will require constant planning to deal with such fluctuations in prices. This is where the local dairy production will prove a boon. Having a dedicated pool of local farmers under contract to sell their production to us will shield us to some extent from short-term price variations. It will also help the farmers, of course. Even when regional or national prices fall, Grameen Danone will provide them with a reliable source of ongoing demand, cushioning them from potential economic shocks.

Our current plans are for the Bogra factory to produce about 6,600 pounds of yogurt daily during the first year. That will increase to 22,000 pounds by the third year.

The lesson: When it is carefully planned, a social business can be very sound business. Just as the business helps the community, the community helps the business. Both can grow and thrive together, lifting families and individuals to higher levels of economic achievement.

Edible Cups?

What is more, Grameen Danone will not stand still. We plan to continue looking for more ways to improve the product and its benefits to the people of Bangladesh.

Here is a small but interesting example. Right from the beginning, we were looking for biodegradable cups for dispensing yogurt. Usually it is sold in plastic cups, which are not biodegradable, and trash disposal is a big and expanding problem. So early in the project, Grameen Danone began working on developing the first "green" containers for yogurt.

By the middle of 2006, Guy Gavelle and his technical team had tracked down a potential supplier in China—a company that makes biodegradable cups from cornstarch. A Danone representative visited the factory in China and reported back: "Cost/kg of the compound is still higher than plastic, but the material resistance is such that the weight per cup could be significantly lower than plastic, which could mean overall savings vs. our current projections." (Lighter packaging saves money both in manufacturing, since less material is required, and in shipping.)

We introduced the brand-new cornstarch containers for Shokti Doi in March 2007. Our Bogra plant even has a specially prepared facility for recycling the used containers—a pit into which the cornstarch cups are put, where naturally accumulating pressure and heat transforms the material into a natural, nutrient-rich substance suitable for fertilizer. It works a bit like the compost heaps many gardeners and farmers have in their yards.

The cornstarch cups are a big step toward green packaging of Shokti Doi. But I am still not satisfied! I would like to find an *edible* cup that we can use—one that kids can scoop the yogurt from, then eat up completely. (Think about how you can eat the ice cream from an ice cream cone, then eat the cone itself.) The cup would offer extra nutrition, the problem of trash disposal would be completely eliminated, recycling would be unnecessary, and everyone would benefit.

Of course, the edible cup must also have all the properties of any good food container: It must be stackable, strong, lightweight, and attractive; it must stand up to shipping and to changes in temperature; and it must be printable with a label, ingredients, and other information. Does this sound impossible? It is—at this moment. But Danone research scientists are working on the problem, and I believe they will come up with a solution. In time, Bangladesh will, hopefully, become a pioneer in introducing the edible food container. Who knows, this may set a trend and a standard for food packaging everywhere.

Bringing Meaning
to Business Life

In October 2006, the Norwegian Nobel Peace Committee announced that Grameen Bank and I would share that year's Nobel Peace Prize. As you can imagine, I received a flood of congratulatory telephone calls, emails, and official messages from heads of states, heads of states and governments, academics, microcredit practitioners, and many other well-wishers. I also received handwritten notes from friends and colleagues around the world.

Among these messages was a formal statement from the Board of Directors of Groupe Danone. Amid many flattering comments about Grameen and our work, the board noted that I had announced that my half of the Nobel Prize money would be invested in social businesses. The board stated that they would match my investment with a Danone investment in whatever social businesses I chose to support.

I also received a more personal message from Emmanuel Faber's office in Shanghai:

Dear Yunus,

It must be the end of one of the longest days in your life . . . and you must have so many emails that you may never find this one down the list on your screen!

I just realized that you met Franck exactly one year ago yesterday, to the day. In that one year, you have changed our corporate life. And thanks to your vision and enthusiasm, we may change a small bit of the way business is done by multinationals. (We have a board meeting on Monday at which we'll discuss our whole new approach to social businesses.)

We'll never thank you enough for bringing meaning to our business life.

Best, Em

This note had a special significance for me. All the things that I have been saying about the immense satisfaction people will derive from social business are now coming to fruition. The same message was conveyed in the title of an article by *Fortune* magazine writer Sheri Prasso, who wrote that we were "Saving the World One Cup of Yogurt at a Time." This idea has also been confirmed by many Danone officials, who have told me that the employees of Groupe Danone find the Grameen Danone joint venture to be an especially important part of their business. They follow its progress with interest, discuss it among themselves continually, and frequently mention it with pride when discussing their company in public.

It's surprising, perhaps, that a small, one-million-dollar business should play such a leading role within a sixteen-billion-dollar corporation. But one of the deep-rooted characteristics of human beings is the desire to do good for other people. It is an aspect of human nature that is totally ignored in the existing business world. Social business satisfies this human craving, and that's why people find it very inspiring.

I can't agree with those who claim that social business will never achieve a significant foothold in the real world. From the reactions I see when people are exposed to the idea of social business, I am convinced that social business will soon take root and flourish in the business world. People want meaning in their lives—the kind of meaning that comes only from knowing that you are doing your part to make our world a better place.

Social business provides this meaning. That's why people respond.

THREE

A World Without Poverty

8

Broadening
the Marketplace

Since the late 1980s, I have been writing and talking about "social-consciousness-driven enterprise" and creating for-profit and not-for-profit companies with very clear social objectives. No desire for personal gain on my part has entered into the equation; I have not created any for-profit company in which I own even a single share. It is the social purpose that motivates me in creating business enterprises.

From my travels and my conversations with people around the world, I know I'm not the only person who feels this way. I am sure many people would like to create social-purpose companies if such entities were recognized by the economic system. It is a major failure of the current economic system that it cannot accommodate this basic human urge.

Over the last few years, I formulated my idea of social business more clearly and began speaking about it wherever I could. I discussed social business in radio, TV, and newspaper interviews, in sessions of the World Economic Forum, in private gatherings of high-net-worth individuals seeking constructive ways to invest their funds, and in meetings like the Skoll Foundation conferences on Social Entrepreneurship at the Saïd School of Business at Oxford University.

At the same time, I realized that it would be important to create a real-life social business in order to demonstrate my ideas in a concrete fashion. That led to our decision to set up a series of eyecare hospitals as a social business. In 2005, four of the Grameen companies—

Grameen Byabosa Bikash, Grameen Kalyan, Grameen Shakti, and Grameen Telecom—stepped forward to be the social investors.

To administer this new business, we created two organizations: Grameen Healthcare Trust (GHT), a not-for-profit company, and Grameen Health Care Services (GHS), a for-profit company. The Grameen companies are directly investing in GHS, while other donors and investors are giving funds to GHT. GHT, in turn, is funding GHS to launch additional hospital projects.

Every month dozens of young people from around the world visit us. As our planning for this venture was taking shape, Tom Bevan and Milla Sunde came. They had met in a songwriting class at England's Liverpool Institute of Performing Arts (LIPA) and founded the music group Green Children, which became the basis for their exciting pop music career. Milla, the lead singer, is from Norway, and Tom, her songwriting and pianist partner, is from the U.K.

When Tom and Milla visited Grameen Bank in 2006, they fell in love with the people and the countryside of Bangladesh. They were so inspired that Tom wrote a song, "Hear Me Now," which tells the story of a Grameen Bank borrower they'd spent time with in a Bangladeshi village. They made a second visit later that year to produce a music video for the song, which you can see and hear on YouTube and elsewhere on the Web.

Tom and Milla also became intrigued by the idea of social business. Milla decided to contribute the full cost of the first eyecare hospital to GHT out of the funds controlled by her own Green Children Foundation. She and Tom also will contribute the entire sale proceeds of the music video to build more eyecare hospitals, each at a cost of nearly $1 million.

The eyecare hospitals will be based on a business plan that may become the simplest and most popular format for social businesses. In order to become sustainable while also achieving the social objective of delivering eyecare services to the poor, the hospital will employ a multiple-pricing policy. It will charge the regular market price to patients who have no difficulty in paying the fee (for a cataract operation, for example), while providing services to the poor at a highly discounted rate or for a token fee. The profit made on the market-rate charges will subsidize the services provided to the poor. This kind of multiple-pricing policy can be applied in many social businesses.

Another opportunity to create a social business came through my meeting with Groupe Danone chairman Franck Riboud in October 2005. As I've described, Grameen Danone company went into operation in early 2007, becoming our first real-life social business. The first eyecare hospital will open at the end of 2007. I hope we'll continue to expand both these social businesses within and outside Bangladesh.

The Grameen Foundation has also launched two more social businesses during 2007. The first is a financial firm, Grameen Capital India, created in partnership with Citibank India and ICICI Bank, to facilitate access to local capital markets for Indian microfinance institutions (MFIs), and its owners have agreed that they will not take any dividend out of this business.

The second is Grameen-Jameel Pan Arab Microfinance, another financial firm that has been formed in partnership with the Abdul Latif Jameel Group of Saudi Arabia. The objective of this company is poverty alleviation in the Arab world through microfinance. The company provides a suite of customized products and services for MFIs, including help with financing. Rather than distributing profits to its shareholders, it will recapitalize them—that is, reinvest them in expanding the business and making its services available to more client institutions.

I hope to keep adding more social businesses to the Grameen roster of companies as we move forward. More important, I expect other institutions to launch their own social businesses, especially after the publication of this book brings the idea into the consciousness of a wider audience around the world.

Who Will Invest in Social Business?

One of the questions I always get when I am explaining the concept of social business is, "Where will the money for social business come from?"

Maybe the question arises because of a fundamental doubt: Why should anybody in his right mind invest his hard-earned money in something that yields no financial return?

It seems to be a reasonable question. Yet people are even crazier than that—they give away their hard-earned money to create foundations and to support charities! People by the millions make such contributions every year, totaling billions of dollars. If one compares this "crazy" behavior with the "craziness" of investing in social business, the latter suddenly looks much saner. After all, when you invest in social business, you get your money back and retain the ownership of a company that supports itself through earned income. So individual contributions, especially from affluent people who want to help improve the world, will be a major source of funding for social business.

There is another ready source of money. Recently the very distinguished head of a major foundation said to me, "We have accumulated an endowment of nearly a billion dollars, and it is growing each year. Yet we don't have enough attractive projects to donate our money to. Can you suggest some projects for us to support?" I've heard similar questions from many other foundation officials over the years.

My quick answer was, "Why don't you think about investing your money in social businesses? You'll retain the flexibility to reuse the money in the future, if you want to. Or you can donate your money to a nonprofit organization that is specifically charged with investing in social businesses, just as the Green Children have done through Grameen Healthcare Trust. Ask for proposals, and see how many fascinating and innovative ones you get. You can do so much with your billion dollars."

Once foundations think about social business as a worthwhile target for support, the possibilities begin to seem unlimited. Microcredit can be a very attractive social business. Health care, information technology, renewable energy, environmental remediation, nutrition for the poor, and many other kinds of enterprises can be other arenas for interesting social businesses.

Foundations, then, can be a great source of funds for social businesses. So can bilateral and multilateral donors, which can create Social Business Funds in each recipient country to provide equity, venture capital, and loans to social businesses. The World Bank and the regional development banks (the Asian Development Bank,

African Development Bank, and Inter-American Bank) can create new lending windows to lend to social businesses. They can offer the same terms as they provide governments for investing the same types of projects the governments undertake—infrastructure, renewable energy, health, education, microcredit, and so on—providing the projects are operated as social businesses.

In addition, commercial lending institutions will be sources of funds for social businesses. Since social businesses are self-sustaining companies just like profit-maximizing businesses, commercial lenders will have no difficulty in funding them, and they will benefit from the good publicity it will bring them.

Finally, new kinds of financial institutions can be created as required to cater to the financing needs of social businesses: social venture-capital funds, social mutual funds, and, of course, a full-fledged social stock market. Each of these will be a mechanism for mobilizing individual and corporate equity in support of social business. The financial markets have a long history of success in developing smart ways to finance business projects, from commercial loans and private equity placements to bond sales and initial public offerings of stock. Some of these existing frameworks will be immediately applicable to social business, while others will need to be adapted in response to the emerging challenges thrown up by social businesses. This is an exciting new area for innovative minds to get busy with, and I have no doubt that the "rocket scientists" of Wall Street will have fun tackling this new challenge.

Financing Grameen Danone

I was thrilled with the way Danone's Franck Riboud enthusiastically accepted the idea of social business and quickly joined hands with Grameen to create the Grameen Danone partnership. But like every CEO of a publicly held company, Riboud is answerable not just to his own conscience but also to his shareholders. As the project was proceeding at full speed in Bangladesh, the management of Danone in Paris was seeking answers to the inevitable question every PMB management will face when they consider launching a social business:

How do we defend ourselves when the shareholders ask, "How dare you invest our money in a project that creates no profit for us? You are violating your mandate in doing so."

Fortunately, Danone's management had been grappling with this question for a long time. Franck frequently reminds the members of his management team about the purpose of Danone's business, citing his father Antoine Riboud's landmark public declaration of more than thirty years ago when addressing his colleagues of the French Conference Board: "There will not be sustainable economic value creation if there is no personal development and human value creation at the same time." Well before Grameen Danone was set in motion, Emmanuel Faber had been taking the lead within Danone in bringing a social orientation to bear on the company's business operations. For several years, Emmanuel had been discussing and debating the challenges of financing a business that has social objectives with friends who work as managers of some of the largest U.S. and European pension funds and mutual funds, as well as with financial analysts and journalists. Many of these fund managers shared Emmanuel's sense of discomfort with present-day capitalism. In view of the world situation, they felt the growing need for a new form of business, one that would do a better job of responding to social needs rather than being riveted to profit maximization only.

When Emmanuel described these debates to me, I was very pleased to hear that even the leaders in the world's financial markets have doubts about what they are doing. "I find this very reassuring," I told him. He laughed and said, "Well, these doubts keep me alive. I am only forty years old. I think I am still young enough to change the world!"

Emmanuel told me that for years he had been trying to solve this dilemma of finding a satisfactory "hybrid" business model. Then he came up with an idea that was different from the idea generally expressed by others in the business world as "double" or "triple bottom line," in which businesses strive to achieve success according to social and environmental yardsticks along with financial ones. Emmanuel's idea of a hybrid business model was that conscious or cause-related investors could be offered specific "social value for money" investment opportunities. The value trade-off would be that investors would agree to "cap" their return from day one under a predefined financial return company policy.

Emmanuel was disappointed when I told him that I don't believe in a hybrid business model, or in a double, triple, or even quadruple bottom line. Companies that espouse these programs often do so in a desperate attempt to assuage the guilt and anguish of executives who genuinely feel uncomfortable over the fact that their social concerns have been left behind in the crush of daily business. Others promote the hybrid or triple-bottom-line concepts as a way of coating their profit-making projects with an attractive public relations varnish.

Yet in the end, the fate of business managers hangs solely on the answer to one question: How much money have you made for us? After you give a satisfactory answer to that question, you may be allowed to do your dance on the second, third, or fourth bottom lines. And the audience at the shareholders' meeting will be very happy to applaud that dance—provided you have already generated a thunderous ovation with your performance on the first question.

Nonetheless, Emmanuel's long quest for the hybrid model prepared him to find a happy solution to the challenge of locating money for Grameen Danone without alienating the company's shareholders. The solution: to create a mutual fund with a special mission and give Danone shareholders the option of joining it if they wish, telling them exactly what they will and will not get out of it.

Emmanuel designed a mutual fund with the French title Société d'Investissement à Capital Variable, SICAV danone communities (Investment Company with Variable Capital, Danone Communities Fund), 90 percent of whose assets will be invested in money-market instruments yielding a predictable market rate of return. The remaining 10 percent will be invested in social businesses, which will pay no return. Taken together, these two pools of money will provide investors with a near-market yield on their money, while at the same time supporting businesses that are bringing specific social benefits to people in need.

Emmanuel had to get his idea cleared by the French regulatory authorities as well as the appropriate officials at the French stock market. Because it was a new concept, we couldn't be sure it would clear either of these hurdles. But on December 14, 2006, Emmanuel sent me the following email:

Dear Yunus,

After two weeks of intense discussions, I got informal indication from the head of the French stock exchange regulatory body that our "social business development fund" will be qualified to be listed as a mainstream money market fund on the French financial market.

The social objective will be stated clearly upfront for investors, and the return to shareholders will be "only" two to three percent, with very limited downside risk or upside potential. So 97 to 98 percent of the profits will be reinvested. People will invest because they want to be associated with the social business projects which will be supported by the fund and that we are working on establishing.

Danone shareholders will be offered the option of a "social dividend" whereby they will be able to get shares in the fund instead of cash from Danone.

The fund will be entirely open to the public and marketed by one of the leading French retail banks. People will be able to buy and sell their shares freely every day.

If we confirm the SEC approvals in the next couple of months, it will mean that we have succeeded in listing a social business on a mainstream capitalist stock exchange.

Looking forward to seeing you next Sunday—

Best,
Em

I'm very excited about the Danone Communities Fund as developed by Emmanuel Faber. It comes very close to embodying the full concept of social business as I have defined it in this book. It would have been a perfect fit if it provided for *no* annual return rather than the modest 2 to 3 percent that Emmanuel projects. In any case, the fund is an innovative way of financing social businesses through the existing stock market—a big step toward creating the Social Mutual Funds of the future.

As I write these words (in mid–2007), the chief regulatory and legal hurdles have been passed. The new mutual fund was officially approved by Danone's shareholders at the company's annual meeting in Paris on April 26, 2007. Underwritten and managed by the French banking group Crédit Agricole, the Danone Communities Fund will draw investment monies from several groups of people: Danone shareholders, who are already enthusiastic supporters of the concept; institutional investors such as banks, pension funds, and insurance companies; and individual investors from the general public of France.

The fund's initial goal is to raise €100 million ($135 million), of which €20 million will come from Groupe Danone. Danone shareholders will be given the option of forgoing annual stock dividends and instead investing the income in the Communities Fund. And over 30 percent of Danone's employees have already opted to invest part of their profit-sharing income in the fund.

The profit earned from the fund will be invested in the expansion of Grameen Danone's outreach throughout Bangladesh, in other Danone social businesses elsewhere in the developing world, and in new social businesses launched by independent entrepreneurs anywhere in the world. Within days of the announcement of the fund's launch, Emmanuel Faber was approached by several such entrepreneurs, eager to find out how they might tap this new source of financing for their social business ventures. The process of evaluating these ventures and selecting worthy recipients of funding has already begun.

Thus, with little fanfare, one of the building blocks of a new economic world in which social business takes its rightful place alongside profit-maximizing business is already falling into place. And the immediate, positive response reinforces my conviction that social business is an idea whose time has come—a concept that will unleash the pent-up creativity of millions of people around the world who have long been eager to apply their talents to solving our planet's most pressing problems but have lacked institutional recognition for doing so.

New Yardsticks for
Evaluating Business

The founding of the Danone Communities Fund is just a hint of the wide-ranging social, economic, and business innovations to come. As social businesses begin to flourish, existing free markets will begin to change in response to the new, broader model of human behavior they embody. A new breed of businesspeople, empowered for the first time to express humanistic values through the companies they found, will demand new institutional structures to support the new kinds of ventures that will emerge. It's not possible to foresee the changes in detail, but one can guess some of what may happen.

To begin with, social businesses will take their place along with profit-maximizing businesses as basic fixtures in the world of business. Social businesses will operate in the same market spaces as PMBs, competing with them and with one another for market share. Consumers will become accustomed to choosing between social businesses and PMBs when buying goods and services. In many cases, they will choose based on traditional criteria—price, quality, availability, brand appeal, and so on. In some cases, they may opt for a social business offering rather than a PMB because they want to support the social mission that will benefit from their purchase. Thus, upholding social values may become a regular part of the equation when consumers make their buying decisions.

Actually, we already see this phenomenon operating in the world of business. Many companies that claim to be managed along "socially responsible" lines try to appeal to the consciences of consumers as part of their overall marketing strategy. For example, clothing manufacturers that pay higher-than-average salaries and take pains to avoid the use of child workers will publicize these labor practices in hopes that concerned customers will choose their garments over those produced by competing companies. Sellers of organic foods promote their products not only by claiming they are more nutritious and healthful but also by saying that natural food-production methods are better for the environment, gentler to animals, and more supportive of local farming communities. There is evidence that a growing number of consumers are responding positively to such claims.

However, there is one problem with such socially responsible marketing in the current economic environment: namely, the lack of any recognized system for evaluating, testing, or enforcing claims of socially responsible products produced by companies. How can a consumer know for sure that a clothing manufacturer is not abusing workers in a factory in far-off Ecuador, Kenya, or Bangladesh? How can she be certain that the chicken or beef she buys in a food store has been produced using methods that are humane and environmentally sound? Standards in these areas are currently vague and difficult for the average person to apply. Consumers must judge based on company claims, advertising and marketing campaigns, statements from consumer groups, and articles in the press, all of which may be a doubtful credibility.

The existence of a social business market will subject these claims to much more serious scrutiny, since now both consumers and investors will be involved. With investors forgoing any return on their money, they will insist on concrete assurances that the social goal of the company is being achieved. In the same way, general consumers who patronize a company because it claims to be helping to reduce poverty, clean up the environment, or provide other social benefits will demand real evidence that the claims are true.

Sooner or later, certification companies and audit firms will have to be created to monitor the claims of social benefits put forth by social businesses. (These certification and auditing firms themselves may be social businesses.) Certification will be needed along two dimensions: financial (that is, to confirm that the company is following the financial standards set by the community of social businesses), and social (to confirm that the company's reports concerning its progress on social objectives are accurate and follow standard guidelines). Social businesses approved by the leading accrediting bodies may display a logo or seal symbolizing that they are backed by the prestige and credibility of the certification board. There may be other specialized rating agencies to certify various aspects of a social business—for example, adherence to labor standards, use of renewable energy sources, and fair practices in selecting suppliers who represent local communities.

The most important thing to remember is that social businesses need to be very well run, with clear, concrete objectives, carefully defined metrics for success, and continual internal and external monitoring. Over time, standardization of procedures, terminology, and accounting practices tailored to social businesses will emerge, just as the so-called Generally Accepted Accounting Practices (GAAP) are now available to PMBs.

To think of the creation of a global regulatory and informational infrastructure for social business may sound at this stage like a farfetched idea, perhaps an unrealistic one. But we are actually fortunate to have a big head start. Much of the groundwork has already been done, because of needs arising from other directions, in particular the need for environmental monitoring. This groundwork was born under a program of the United Nations Environment Program (UNEP) and the Coalition for Environmentally Responsible Economies (CERES) known as the Global Reporting Initiative (GRI). A well-known and widely used system for measuring and monitoring corporate behavior in relation to social and environmental goals, GRI may be seen as an early version of the kind of evaluation system that social business will benefit from.

The GRI guidelines were officially released at the World Summit on Sustainable Development in Johannesburg, South Africa, in 2002. The GRI idea was conceived in 1997 by CERES, which represents a number of socially responsible investment groups and funds. There are over 200 such funds, collectively holding some $179 billion in assets. Many of these funds were using different, home-grown systems for measuring sustainable business practices. To save time and energy, they wanted to create a shared set of universal protocols. GRI is the outcome of this desire. Today, more than 3,000 corporations issue periodic environmental or social responsibility reports, and over 700 use the reporting guidelines formulated by GRI.

Several other efforts have been undertaken to create systems for measuring and monitoring the social performances of PMBs. Asset 4, a research firm, has created a set of over 250 "extra-financial" indicators on which it tracks almost 1,500 companies on behalf of institutional investor clients. For each company it monitors, Asset 4 produces an economic rating, an environmental rating, a social rating, and a governance rating (the last of these evaluates a company's decision-making processes to determine whether they are designed to ensure responsible corporate behavior).

In April 2007, *Fast Company* magazine unveiled its first HIP (Human Impact + Profit) scorecard, a systematic rating of companies based on social, environmental, and financial performance. Both Asset 4 and HIP are designed for use by profit-seeking investors who are looking for companies that are both "economically successful" and "socially responsible" to invest in.

In creating objective, standardized systems for measuring social impact in the context of the objectives of social business, we may learn from the evaluation methodologies of the PMBs. However, we must design the new social business monitoring systems independently. In a PMB, social benefit is a by-product whose measurement must be consistent with the prime objective—profit. In social business, social impact is the prime objective, while profit forms a part of company's strategy for managing in a financially prudent way. Thus, the methodology for measuring the social impact of a social business must fit the purpose of the business.

Tax and Regulatory Issues

As social businesses multiply, it's likely they will demand tax benefits from the government to facilitate their work and reach out to more people. On the surface, these claims will appear legitimate. After all, if a social business is providing low-cost health care to the poor, why should it not be tax-exempt, just as a nonprofit with the same objective would be? The money not paid in taxes by the social business can be used to provide health services to more poor people, and the burden on tax payers to meet the needs of the poor will be lessened by the same amount.

To avoid confusion and controversy, governments will need to develop their own criteria detailing under what conditions social businesses will be eligible for specific types of tax benefits. Through appropriate tax policies, governments may encourage businesses, individuals, and institutions to create social businesses and bring beneficial innovations to the sector.

If government is convinced that social businesses are filling a role that the state is usually expected to fill, then it would make economic sense to encourage social businesses through tax exemption. It seems reasonable to give social businesses favorable tax treatment as a reward for reducing the burdens that taxpayers would normally bear. Under these circumstances, investment in social businesses could be treated like a donation to a tax-exempt charity or foundation and be exempted from income tax. Again, the purpose of encouraging the creation and support of social businesses would be served.

Some will argue that it is unfair to ask tax-paying profit-maximizing companies to compete against tax-exempt social businesses. That might be so if it were impossible for one type of business to be converted into the other. But as I envision it, there would be no such restriction. A PMB that is willing to follow the criteria for a social business—in particular, by forgoing the payment of dividends to shareholders and by dedicating itself to achieving a social benefit—should be able to easily convert itself into a social business. This provides a ready response to the complaint of unfair competition: If you can't beat social businesses, join them!

In any case, the creation of social businesses is not dependent on whether or not governments provide tax exemptions. People will create social businesses to fulfill their inner urge to shape a better world. A supportive tax policy will merely make it easier for them and encourage more investments. But initiating a basic structure of tax policy for social businesses is important from another perspective. Tax laws will create a credible regulatory environment for social business. The moment we set about designing a tax policy, we'll have to start defining key concepts in a concrete way: What is a social business? What activities by an organization disqualify it from being considered a social business? What must a PMB do in order to convert itself to social business status? What specific organizational and financial characteristics distinguish the not-for-profit organization from the social business?—and so on.

Having a set of clear, government-enforced definitions of social business will prevent unscrupulous business people from creating fake social businesses to fool investors and consumers.

One way dishonest people might try to deceive investors will be to claim social benefits from businesses that produce none. A company that does nothing to help the environment may create an image as a champion of green business through a clever and deceitful media campaign, thereby misleading innocent investors who may remain in the dark. Thus, developing institutional facilities and methodologies for credible impact evaluation of social businesses will be critical to the success of the social-business concept. The role of independent agencies in undertaking impact studies and designing methodologies for internal evaluations will be very important. Putting the results of impact studies in the public domain through the Internet will be immensely helpful in eliminating false claims.

Another challenge that the social-business movement will need to address is the problem of wrong delivery, in which a product or service meant to help people at the bottom of the social and economic pyramid does not reach them and instead goes to those of middle-class or affluent status. If this happens, the benefits produced by the sacrifices of the investors will end up in unintended places. For example, Grameen Danone yogurt is designed to help the malnourished children of the villages of Bangladesh. But suppose, through corruption or simple failure of the company's marketing system, the yogurt shows up instead on the tables of the rich. The whole idea of Grameen Danone as a social business could be destroyed.

We've faced this problem in designing the Grameen microcredit programs, which are intended primarily for the poorest women in Bangladesh. One way we address it is by making sure that our marketing and managerial staff are immersed in the local communities they serve and are able to put demands for services into a specific social and economic context.

For example, on rare occasions, a well-off woman might try to join a Grameen Bank group and receive a loan intended for a poor woman. Our staff members are trained to deal with this problem. Since we do all our discussions at the homes of our potential borrowers, we visit the house of this well-to-do woman and tell her how lucky she is—luckier than many others in the village, whose economic situation is much worse. Generally speaking, the prospective borrower readily agrees with this observation.

Then we ask for her assistance to identify women in her neighborhood who are really destitute. In most cases, she takes this task very seriously and leads us to the women whose economic situation is miserable. In the end, she does not resent the fact that we are not giving her a loan. Rather, she is happy that she is helping her poorer neighbor become a member of Grameen Bank. Her own self-esteem and her status is the community are enhanced by the positive role she is now playing as a leader among her peers.

Grameen Bank also uses multiple pricing as a way of ensuring that economic benefits go to those who need them the most. We charge 20-percent interest for our regular borrowers. This is an unsubsidized interest rate. Recently, we began serving another class of borrowers—the beggars. Loans given to them are interest-free—in other words, 100 percent subsidized. We find no problem in keeping these two markets separate from each other as well as separate from the broader credit market.

Obviously, the social circumstances of countries around the world are all unique. Methods for evaluating the economic need of individuals will need to be tailored to local conditions. If I were operating a microcredit program in a country like the United States, I might require prospective borrowers to provide a copy of last year's income tax return as a way of verifying their eligibility for a subsidized loan, much as families do when applying for a low-cost student or housing loan. In other societies, different methodologies might be necessary.

The broader point is that, in designing a social business, one has to be innovative in keeping multiple markets effectively separated. Sometimes it will be done through packaging and pricing, making the same product look very different depending on the target market. Most middle-class or affluent people would feel uncomfortable buying products clearly packaged and designed for the poor, sensing that they are unfairly taking goods intended to help the unfortunate as well as lowering their own status by buying such goods.

In other cases, markets can be separated by the place and method of sale. When designing the Grameen Danone operation, we decided to locate our first yogurt factory in a remote rural area so that Shokti Doi would reach the poor first rather than showing up in the markets of the capital city of Dhaka. Local Grameen borrowers—poor women—are selling the product to their friends and neighbors, who are also poor women. In time, we'll introduce another version of Shokti Doi, which will be marketed to well-off urban consumers at a much higher price. But for now, the geographic location and marketing methodology associated with Grameen Danone should assure that the benefits of the product are reaching the intended audience.

In social business, market segmentation will remain an essential feature. That is its strength as well as its weakness. That's why we need innovative marketing methods to achieve our social goal while ensuring our economic success.

Social Business and a World Transformed

In time, more institutions to support the burgeoning universe of social businesses will emerge. We'll need formal systems for the financing of social businesses, and social mutual funds like the Danone Communities Fund represent just one of many possible options. Others include the creation of new commercial and savings banks that specialize in financing social business ventures, the emergence of social venture capitalists, and the birth of an after-market in social business investments. Investors will be able to buy and sell shares in social businesses just as they currently buy and sell shares in conventional PMBs. In time, all of these financing mechanisms and more will fall into place.

A full-fledged social stock market dedicated to trading social business shares will soon be needed. Again, it will be important to clearly define social business for the purpose of determining which companies are eligible to participate in this market. Investors must have confidence that companies listed in the social stock market are truly social businesses, not PMBs masquerading as social businesses.

As the social stock market grows, eventually attracting thousands of companies that use business practices in pursuit of social objectives, millions of people around the world who care about the future of our species will devote time and energy to analyzing, tracking, and participating in this market. The prices of shares on the social stock market will reflect the consensus of social investors as to the long-term value of the company whose ownership they represent. However, that value will not be measured in terms of profit expectations, but rather in terms of the social benefit produced, since that is the primary objective the social investor seeks.

It's easy to imagine how the social stock market will bring new visibility and prominence to human, environmental, and economic goals, and to the organizations that work to pursue them. Every day, *The Social Wall Street Journal* will report the latest news about the progress and setbacks experienced by social businesses around the world. We'll read stories like this:

DHAKA, BANGLADESH: The CEO of People's Sanitation, a social business devoted to providing high-quality sewer services, water treatment facilities, and environmentally friendly garbage disposal in urban areas throughout South Asia, announced the results of a new study showing that rates of infectious disease have fallen by 30 percent in cities served by the company. Shares of People's Sanitation rose from 12.00 to 14.50 on the London Social Stock Market as a result. . . .

Or this:

NEW YORK: At today's annual investor's meeting of Health Care for All, a social business that provides affordable health insurance for poor people in the United States, a new board of directors and executive vice president were elected by dissatisfied investors. "Over the last year, we've seen some progress toward achieving our goal of providing health insurance for every poor American," the spokesperson of the major investors said. "But we think we can do better in the coming year. The new leadership we've selected today will help us reach that goal. . . . "

Or this:

TOKYO, JAPAN: Executives from two of the world's leading social businesses, Global Water Supply, based in Tokyo and Agricultural Irrigation Industries, headquartered in Seoul, Korea, today announced plans to merge their organizations. Observers say the merger will produce greater efficiency and assist both companies in pursuing their mission of providing pure water at low cost to poor families and farmers in sixty countries of the developing world. Investors appear to agree, as shares of both companies rose on the Tokyo Social Exchange by over 30 percent in the wake of today's announcement. . . .

There will be a Social Dow Jones Index, reflecting the share values of some of the world's largest, most important, and most broadly representative social businesses. The value of this index will rise and fall in response to news from the world of social development. As poverty, disease, homelessness, pollution, and violence decline, the popularity and value of the social businesses active in those causes will grow—and so will the value of the Social Dow Jones Index. Smart investors will listen for *two* numbers on the daily news report, and a good day will be one in which both the PMB Dow Jones and the Social Dow Jones finish on the upside. That will mean a day in which our world is getting richer in both economic terms and human terms.

Magazines devoted to social business will appear on newsstands, and television programs featuring leading experts on social investment will pop up on the news networks. Managers of social mutual funds will compete to find companies that are developing the most innovative and powerful tools for promoting social progress, and those with the best investment records will find themselves honored with cover stories in publications that might be called *Social Business Week* or *Social Fortune.*

Executives of leading PMBs like General Electric, Microsoft, and Toyota will continue to be lionized in the conventional business press. But their counterparts from the world's top social businesses will now become equally famous. The CEOs of organizations that combat hunger, clean the air we breathe, and provide vaccinations for poor kids will become heroes to millions of people, students, and aspiring managers, their leadership strategies scrutinized and their exploits recounted in best-selling books. They'll be receiving prestigious national and international awards and honors.

Principles for managing social businesses will become an important part of business education. Students pursuing a Social MBA will be expected to master many of the same skills as their classmates in a traditional MBA program: finance, management, marketing, human resource development strategy, and so on—but designed from a completely different perspective. In addition, they will also take courses in topics that are relevant to the social business program, courses with titles like The Economics of Poverty, Maximizing Social Benefits to the Poor, Important Issues in Designing Social Business Programs, and Finding Solutions to Social Problems through the Free Market. Graduates of such programs will be in great demand—by social businesses, of course, but also by PMBs, nonprofit organizations, and government agencies, because of their unique combination of powerful analytic and quantitative skills with sophisticated, compassionate understanding of human beings and their needs.

More Than a Fantasy

Perhaps, to some, the idea of social business sounds purely fanciful, a fantasy of a world that can never be. But why? Who has given the ultimate verdict that people are motivated only by money—that the desire to do great things for the world can't be just as powerful a driving force in human behavior?

People get excited about all kinds of goals and activities. There are millions of young people around the world today for whom video games, hip-hop music, soccer, snow-boarding, and posting content on the Internet are all-absorbing pursuits. They spend countless hours enjoying these activities, honing their skills, and discussing them with friends and strangers, and would gladly devote their lives to them if they could earn a living by doing so. They love these pursuits, which some people might consider trivial or foolish, because, to them, they are challenging, creative, competitive, and social.

I'm convinced that most people, particularly young people, will become enormously excited about social business and its potential to transform the world. All that is lacking is the enabling social and economic structure that will make it possible, to teach the necessary skills, and to encourage participation. I hope all of these elements will be in place soon.

The existence of social businesses will offer an alternative career and life path to students and others who are hungry for a life rich in meaning beyond profit. Non-financial motivations will finally be recognized as the important drivers of human behavior that they are; the desire to do good for our fellow humans will be acknowledged as a legitimate and powerful factor in the world, rather than relegated to "charity" as it is today.

Most important, the new social business arena will allow the poor themselves to express their enormous gifts for entrepreneurship, creating newfound abundance not only for themselves and their families but for the communities in which they live.

9

Information Technology, Globalization, and a Transformed World

As we are all witnessing, the world is going through a revolution driven by information technology (IT). Business, government, education, the media—all are being transformed by the Internet, wireless telephony, access to powerful yet inexpensive computing technology, cable and satellite television, and other elements of the new IT. But what is less well understood is the enormous potential of the new IT for transforming the status of the poorest people in the world.

It is not the huge size of the annual addition to the GDP that characterizes the new society being created by the information revolution. It is not about the wealth that certain people or companies are accumulating by using this technology. The new IT's unique contribution comes from one fundamental fact: It is creating new relationships among people. And this transformation will inevitably have a profound impact on the lives of the poor, particularly poor women and children.

How will IT affect the world's poorest economies? Broadly speaking, there are two possibilities.

One possibility is that, with the emergence of new economic forces driven by IT and their ever-increasing strength in the world economy, nations that were small, weak, and poor under the old

dispensation will be further marginalized, making it even more difficult for them to compete. Under this scenario, IT will make the
current rush toward uncontrolled globalization even stronger and
more unstoppable. Global corporations will dictate terms to the weak
economies, which will have no choice but to submit. Their role in
the new information-driven economy—if any—will be to provide the
most menial services and the cheapest, least-differentiated products,
while the lion's share of the economic rewards will go to their better-
educated, richer, more advanced, and more powerful counterparts to
the north.

But there is another possibility, one that is just the opposite of
the pessimistic scenario. It's possible that the new IT will spread
into the sleepy, backward economies of the global South so quickly
that they will no longer remain sleepy. If the leaders of the developing
world are wise and the people are eager and energetic, the new IT can
be turned into a magic wand. The distance- and time-annihilating
properties of electronic information management and communications can be used to eliminate many of the barriers that blocked the
developing nations from full participation in the global economy.
The new IT can become a great leveler, allowing people and companies in countries from Bangladesh to Bolivia to compete on an equal
basis with their counterparts in the United States and Europe.

It is this second scenario that I believe can and will happen—
provided we have the will to *make* it happen.

There are skeptics who think the poor economies are incapable of
using IT as a fulcrum for growth. In this chapter, I'll illustrate how
the new IT can enable poor economies to leapfrog past patterns of
economic development and become successfully integrated into the
world economy much faster than anyone might have predicted. I'll
also list some of the practical, concrete steps that can be taken by
both the rich countries and the poor to ensure that the benefits of IT
are enjoyed by all, including those who today are among the least
privileged people in the world.

Globalization is another trend that is transforming our world,
both economically and socially. And like IT, it can be either a force
for positive change for the poor or yet another way to marginalize and
exploit them.

Open markets are crucial to economic growth. Free trade can potentially benefit all peoples. But we need well-designed global rules if we are to achieve this outcome. Without such rules, the richest and most powerful companies and countries will dominate those that are poorer and weaker. Instead, globalization can be managed in such a way that less-developed societies and individuals can find their own place and, in time, catch up to their more powerful neighbors.

If these two trends—the IT revolution and the advance of globalization—are guided into productive channels, a social revolution will take place on the heels of the current revolutions in technology and economics. There will be an unprecedented explosion in the personal and economic freedom enjoyed by humans around the globe.

Two groups that can play an important role in this revolution and will be among its main beneficiaries are women and youth. Newly empowered to unleash the creativity that has formerly been repressed, these two groups can lead the world toward a new era of growth and prosperity. It's the job of the current generation of leaders to ensure that this happens.

The Power of IT to Help the Poor

In several major areas, IT can play a powerful role in bringing an end to poverty. Here are some of the unique capabilities of the new IT for serving the world's poorest:

- The new IT can help to integrate the poor in the process of globalization by expanding their markets through e-commerce. Traditionally, the poor have been victimized by middlemen who have controlled their access to markets, dictated business terms, and siphoned off profits. Properly applied, the new IT can largely eliminate middlemen who fail to add unique value, allowing people in the poorest countries to work directly with consumers in the developed world and creating international job opportunities through electronically enabled outsourcing.

- The new IT can promote self-employment among the poor, liberating them from reliance on corporate employers or government make-work programs and unleashing their creativity, energy, and productivity. Armed with a cell phone and an Internet connection, a Bangladeshi villager can launch an enterprise that serves customers in Dhaka or Mumbai, London or New York, transcending the vagaries of local economic fluctuations and market conditions.

- The new IT can bring education, knowledge, and skill training to the poor in a very friendly way. One huge barrier to economic advancement for those in the developing countries has been the sheer difficulty, cost, and inconvenience of bringing teachers, consultants, and other suppliers of outside expertise into remote villages that are separated from capital cities by mountains, rivers, jungles, deserts, or hundreds of kilometers of inadequate roads. For many purposes, the Internet eliminates such barriers, making it possible, for example, for a dairy farmer in a remote region of Bangladesh or Peru to consult with an agricultural expert in Beijing or Chicago about the latest techniques for improving the health of his cattle and increasing their yield.

The best aspect of the new IT is that it cannot be controlled by a single owner or authority. It is an empowering tool that enhances options and brings all the world's knowledge to everyone's doorstep. When IT enters a poor economy, it creates wider choices and new relationships, replacing the traditional uni-directional relationship between the rich and poor with a set of multi-dimensional and global relationships in which the poor have an equal footing.

Many people in the developed world believe that IT is totally irrelevant to the problems of poor people. According to this view, IT is too complicated, too expensive, and too impractical for the poor.

This attitude sounds hard-headed and sensible at the abstract level. Yet I've experienced the power of visionary technology to transform the lives of the very poor—in the face of negative predictions by the skeptics.

When we launched our cell-phone company, Grameen Phone, in 1996, the skeptics essentially said, "You must be crazy to think of selling cell phones to poor, illiterate women in the villages of Bangladesh. None of them have even seen a conventional telephone in their lives! They can't afford a phone, they won't know how to dial a number, and anyway whom will they call? The whole idea is insane! You should stick to what you know, and leave the high-tech stuff to the big corporations and the engineering experts."

Yet the Grameen telephone ladies have emerged as a major force for social, economic, and technological transformation in Bangladesh. They are serving as information lifelines for their villages and creating businesses that benefit themselves and their families. Their telephones also provide Internet services. They are now moving in the direction of becoming "Internet ladies" as well. As the technology continues to evolve, they will be the first ones to bring the super-powerful digital genie into the remote, once-isolated villages of Bangladesh, helping their neighbors solve problems and discover opportunities formerly reserved for the highly educated and the wealthy. Through the Internet, the villagers will gain access to all the information, services, and economic networks of the world.

As for those who doubt the ability of poor, illiterate women to play such a role: I remember asking some of the very first batch of telephone ladies, "Do you have any difficulty dialing telephone numbers?"

They all told me that they had no such problem. One stood up and declared, "Put a blindfold on me and tell me a number to dial! If I can't dial it correctly the very first time, I'll turn in my phone and get out of the business."

I was astounded by her confidence in her newfound skill. But this is what happens when you give the poor an opportunity to show what they can do—almost always, they seize the opportunity and run with it.

Already another Grameen company (Grameen Communications) is setting up Internet kiosks in the villages and running them on a commercial basis. We've been pleasantly surprised to see the response from the villagers to the opportunity to use the Internet and other computer services. Many young people are signing up to learn

computer skills for a modest fee. In villages that the national electrical grid doesn't reach, solar panels marketed by Grameen Shakti are
powering the cell phones and computers.

Both Microcredit and IT can empower poor people, particularly
poor women, in ways that go far beyond what dollars and cents can
measure. I am convinced that the best way to combat poverty is to
give dignity and self-reliance to poor women. Both IT and microcredit
do this very effectively and mutually reinforce each other in the effort.

This is not to say that the challenges raised by the skeptics are
completely wrong. The ability of the poor and the illiterate to afford
and use the new IT depends on the appropriateness of the institutional environment around the poor and the rate of return on the investment they must make. Microcredit can provide an appropriately
supportive institutional environment, as demonstrated by the success
of the thousands of village phone ladies who purchased their equipment through loans from Grameen Bank and have transformed their
small bits of technology into thriving local businesses.

Another misconception is that developing nations must recapitu-
late the path of development followed by developed countries decades
or even centuries ago. New technologies hold out the potential for
leapfrogging steps in the process. It is not necessary for a developing
country in Asia, Africa, or Latin America to build a network of land
lines to provide telephone service, as was done in Europe and North
America in the late nineteenth and early twentieth centuries. Instead,
those regions can jump directly to wireless cellular telephone service,
saving vast amounts of money, years of development time, and precious nonrenewable resources (such as the copper once used in making telephone lines) in the process.

China, India, Bangladesh, and many other countries have made
exactly this leap. Cell-phone outreach is expanding in these countries
like a tidal wave. Now the real challenge is to discover all the many
ways these phones can improve the lives of the people who own them.

Similarly, it may not be necessary for a developing country to go
through a heavy industry phase in which businesses like steel, autos,
and machinery are emphasized. Instead, such a country may be able
to develop its economy around information-age technologies such as
software development, IT support services, and production of a host

of consumer goods. Fresh, unprejudiced thinking reveals a range of such opportunities for integrating the developing countries into the world economy with amazing speed and effectiveness.

Tailoring Technology
to the Needs of the Poor

There's a lot of talk about the digital divide—the huge gap between the rich and the poor in terms of their access to and ability to use the latest information and communications technology. I share this concern. Left unchecked, the digital divide will increasingly add to the knowledge divide, the skill divide, the opportunity divide, the income divide, and the power divide.

However, there's no reason to assume that the digital divide is permanent and inevitable. Much can be done to alleviate the problem.

The effort must start with a new approach to developing IT products and services. Companies can't simply take their traditional offerings, eliminate a few bells and whistles, and then try to sell the cheapened versions to people in the poorer nations. Instead, IT for the developing world has to be designed from the ground level up, keeping the picture of a poor woman in a poor country in the forefront of the IT product and service designer's consciousness. What are her daily problems? How can my device, appliance, or service help her find solutions to these problems? The answers to these questions will help create products and services that can truly revolutionize the world of the poor. The solution may involve designing a brand-new chip, a new device, a new Internet link, a new operating system, a new interface—a new everything.

The ultimate power tool for the developing world that I want to see IT companies working to create is a device that can be a constant companion to the poor woman in the developing world. It could be a new kind of device—not a laptop computer, a personal digital assistant (PDA), or a cell phone. It could be some new kind of gadget that currently exists merely as a gleam in some visionary designer's eye.

Whatever its precise form, this new device would have the potential to transform the poor woman's life. It could become her constant friend, philosopher, guide, business consultant, health, education and marketing consultant, trainer—her link to the larger world, her digital Aladdin's lamp. She'll touch the lamp or utter a magic word of her choice, and the digital genie will emerge from this lamp, ready to help her find the solution she is looking for. With the help of this technological friend, she'll come out of her shell, step by step, discover her talents, and lift her family out of poverty. Her children, in turn, will grow up with the IT genie as their best friend and mentor.

There are many resourceful people and organizations in the world who are committed to ending poverty. We need them to use their influence to inspire the IT industry to develop infrastructure, products, devices, protocols, activities, systems, and services that fit the needs of poor men and women around the world.

The One Laptop per Child project and Intel's Classmate PC project are promising examples. Giving a laptop to a child sends a powerful message: Discover yourself, discover the world, and create your own world. There is no reason why every developing country can't participate in this exciting program. Letting all children—rich and poor, boys and girls, urban and rural—have access to computers and the Internet will help compensate for the current vast discrepancy in quality between the educational facilities available to the rich and the poor.

But more such projects are needed. For example, why can't the brilliant minds of Silicon Valley design a voice-based IT terminal for an illiterate poor person that requires little or no training for use? The IT gadget itself would guide the person in learning the possibilities it offers. The user of this device would simply have conversations with it, just as he or she does with any of his or her friends. I find it hard to believe that such a challenge is beyond the reach of creative geniuses like those who developed the graphical user interface, the World Wide Web, and the iPod.

Another exciting challenge waiting in the world of IT is the language problem. The vast array of content and resources on the Internet are now available mainly in English, Chinese, and a handful of other major languages. In fact, it is estimated that some 80 percent of Internet content is in English, which automatically excludes an enormous portion of the world's population.

In the ideal IT world, there will be only language—your own. All information and ideas will come to you in your language, whatever that is. As an IT user, you won't even need to know that other languages exist. When you browse the Internet, you'll see everything in your language; when you receive a phone call from anywhere in the world, you'll hear the voice at the other end speaking your language, with simultaneous interpretation and translation provided automatically without your even knowing it. Conversely, you will talk to the computer in your own language and have the computer convert it into any language you desire.

Does this sound incredible? Visionary? Impossible? No more so than the Internet itself, which would have been deemed an absurd fantasy if anyone had dared to describe it fifty years ago.

The new IT is still in its infancy. We can't even imagine where it will take us in the next generation or two. But I don't even want to think in terms of "where it will take us." That's a very passive view of life. I would rather think about "where we want IT to take us." It's our job to figure out where we want to go and to guide the world's IT makers, designers, and marketers toward those goals.

One of the potential benefits of the new IT is its power to alleviate the terrible problem of overcrowding and infrastructure collapse in the cities of the developing world. E-commerce can help to make crowding in the cities unnecessary. When every point on the planet is connected by the Internet to every other point, an ambitious, poor young person from a remote village will no longer have to migrate to the big city for a better job. He can do the same job—or launch his own business—out of his home in the village. Of course, purchasers of services will also benefit from the new interconnectivity. For example, a medical patient will be able to decide whether to consult with a doctor in his own city, one in Bangladesh, one in Japan, or one in any other country in the world. Borders and distances will mean almost nothing; knowledge, talent, and ability will mean everything.

The new, electronically enabled interface between a government and its citizens has the potential to change the entire governance structure. The idea of a "capital city" may be altered beyond recognition. With the new IT, all government offices do not need to be located in a single city—or even in a city at all. They could be located in small villages scattered throughout the country, providing jobs for thousands of people who need them.

The idea of a university campus will also have to be redefined, because neither the students nor the faculty will have to be located in a single place. The best student in Harvard Business School's class of 2020 may be a young woman who has never left her village in Ethiopia.

The new IT may provide the magic platform to create dramatic changes in any area of our interest: health, nutrition, education, skill development, childcare, marketing, financial transactions, outsourcing, and the environment. The power of the new IT is limited only by our imaginations.

Obviously, concrete actions are needed to make these dreams come true. One such opportunity arose with a visit to Dhaka by Craig Barrett, chairman of Intel Corporation, in September 2007. We agreed to create a joint venture social business to be named Intel Grameen. We are now working to set up this company, which can address many unexplored issues related to IT.

Social Business and the IT Revolution

Technology should be harnessed to create a better life for everyone, not just the wealthy few. But in a free-market economy, it is the profit-maximizing companies who decide the uses to which technology is put. Corporate strategists decide where research and development funds are invested; they choose the products and services that are created, and they develop marketing campaigns to convince consumers that the offerings their companies are promoting are exactly what everyone needs.

When it comes to the new IT, however, "business as usual" is not acceptable. The emerging technologies will be so overwhelmingly important in shaping our future lives that we cannot leave the development of tomorrow's IT to the board-room decisions of profit-maximizing businesses alone. Instead, social business must step up to take an important role in creating the next generation of IT.

I see individuals as the best bet for starting this effort, particularly individuals who are IT enthusiasts and have a foothold in the worlds of business, technology, science, the arts, and academia. There are thousands of brilliant, idealistic people like this around the world who would like to devote their time, energy, and talent to finding ways of using IT to help poor people escape poverty. IT itself can bring these individuals together, using the Internet to build a strong global force of people dedicated to applying the power of information to the world's most serious social problems.

I propose giving this potential movement a structure by creating an umbrella organization to embody and support it. It might start as a virtual organization, then later add one or more physical locations as the movement grows in strength, wealth, and importance. Let's call this organization the Center for International Initiatives for IT Solutions to End Poverty—or, in brief, IT Solutions to End Poverty (ISEP).

How will ISEP get started? Any individual, group of individuals, or organization (business, NGO, foundation, or academic institution) can start it by presenting a mission statement on the Web and asking others to join in the network. Once it starts rolling, there might be a conference (virtual or physical) to build a leadership team, to sort out the management issues, and to establish a legal entity that can accept funds and represent the network to the public.

ISEP will probably have a group of paid staff as well as volunteers and interns devoted to the network's program. However, its true legitimacy and authority will come from its membership—high-powered, imaginative people and organizations who are committed to contribute their talents to designing, developing, testing, implementing, and marketing IT solutions for the poor. Instead of having only one physical location, ISEP could maintain a number of centers located in different parts of the world, which would network and compete among themselves in pursuit of the same objective—ending poverty.

Funding will be needed for hiring staff, for maintaining one or more offices, for developing systems, processes, solutions, and product prototypes, and for field trials and experimentation for projects undertaken by the network, and the management team will be responsible for finding these funds. Grants from foundations, businesses, and governments would be likely initial sources. Later, an endowment fund could be created by a consortium of donors and contributors to support the core programs of ISEP, and all businesses that produce and market IT products and services—the Microsofts, Apples, Googles, Dells, Infosys, Intels, and eBays of the world—could be invited to contribute each year. And perhaps ISEP could

receive project grants from governments, companies in the IT industry, other businesses, foundations, and wealthy individuals. Eventually, ISEP will generate funds by selling intellectual property rights to
the products and services that it develops, and it can earn money by
selling its services, publications, and products.

The money to create ISEP certainly exists. What is needed is the
focus on IT for the poor, the will to establish a worldwide network of
people devoted to that focus, and the visionary leadership of a few
strong individuals who will drive the process.

I could make a long list of projects that ISEP members or centers
could spearhead. Here are just a few of them:

- ISEP could generate ready-to-apply social-business ideas
  for using IT to bring services to the poor as well as to take
  products and services from the poor to the broader market. ISEP should also publicize such ideas as widely as
  possible so that social investors will be attracted to translate these ideas into concrete social businesses.
- ISEP members could develop prototypes for IT infrastructure and information systems for anti-poverty programs and services anywhere in the world.
- ISEP members could study the interface between the informational needs of the poor (especially those related to
  their productivity at work) and existing IT capabilities,
  and then proactively create applications or systems needed
  to better serve the poor.
- ISEP could identify IT infrastructure imperatives for the
  delivery of education, health care, good governance, and
  legal services to the poor, and provide consulting services
  to governments, NGOs, and businesses that are interested
  in producing the necessary infrastructure.
- ISEP could create informational networks based on geographic areas (national or regional), causes and correlates
  of poverty (agriculture, product marketing, health, education, legal, women, children, destitute, indigenous people,
  and so on), and type of participants (individuals, NGOs,
  governments, businesses, and so on).

- ISEP could create a data base of skills, knowledge, and technologies for governments, international institutions, businesses and NGOs that are working or planning to work in poverty elimination programs and social businesses, and become a clearing house for connecting people and ideas.
- ISEP could provide electronic capabilities to assist in the promotion and preservation of the art and culture of indigenous and poor peoples around the world.

ISEP will be a dynamic network of institutions and persons around the globe, all working toward common goals as articulated, defined, and monitored by a management and steering team. ISEP will build strategic partnerships with leading IT companies and their staffs, research and academic institutions, social activist groups, financial firms, microcredit institutions, development agencies, health and educational institutions, and professionals from many walks of life.

I am hoping that somewhere in the world someone reading this book will accept the challenge of launching this ISEP initiative around the world.

The IT Revolution and Democracy

IT has the potential to impact the world on many other planes besides the economic. Perhaps the most important of these is the political realm. It's a topic I consider vitally important, since the elimination of global poverty can never truly take place until the poor take their rightful place as fully empowered citizens of free societies.

Unfortunately, the political process in many countries has been very frustrating, to say the least. Investing huge sums of money to buy government offices, manipulating the media to create false images of candidates, and dirty tricks designed to smear opponents and even steal elections have become all too common. In some countries, units of the armed forces or private militias have seized control of the mechanisms of government. All too often, "people power" seems to have disappeared from politics, replaced by money power, muscle power, and even firepower.

We see these troubles with democracy in some of the world's largest and most powerful countries, from the United States to Russia. Similar problems exist in Bangladesh, where political corruption, distortion of the very purpose of governance, and self-dealing have been rampant. (Now, in 2007, a non-political caretaker government under an emergency rule is trying to create an opportunity to clean up the political parties and the system. So far, they seem to be succeeding, although much remains to be done to bring true, responsive, and vibrant democracy to Bangladesh.)

As a result of the problems of democracy, people around the world are losing faith in the political process. Young people especially have been turning apolitical, rejecting a system they regard as hopelessly compromised. In this climate, politicians feel driven to consolidate their power by stoking hatred between citizens, ethnic groups, religions, and nations. Visionary leaders who can bring people and nations together are becoming more and more rare. If we had a few such visionary leaders in South Asia, problems like Kashmir and other issues would long ago have been peacefully resolved.

Democracy is the best political framework to unleash the creative energy of the people, particularly the young. True democracy empowers individual citizens. When the citizens are forced to confront their own governments in an antagonistic way or must struggle to surmount needless barriers built by the state just to live productive lives, then neither freedom nor free enterprise can flourish.

Today, the new IT offers a powerful tool in support of real democracy.

Information is power. This is why governments that seek to *rule* the people rather than *serve* them are so eager to maintain their control over information. By making such centralized control far more difficult, the new IT—especially the Internet—creates enormous obstacles for would-be tyrants.

IT eliminates middlemen. As a result, both economic and political power brokers are equally threatened by IT. Thanks to the Internet, a single individual can now speak out to the whole world without the control of any intermediary (including the traditional news media, which, in weak democracies, are often biased or government-controlled). This makes IT a powerful amplifier for the voices of the people, especially minority groups, the poor, and the geographically isolated. It also reduces the costs in time, energy, and money of communicating with a large number of people. Gone are the days of hand-printed flyers, surreptitious radio broadcasts, or individually typed *samizdat* manuscripts circulated at great danger and expense. Once I post a message or a photograph or a video clipping on a website, it is there for anybody in the world to see. Networking among like-minded people has never been easier.

These features are very important for democracy anywhere. But they are particularly important in emerging nations that are struggling to achieve true democracy.

The new IT also serves to empower individual citizens by giving them direct access to their governments. In Bangladesh, we have tried this in a small way through our telephone ladies. Each time a new Grameen telephone lady launches her business, she is given a list of important telephone numbers, including the phone number of the local member of parliament, the head of the local government administration, the police chief, the local health service facilities, and other relevant officials—up to and including the prime minister of Bangladesh. We explain to her that these numbers are for her use whenever she or the people of her village have a problem and need government help. It's a symbolic gesture, but also a very real indication of the power that being connected electronically can bring to individual people.

There are instances when Grameen phone ladies have actually used that power. A favorite story of mine involves a phone lady in a village where a crime had occurred—an assault on a local person by an unknown stranger who quickly disappeared. The people of the village were angry and distraught, and the fact that the local police chief remained totally indifferent to their calls made them all the more angry.

In the past, they would have had no real recourse. But the phone lady said, "Don't worry. I'll call the police chief." She rang him up and said, "People in our village are really getting very angry because you refuse to respond to our calls. I request you to send some police to our village right away to investigate this crime. Otherwise, I'm going to call the prime minister's office—I have her number right here!"

The police arrived within an hour.

Finally, the new IT can strengthen democracy by providing a platform for citizen activism. This power of technology was vividly demonstrated in 2001 in the largest democracy of the world—India. Using a cleverly concealed video camera, two young journalists filmed an apparent case of bribery, in which a government official was seen accepting a wad of bills amounting to 100,000 rupees (about $2,000) in exchange for a defense contract. Then they posted the film on an Internet news site called Tehelka.com. The country was so outraged that the defense minister and several of his colleagues had to resign immediately to stave off a complete collapse of the ruling government.

It's funny—most Indians assume that millions of dollars' worth of bribes change hands behind closed government doors every year. But actually *seeing* $2,000 being exchanged had an incredible impact on public opinion.

That's the power of IT. It can give voice to the voiceless, eyes to the politically blind, and ears to the politically deaf. It's yet another reason why governments, businesses, NGOs, and ordinary citizens need to join forces in an effort to make sure that the power of technology is put within reach of everyone in our world—including the poorest among us, who need its help the most.

10

Hazards of Prosperity

In recent years, as a scientific consensus has developed about the growing threat of global warming, people around the world have begun to take this problem seriously. However, in many cases, although the concerns are genuine, people are not worried about the planet as a whole. Instead, their immediate personal responses are centered on threats to property and income rather than to life itself. People worry: Will climate change increase the number and severity of hurricanes in the Caribbean? Will the value of my beachfront property in Florida or the Bahamas be destroyed? Will new forms of insect or crop infestations ruin my garden or drive up the cost of the food I buy at the supermarket? Will my children miss out on the opportunity to enjoy the splendor of Australia's Great Barrier Reef?

In Bangladesh, the situation is more immediate: Global warming is a threat to our very lives and livelihoods. Bangladesh will be on the front lines of the catastrophic changes that many scientists now foresee. In this respect, the troubles of Bangladesh represent those of the entire developing world. Problems ranging from climate change and water shortages to industrial pollution and high-priced energy, which are mere nuisances to people in the global North, pose life-and-death difficulties for those in the global South.

Even under normal circumstances, about 40 percent of the land surface of Bangladesh is flooded during the annual monsoon season. Like the fabled flooding of Egypt by the Nile River, this yearly phenomenon has a benign aspect, as it makes our land extremely lush and fertile. But when small shifts in weather patterns intensify the floods, the destructive power of nature is unleashed. Villages and sometimes entire districts are washed away, and hundreds of thousands or even millions of people are left homeless. Many die in the most severe flooding, particularly children. Because we lack the major resources it would take to manage and control the flooding (the way the Dutch have controlled the high seas that threaten their own low-lying country), these periodic disasters have helped perpetuate the poverty of Bangladesh, as our people must spend years simply rebuilding after each inundation.

Global warming holds the threat of greatly multiplying the destructive forces aimed at Bangladesh. If the vast ice fields of Greenland continue to melt, global ocean levels will rise, gradually covering large portions of some of the world's low-lying land masses, including Bangladesh.

Imagine the scale of the human crisis this would produce in our vulnerable, extremely crowded nation. The results would include devastating reductions in rice harvests, terrible loss of life, and a flood of refugees that could dwarf most previous mass migrations.

This tragedy may happen sooner than you think. Scientists report that the sea level in the Bay of Bengal is already rising. Recent studies measure the rise at between three and eight millimeters a year. It doesn't sound like much, until you realize that about 20 percent of Bangladesh, home to some thirty million people, lies three feet or less above sea level. Kofi Annan, former Secretary General of the United Nations, has warned that a significant part of Bangladesh is likely to disappear completely by the end of this century.

We Bangladeshis can do a lot to fight poverty on our own. But how can we fight the effects of global warming on our own?

Obviously, we can't. The brunt of the coming disaster will be borne by the poor people of Bangladesh, along with poor people in many other affected regions, from the Pacific Rim to the drought-prone regions of Central Africa. But solving this crisis will require a unified effort by all the peoples of the world. If this effort is not mounted—soon—I'm afraid that all of our work to alleviate poverty and improve life for the world's poorest will be in vain.

And of course the world's poorest will not be the only ones affected by global climate change. Like the fabled canary that coal miners used to alert them to the presence of dangerous gases underground, the people of the developing countries will be the first victims of the coming changes, but not the last. Our fate will be a harbinger of what millions in the developed world can expect to suffer in their turn.

Economic Inequality and the Struggle over Global Resources

To understand what must be done to solve this crisis before it devastates the world, we must understand its roots in economics, social and political circumstances, and human nature.

In the decades since World War II, the world economy has been growing at an unprecedented pace. This is a good thing in most ways. The wealth generated by new technologies, liberalized markets, and increased trade has improved the standard of living for hundreds of millions of people in the developed nations. It has also begun the process of lifting hundreds of millions more out of poverty in the developing world.

But growth also creates problems. Nonrenewable resources are rapidly becoming depleted as the demand for them increases exponentially. Fossil fuels such as oil, natural gas, and coal are the primary examples, but industrial metals and minerals, hardwoods, fish, potable water, and many other essential commodities are also becoming increasingly scarce.

Thus, in the form of capitalism under which most of the world is currently organized, there is an unhealthy connection between the environment and economic growth. The bigger the world economy, the bigger the threat to planet Earth—and, in the long run, to the survival of our species.

In these early years of the twenty-first century, the threat to the world's natural order comes mainly from the economies of Europe and North America, which were the first to industrialize and therefore have had the longest time to develop a large, heavy footprint on the planet we share. Today, these powerful economies are continuing to use up resources at a rate that far outstrips the portion of the world's population they represent. In general, the higher the level of income in a country, the higher the contribution to the world's environmental risks.

Probably the most obvious result of this hyper-industrialization is global warming. This phenomenon is driven by dangerous and ever-increasing levels of greenhouse gases in the atmosphere, produced primarily by the burning of fossil fuels. These gases are trapping the sun's heat and altering the world's climate in ways that are not fully predictable. Although scientists differ about the precise extent and rate of global climate change, virtually all agree that such change is already occurring and is likely to accelerate in the years to come. A prestigious study by the United Nations says that average global temperatures can be expected to rise between 2.5 degrees and 10.4 degrees Fahrenheit by the year 2100.[1]

And who are the largest creators of the greenhouse gases whose impact will be felt in every corner of the globe over the next three generations? Overwhelmingly they are the wealthy nations of the developed world, which burn the vast bulk of the planet's fossil fuels to drive their automobiles, light and heat their homes and offices, and power their factories. For example, the United States, with only 4.5 percent of the world's population, currently produces 25 percent of the total greenhouse gas emissions.

What's more, these uses of fossil fuels are not the only way in which the lifestyle of the developed nations is damaging our environment. For example, it has been estimated that the equivalent of some 400 gallons of gasoline is expended each year to feed every American. Of this total, fully 31 percent is due to the use of fossil-fuel-derived fertilizers. Much of the rest goes to operate machinery, irrigate the soil, and produce pesticides.

All of this is tremendously wasteful. As one critic has put it:

In a very real sense, we [Americans] are literally eating fossil fuels. However, due to the laws of thermodynamics, there is not a direct correspondence between energy inflow and outflow in agriculture. Along the way, there is a marked energy loss. . . . we have reached the point of marginal returns. Yet, due to soil degradation, increased demands of pest management and increasing energy costs for irrigation . . . modern agriculture must continue increasing its energy expenditures simply to maintain current crop yields. The Green Revolution is becoming bankrupt.[2]

Industrial-style agriculture as practiced in the United States has been very effective at raising crop yields (as well as generating huge profits for agribusiness). But in the long run, it is not sustainable.

It's obvious that the imbalance between the relatively modest populations of the wealthy developed nations and their profligate use of resources is neither just nor indefinitely sustainable. With every passing year, more and more people in both the developed and the developing worlds come to recognize and appreciate this reality.

Unfortunately, however, the principle response by those in power has been to seek ways to consolidate and retain that power. Governments in the developed nations consider it their mandate to make sure that they control the world's most vital resources, no matter where those resources are found. They work hand in glove with big companies operating in the developing countries to make sure that the availability of crucial resources such as oil, gas, and minerals continues uninterrupted. And when control over resources is being negotiated among corporate leaders, trade representatives, and global diplomats, these major companies bring to the table their own financial power as well as the political and military power wielded by their home governments.

It's no accident that certain regions of the world that are resource-rich have long been centers of political, military, and economic intrigue as leaders of the rich nations vie for long-term control of those resources. The Middle East is the leading example. Thus, the growing anxiety around the world over steadily dwindling supplies of vital resources—especially oil—also poses a serious threat to global peace.

Americans and others among the world's wealthiest may enjoy their lavish lifestyles today. But in the long run, how great a price in environmental destruction and military conflict are they willing to pay to sustain those lifestyles indefinitely?

Spreading the Wealth and the Growth Dilemma

No one who cares about humanity is satisfied with a world in which a few hundred million people enjoy access to all the resources of the planet, while billions more struggle just to survive. Yet, of course, that is exactly the kind of world in which we live today.

Consider just a few of the grim statistics concerning economic inequality. According to a study by the World Institute for Development Economics Research at United Nations University, in the year 2000, the richest 1 percent owned 40 percent of the world's assets, and the richest 10 percent owned 85 percent. By contrast, the bottom half of the world population owned barely 1 percent of the planet's assets.

Similarly gross inequities exist when we look at income. Five countries—the United States, Japan, Germany, France, and the United Kingdom—contain 13 percent of the world's population and enjoy 45 percent of the world's income. By contrast, three giant countries in the developing world—India, China, and Indonesia—have 42 percent of the world's population but receive only 9 percent of its income. To put it another way, the 50 million richest people in the world—the top 1 percent—receive as much income as the bottom 57 percent, numbering over three billion individuals.

It sounds very cruel—but that's the reality. And even with the world economy growing fast, income inequality is not diminishing at anything like the rate most caring people would want to see.

The reduction of inequality, and the expansion of the global middle class to include billions of people who today must eke out a miserable existence on incomes of $2 per day or less, is therefore a very high human priority. It is the cause to which I have devoted my life. But we must also recognize that solving the inequality problem will bring with it serious new challenges, whose impact and severity are already becoming apparent.

One of the hopeful stories of the era in which we live has been the steady economic growth of some of the largest countries in the developing world, particularly the two Asian giants, China and India. Tens of millions of people in those countries have already emerged from poverty as a result. But as these countries expand their industrial base and their consumption of resources, they are becoming major contributors to the global pollution and climate change problems. And the higher the growth rate they enjoy, the higher the probability that environmental issues will be ignored in the hopes of perpetuating that high growth.

Already China and India are increasing their contributions to greenhouse gas emissions at an alarming rate. During the years

1990–2004, according to a UN study, developed nations such as the United States, Germany, and Canada increased their emissions by amounts ranging from 16 to 27 percent, while the United Kingdom actually *decreased* its emissions by 14 percent. Meanwhile, China's emissions were growing by 47 percent, while India's increased by 55 percent.[3]

In more recent years, as China's economic growth has accelerated, the problem has gotten even more serious. In 2006 alone, China increased its energy-production capacity by an amount equal to the entire power systems of the United Kingdom and Thailand combined. Most of the new power plants going online in China are based on "dirty," coal-powered generators, adding enormously to the air and water pollution problems faced by the country. The International Energy Agency has predicted that, by 2009, China will have surpassed the United States as the largest producer of energy-related greenhouse gases. Other researchers say the story is even more alarming; according to the Netherlands Environmental Assessment Agency, China actually overtook the United States in 2006.

Of course, climate change is not the only environmental problem caused by uncontrolled growth. The direct effects of pollution can be equally deadly. And, again, the rapidly growing giants of the developing world vividly illustrate the problem and its effects. China today is home to sixteen of the world's twenty most polluted cities. The situation in India may be even worse. A 2004 study of air quality in eighty-three Indian cities found that more than 84 percent of the population is breathing dangerously polluted air.

And, of course, the human destruction caused by pollution also takes an economic toll. Premature deaths, hospital stays and doctor visits, days missed from work, and the expense involved in trying to remedy environmental problems (which are much cheaper to prevent in the first place), all add up to a tremendous drain on the economy. Depending on which study you accept, the estimated cost of environmental degradation to the Chinese economy is somewhere between 7 and 10 percent of that country's GDP.

We live in a world where economic inequality is causing enormous human suffering for the billions of have-nots. Yet the apparent solution to the inequality problem—rapid economic growth in the developing world—appears to bring with it catastrophic dangers of its own. We might call this double-bind the Growth Dilemma.

The Logic of Uncontrolled Growth

What are the root causes of this painful dilemma in which we seem to be trapped? Ultimately, I believe, they can be traced to the same incomplete and flawed view of society and human existence that underlies our entire economic system.

Here, in a nutshell, is the philosophy of capitalism that virtually every economist, corporate executive, policy expert, and business writer takes for granted:

- A better way of life for the people of the world—including a reduction in the suffering caused by inequality—can be produced only through robust economic growth.
- Economic growth can be fueled only by capital investments through the competitive free markets.
- Investment money can be attracted only by companies that are managed so as to maximize their return on capital.
- Return on capital can be maximized only by companies that make profit maximization their only objective.

This logic brings us back to the same conclusion we reached earlier, based on the assumption that human beings are one-dimensional creatures for whom money is the only source of motivation, satisfaction, and happiness—namely, that profit maximization is all.

In its own terms, the logic seems irrefutable. Yet when we look at the real world, the results are not satisfactory. Businesses in the developed nations are diligently maximizing their profits—and as a result, resources are being squandered, the environment is being despoiled, and generations to come will have an increasingly grim future to look forward to. As the capitalist philosophy spreads, developing nations like China and India are growing their own classes of business people who are also diligently maximizing their profits, following their models in North America and Europe—and as a result, hundreds of thousands of people are afflicted with diseases and dying prematurely due to pollution, and the global problem of climate change is rapidly moving toward a point of no return.

Obviously there is something wrong with the "irrefutable" logic of uncontrolled growth.

Think about what the philosophy of uncontrolled growth dictates when it comes to natural resources. If it is right and proper for businesses to maximize profits at all costs, how should they behave in regard to those resources? Obviously they should follow the principle of "First come, first served." Whoever has the money or the muscle power (in the form of military support) to seize and control resources should do so. Then those resources can and should be used to support businesses that will maximize the profits of their owners, who have the sole legitimate voice in determining how the resources will be allocated.

In fact, this is a very accurate description of how resources from oil, gas, and coal to farmland, fish, timber, minerals, and even fresh water are currently controlled and utilized. In some cases, private companies exercise the control at their sole discretion. In other cases, businesses wield power in collaboration with their governments. In almost no case is there a seat at the table for the vast mass of people whose very lives depend on access to a share of the resources. After all, according to capitalist logic, why should they be considered? How do their needs contribute to profit maximization?

This system, under which plundering nations and companies are allowed to grab resources and use them to maximize their immediate profit, would probably continue unchecked were it not for the fact that life on earth is approaching a crisis point. As nonrenewable resources continue to shrink—as the rate of their consumption continues to increase—and as the danger from climate change continues to advance—even the most ardent capitalist must accept the fact that pure pursuit of profit is no longer an acceptable principle on which to base our environmental policies. How will even the world's greatest billionaire enjoy his wealth if the air around him is too dangerous to breathe?

How Much Consumption?

I am a firm believer in personal freedom. Each individual person on this planet is packed with limitless capabilities. An ideal society should create an enabling environment around each individual so that all of his or her creative energies can be unleashed to the very fullest. A maximum of personal freedom is vital to the creation of such an enabling environment.

At the same time, we all realize that there are circumstances in which sacrificing some part of our personal freedom is necessary to enhance our own security, safety, and long-term happiness. That's exactly the reason why we have traffic rules in the streets. Of course, having to stop my car at a red light diminishes my personal freedom to a small extent. But if there were no traffic lights, it would be highly risky to drive at all, never knowing whether a careless driver might come barreling through the next intersection without regard to the presence of other cars. Most people in civilized societies willingly accept reasonable regulations on business and other personal activities for much the same reason—that in the long run they enhance the quality of life for all without imposing an unfair burden on any individual.

In the circumstances we face today as a species, I think it is time to consider limiting the freedom of the individual nation to consume or waste natural resources. To begin with, I would urge nations to think about restricting their own consumption voluntarily. If this proves inadequate, I would move—reluctantly—toward restrictions defined and enforced under global treaties.

Through their current, virtually unrestricted consumption, waste, and despoliation of natural resources—including both nonrenewable resources like oil, gas, and coal, as well as essential shared goods such as clean air and water—the citizens of the wealthiest countries are depleting assets that should be the shared patrimony of all humankind. In the process they are short-changing future generations of an equal chance to enjoy a full, satisfying life as well as depriving people from the developing world who aspire to a better way of life. Someday, when the people of Bangladesh and other developing countries reach the stage where they are ready to enjoy a similar level of consumption to that enjoyed in North America and Europe, it may be impossible for them to do so because the necessary resources have been sequestered for use by the richest countries—or even completely used up.

People and nations have a right to enjoy their lives as fully as they want. I endorse Jefferson's ringing words in which he declared "the pursuit of happiness" to be an unalienable human right. But does this mean all nations have a right to waste as much as they want, to use up resources that others need to survive, or to leave behind a planet that our children and our children's children will find unlivable?

The urge to consume without regard to the long-term social costs is a natural, even inevitable outgrowth of the breakneck quest for profit maximization. When we put profit first, we forget about the environment, we forget about public health, we forget about sustainability. The only question we consider legitimate is: How can we buy and sell more goods, at a higher rate of profit, than last year? Whether those goods are actually "needed" by the people or are beneficial to them in the long run is considered irrelevant. In this mad rush for profit maximization, what gets lost is environmental quality, long-term sustainability, and even the health of individual consumers. Agencies like the Food and Drug Administration in the United States can only oversee the purity of what consumers are eating; it cannot oversee how much they are eating and how it will affect their health over decades. Meanwhile, marketing experts are busy urging consumers to devour more than they need.

Making Space for a New Set of Voices

Today the marketplace is dominated by the voices of traditional capitalism. Many of these voices speak on behalf of corporations, urging consumers through advertising, marketing, publicity, and consumption-oriented media (such as magazines devoted to cars, fashion, home decorating, and vacations) to buy more goods and services as quickly as they can. The sole messages are: Buy More! Buy More! Buy More! And Buy Now! Buy Now! Buy Now! And we wonder why so many young people are alienated, and why older people often feel their lives have been less than fully satisfying.

The only voice in the marketplace is the voice of profit-maximizing businesses, geared to making sure that the objective of ever-increasing consumption is achieved. This voice follows consumers everywhere— when they are reading newspapers, listening to the radio, watching TV, driving their cars, or surfing the Internet. A seamless stream of messages urging consumption keeps flowing every second of their waking hours. Businesses are finding ever smarter ways to grab consumers' attention in every possible situation and persuade them to buy their products. No wonder virtually everyone finally surrenders and makes the purchase. But even then the commercial propaganda does not stop. Businesses then want consumers to buy more, to abandon the first product in favor of a newer, more expensive model, or to buy more simply for the sake of buying.

This process of promoting consumption is supposed to be a driving force behind economic growth. But what about global sustainability? What about restraining wasteful consumption? What about the personal satisfaction to be derived from enjoying what one has rather than constantly striving to seize the lead in a endless struggle for economic dominance? Don't these values deserve a hearing, too?

I strongly feel that we need a parallel voice in the marketplace, offering consumers a different set of messages—messages like:

- Think about whether you really need it!
- The more you buy, the more likely it is that you are exhausting earth's nonrenewable resources.
- Check the packaging—is it wasteful?
- Buy from a company that will take back your last purchase and recycle it.
- Create a socially responsible home.
- Are you spending like a citizen of the world?

Where the voice of the PMB urges consumers to damage their health through excessive consumption ("Why not super-size it?"), the parallel voice will send messages about the pleasures of being healthy and the steps required to achieve good health: what to eat and what not to eat, how to help kids become interested in nutritious foods, how exercise and activity contribute to well-being, why natural and locally produced foods taste better and are better for you, and so on.

Some might complain that I am urging the use of "propaganda" to manipulate people, or that I am trying to turn society into a "nanny" that nags people about proper behavior. But the people of the world are already being inundated by propaganda and by the nagging of a nanny—except the propaganda and the nagging come from the corporate profit-makers, whose only motive in spending huge sums of money is to cajole consumers into providing them with even bigger profits. We need a parallel voice to provide at least a semblance of balance.

Where will this parallel voice come from? Social business can play a crucial role.

Even today, parallel voices like the one I've described are available. They come from schools, NGOs, charities, foundations, faith groups, and other not-for-profit organizations. But these voices are faint and hard to hear. Short on money, the groups that provide these voices lack the giant platform and the powerful media megaphone that mainstream businesses enjoy. No wonder they reach only a tiny audience and are generally drowned out by pro-consumption hype.

If this voice comes from mainstream business as a business message in a business campaign format, it will reach a much bigger audience. An important part of the campaign will be to make social business understood and appreciated by people. I believe that the core idea of social business is already embedded in every human mind, waiting to find expression—only our existing theoretical framework does not recognize it.

As I travel the globe speaking about microcredit and social business, I've met countless young people in schools, colleges, and universities throughout the world. I've been impressed by their idealism, their compassion, and their creativity. I believe they are ready and willing to do the right things for themselves and for the world.

Social businesses may become a source of the strong countervoice that we are looking for. They can be a credible source that people can believe, because they know that those who speak aren't trying to manipulate them in search of personal gain.

A social business dedicated to environmental objectives can highlight how PMBs are harming the planet and how consumers can alleviate the climate crisis by using environmentally friendly products. A social business running a microcredit program can explain why this program is necessary and how the mainstream banking system needs to be reformed. A social business offering low-cost health insurance can inform people about ways of staying healthy without spending money on doctors or medications, through preventive care, sound nutrition, and exercise. Providing consumers with unbiased advice and information can itself be an attractive area of social business.

Because social businesses are, above all, *businesses,* they will have the incentive, the resources, and the market clout necessary to bring their out-of-the-mainstream messages to a broad, mainstream audience for the first time. And social businesses will have a competitive advantage in the marketplace of ideas because everyone will know they have no incentive to lie. Because there are no dividend-takers in a social business, the only objective of the company is to create a social benefit. Consumers who hear about the cause and share the values behind it will support the business—and spread the message.

The voice of social business will find ready listeners because many people feel harassed, abused, and manipulated by the marketing techniques applied by PMBs. Many people, particularly the young, will listen because they want to find a way of life that is healthy, sustainable, environmentally friendly, generous to the poor, and conducive to peace of mind.

The ultimate result, as the efforts of thousands of social businesses accumulate, will be an unmistakable shift in the tone and content of the public conversation. Values other than money will have a place in the discussion and be recognized for what they are: important guides and stepping stones toward a more meaningful and satisfying life.

Solving the Growth Dilemma

Meanwhile, what can we do about the Growth Dilemma—the conflict between the absolute need to improve the living standards of the billions of poor people in the world and the equally absolute need to prevent economic growth from accelerating the destruction of our global environment and producing devastating climate change?

It seems clear that we must make progress on several fronts. Over the past two centuries, since the advent of the Industrial Revolution, the rich nations have enjoyed the use of world's nonrenewable resources without any restrictions. Now it is time to decide how the world's remaining resources are to be allocated.

We often hear that the fast-growing economies of the South (India, China, Brazil, Indonesia, and expanding economies in Africa) must not fall into the same consumption style as the North; instead, they must develop a better and more environmentally sustainable lifestyle and value system for themselves. This is true, but it's also insufficient. We should not be talking about two lifestyles—one for the North and one for the South. That is neither desirable nor sustainable. Instead, we should move toward one converging lifestyle the world over.

Of course, there will always be cultural, historical, and religious diversity in lifestyles. But as products become global, company operations become global, and information technology turns the whole world into a global village, there is no way to maintain the current divide between North and South. What the North does affects the people in the South—which is why countries like Bangladesh are already suffering the effects of global warming created mainly by consumption in Europe and in North America. Soon the North will start feeling the impact of damage done to the planet by the peoples of the South. We are in the same boat, and we must all learn to live responsibly— or we will sink together.

We need to put our minds together to outline the basic features of a new, globally sustainable lifestyle so that we know in what direction our technology, our innovations, and our creativity have to be directed. Technology blossoms only in the directions where our minds direct it to go. If we are not thinking about something, technology will not flourish in that direction. But if we want to get somewhere, technology will be developed to get there. So if we truly set our sights on making a sustainable global lifestyle for the entire planet, the technologies we need will begin to appear.

Unfortunately, our current efforts are in the opposite direction. Most of the creativity of the developed world is focused on spreading the unhealthy, non-sustainable lifestyle of the North into the growing nations of the South. Through their skillful marketing campaigns, powerful companies in North America and Europe are extending their influence into every corner of the world. Even people in the remotest villages in poor countries want to drink Coke and Pepsi, to smoke Marlboro and Camel cigarettes, to use Tide detergent and Crest toothpaste. People in those remote villages dream of using these products and enjoying the "good life" they represent. This is another reason why a compelling alternative voice must be heard in the global marketplace.

Government regulation on both a national and international level must also play a role in solving the Growth Dilemma.

The dynamic of capitalist competition among businesses is such that firms that operate in a socially or environmentally friendly fashion may have a disadvantage in the marketplace, at least in the short term, while those that save money by polluting at will may gain the upper hand. The same is true at the global level, as countries with lax or weakly enforced environmental standards may attract companies eager to do business unconstrained by government regulations.

This is why international agreement on guidelines to protect the environment is so crucial. It is the only mechanism to prevent a "race to the bottom" by countries competing for business in a global marketplace.

The Kyoto Protocol was born out of this necessity. The chief goal of this international accord is the reduction of greenhouse gas emission levels by the year 2012 to an average level of 5 percent below the 1990 levels—a reduction of up to 15 percent below expected levels in 2008 and of almost 29 percent compared to predicted levels in 2012 if no attempt to limit greenhouse gases was made.

Although opponents of the Kyoto plan decry its rigidity, the use of flexible market mechanisms to facilitate these reductions is an important part of the protocol. Countries in the developed world (known in the terms of the protocol as "Annex I economies") that find it difficult to achieve the mandated reductions may purchase equivalent reductions from financial exchanges or through the so-called Clean Development Mechanism, which reduces emissions in the developing world. This "cap and trade" system gives countries several options they can consider in pursuit of the overall goal of reducing carbon emissions at both the national and global levels.

The Kyoto Protocol was negotiated in 1998 with a provision that it would go into effect once it was ratified by at least 55 nations, representing producers of at least 55 percent of the world's greenhouse gases. That point was reached with the ratification by Russia in November 2004. As of December 2006, 169 countries that collectively produce over 61 percent of the world's greenhouse gases have ratified the protocol. However, the United States remains a holdout. In 1998, Vice President Al Gore, representing the Clinton administration, signed the Kyoto protocol, but it has not been ratified by the Senate, and without such ratification it is not binding.

This is a sad case of failure to lead by the nation with the most important leadership role to play. And the rest of the world has taken note of the American attitude. Leaders in China and India point to the failure of the United States to ratify Kyoto as ground for their reluctance to make international commitments to take strong steps on environmental protection. In the spring of 2007, a new report by the UN Intergovernmental Panel on Climate Change highlighted the growing importance of the two Asian giants in the effort to stem climate change and led to fresh calls for action on their part. But the official newspaper of China's ruling party pushed back with an editorial that said, "As the biggest developed country and the biggest emitter of greenhouse gas, the irresponsible remarks and behavior of the US government will only leave an impression of its being 'heartlessly rich.'" This language, which many in the developing world would surely support, illustrates the degree to which the United States since 2001 has lost the moral high ground in the battle to protect the global environment.

I am not saying that the Kyoto Protocol is a perfect document. Very few treaties developed through negotiations among dozens of independent states are. Environmental scientists disagree over the precise details of the best plan for halting the onset of devastating climatic changes. And the fact that the Kyoto Protocol places no immediate emission reduction requirements on the nations of the developing world, including the rapidly growing giants China and India, is a flaw that will ultimately need to be remedied. Supporters of Kyoto have always acknowledged that the current protocol is simply a first step that must be supplemented by new measures as the world's environment and economic situation evolves.

Kyoto represents an important and useful starting point for addressing the problem. It is short-sighted and tragic that, even as the U.S. government rejects the approach presented by Kyoto, the current administration is unwilling to offer any serious alternative plan for getting greenhouse gas emissions under control.

Other efforts are being made to address the climate change problem, but with mixed results. In January 2006, the Asia-Pacific Partnership on Clean Development and Climate was launched. Under this agreement, Australia, China, India, Japan, South Korea, and the United States have announced nearly 100 projects aimed at clean energy capacity building and market formation. The pact calls for the setting of national goals for greenhouse gas reduction, but envisions no enforcement mechanism. China has set its own internal targets for pollution control, aiming to increase energy efficiency by 4 percent per year, but it has so far failed to achieve these goals.

Thus, the way forward on global pollution and climate change is far from clear. Along with millions of other concerned citizens of the developing world, I can only hope that a change of heart among the leaders of the wealthiest nations—especially the United States—will create an opportunity for the people of those countries to show some real leadership in the quest to develop new ways of life that will be less destructive, more sustainable, and more rewarding in the long term.

The Kyoto Protocol's first commitment period ends in 2012. Before that, the world must get ready to adopt an enforceable global treaty on climate change issues. At their meeting in Germany in 2007, the G8 countries agreed to "consider" reaching a global agreement to reduce greenhouse gas emissions by 50 percent by 2050 within the framework of the United Nations. (However, many environmental groups around the world are demanding a reduction of 90 percent by 2050.) I hope there will be enough political will generated within the United States so that it not only agrees to this goal but also takes the leadership role in making it come to pass.

We see, then, that the problem of global poverty is deeply interwoven with many other challenges faced by humankind, including some that may threaten our very existence as a species. This makes the necessity of reforming the capitalist system and making room for the new kind of enterprise I call social business even more urgent. "Doing the right thing" is no longer merely a matter of making ourselves feel good; it's a matter of survival, for ourselves and for generations to come.

And while we continue to bring pressures on the policymakers to make tough decisions to save the planet, I urge young people to make up their minds as to what they will do as they grow up. Are they willing to distinguish the products they consume as "red" products, "yellow" products, and "green" products, depending on their negative or positive contribution to the survival of the planet? Are they willing to adopt the principle that each generation must leave the planet healthier than they found it? Are they willing to make sure that their lifestyle does not endanger the lives of others? I hope so—and I believe they are.

Notes

1 United Nations, Intergovernmental Panel on Climate Change, *Climate Change 2001: The Scientific Basis.*

2 Dale Allen Pfeiffer, "Eating Fossil Fuels," *From the Wilderness,* October 2003. Online at http://www.fromthewilderness.com/free/ww3/100303_eating_oil.html.

3 United Nations Framework Convention on Climate Change: Changes in GHG emissions from 1990 to 2004 for Annex I Parties.

11

Putting Poverty
in Museums

In 2000, all the nations of the world gathered at the United Nations headquarters in New York City and declared their determination to achieve eight important goals by 2015, including the reduction of poverty by half. It was a daring declaration. Not every nation will achieve the goals by 2015, but many will. Their success will bring us to the threshold of another bold decision—to end poverty on the planet once and for all. It can be done if we believe it can be done and act on our belief.

Once poverty is gone, we'll need to build museums to display its horrors to future generations. They'll wonder why poverty continued so long in human society—how a few people could live in luxury while billions dwelt in misery, deprivation, and despair.

Each nation will have to choose its own target date for building a national poverty museum. The initiative could come from government, foundations, NGOs, political parties, or any other section of society. Civil society groups and students may form a citizens' committee to build the national poverty museum by a specific future date. This date will express a desire and a commitment to eradicate poverty in the country within a specific period. Fixing a date can build the national will and energize the nation to put plans into action to make it happen.

But does this sound real? Can we really have poverty in the museums?

Why not? We have the technology. We have the resources. All we need is the will to do it and to put the necessary institutions and policies in place. I have tried in this book to explain what steps are needed to create a safe world without poverty. In this final chapter, I'll present some ideas relating to how individuals and organizations can actively participate in building the world that we would all like to create.

A Better World Starts with Imagination

The world in which we live is changing faster and faster. It is particularly true in the realms of economic development and technology.

As recently as the 1960s, all developing countries looked almost the same: massive poverty, rampant disease, periodic extreme economic crises, high population growth, low levels of education and health care, low economic growth, absence of infrastructure, and so on. There seemed little basis for optimism. But in the next thirty-five years, the economic map changed dramatically. Taiwan, South Korea, and Singapore joined the ranks of the developed countries. The economies of China, India, Malaysia, Thailand, and Vietnam began growing very fast. In the past eighteen years, the poverty rate in Vietnam has fallen from 58 percent to 20 percent. Globalization, despite its shortcomings, is producing changes around the world that could not even be imagined a generation ago.

We can always make educated guesses about what the future holds for the nations of the developing world. But past experience shows that, when countries are ripe for change, they can improve far faster than our educated guesses suggest. In particular, dramatic changes in technology are driving today's ultra-rapid rate of change. In the past, it took entire generations for social and political changes to impact people's thinking. Now new ideas can spread across the globe not in years but in months, even days, even seconds.

This is good news and also bad news. Improvements in technology, advances in democracy, and new problem-solving techniques can spread faster than ever, bringing benefits to millions of people. But we can create disasters very fast, too. If we are lucky enough to have a great leader in a major country of the world, people around the globe can benefit from his leadership immediately. If we are unlucky and have a bad leader in a highly influential country, the whole world may suffer from turmoil, economic dislocation, and war. Soundness of governance, global as well as national, is more important in today's fast-moving, interconnected world than ever before.

Today's rapid pace of change makes it crucial that we, as individual citizens, have a clear idea as to where we want our world to go. If we hope to find and stay on the right course, we must agree on the basic features of the world we want to create. And we must think big, as big as we dare to imagine—lest we waste the unprecedented opportunities that the world is offering us. Let us dream the wildest possible dreams and then pursue them.

Let me give a wish list of my dream world that I would like to see emerge by 2050. These are my dreams, but I hope that many of my dreams will coincide with yours. I am sure I would love many of the dreams on your list so much that I would make them my dreams too. Here is my list:

- There will be no poor people, no beggars, no homeless people, no street children anywhere in the world. Every country will have its own poverty museum. The global poverty museum will be located in the country that is the last to come out of poverty.
- There will be no passports and no visas for anybody anywhere in the world. All people will be truly global citizens of equal status.
- There will be no war, no war preparations, and no military establishment to fight wars. There will be no nuclear weapons or any other weapons of mass destruction.
- There will be no more incurable diseases, from cancer to AIDS, anywhere in the world. Disease will become a very rare phenomenon subject to immediate and effective treatment. High-quality healthcare will be available to everyone. Infant mortality and maternal mortality will be things of the past.
- There will be a global education system accessible to all from anywhere in the world. All children will experience fun and excitement in learning and growing up. All

children will grow up as caring and sharing persons, believing that their own development should be consistent with the development of others in the world.

- The global economic system will encourage individuals, businesses, and institutions to share their prosperity and participate actively in bringing prosperity to others, making income inequality an irrelevant issue. "Unemployment" and "welfare" will be unheard of.
- Social business will be a substantial part of the business world.
- There will be only one global currency. Coins and paper currency will be gone.
- Technology will be available with which all secret bank accounts and transactions of politicians, government officials, business people, intelligence agencies, underworld organizations, and terrorist groups can be easily detected and monitored.
- State-of-the art financial services of every kind will be available to every person in the world.
- All people will be committed to maintaining a sustainable lifestyle based on appropriate technologies. Sun, water, and wind will be the main sources of power.
- Humans will be able to forecast earthquakes, cyclones, tsunamis, and other natural disasters precisely and in plenty of time to minimize damage and loss of life.
- There will be no discrimination of any kind, whether based on race, color, religion, gender, sexual orientation, political belief, language, culture, or any other factor.
- There will be no need of paper and therefore no need to cut down trees. There will be biodegradable reusable synthetic papers, in cases where "paper" is absolutely needed.
- Basic connectivity will be wireless and nearly costless.
- Everybody will read and hear everything in his own language. Technology will make it possible for a person to speak, read, and write in his own language while the listener will hear and the reader will read the message in his own language. Software and gadgets will translate simulta-

neously as one speaks or downloads any text. One will be able to watch any TV channel from anywhere and hear the words in his own language.

- All cultures, ethnic groups, and religions will flourish to their full beauty and creativity, contributing to the magnificent unified orchestra of human society.
- All people will enjoy an environment of continuous innovation, restructuring of institutions, and revisiting of concepts and ideas.
- All peoples will share a world of peace, harmony, and friendship devoted to expanding the frontiers of human potential.

These are all achievable goals if we work at them. I believe that, as we proceed through the future, it will be easier and easier to get closer to our dreams. The difficult part is making up our minds now. As more of us can agree on what we want to achieve, the quicker we can reach our goals. We tend to be so busy with our everyday work and enjoying our lives that we forget to look through the windows of our lives to find out where we are right now in our journey, and take time off to reflect where we wish to go ultimately. Once we know where we want to go, getting there will be so much easier.

Each of us should draw up a wish list of our own—to reflect on what kind of world we would like to see when we retire. Once it is done, we should hang it on our walls to remind us daily whether we are getting closer to the destination.

Then we should insist that the drivers of our societies—the political leaders, academic experts, religious teachers, and corporate executives—take us where we want to go. Remember, we each have only one life to live; we must live it our way, and the choice of destination should be ours.

This process of imagining a future world of our liking is a major missing element in our education system. We prepare our students for jobs and careers, but we don't teach them to think as individuals about what kind of world they would like to create. Every high school and university ought to include a course focused on just this exercise. Each student will be asked to prepare a wish list and then to explain to the class why he wants the things he wants. Other students may endorse his ideas, offer better alternatives, or challenge him. Then the students will go on to discuss how to create the dream world they imagine, what they can do to make it happen, what the barriers are, and how partnerships and organizations, concepts, frameworks, and action plans can be created to promote the goal. The course would be fun, and, more important, it would be a great preparation for an exciting journey.

Practical Steps toward the Dream-World of the Future

Dreaming about a better world is fun. But what can individuals do to help bring that world closer to reality? One practical step is to create a small organization to realize part of the goal—something I call a "social action forum."

A social action forum can be as small as three people who band together to address a single, manageable, local problem. If others want to join, that is fine, too. But if you feel comfortable with three, don't try to expand the number. You can give your forum an interesting, funny, bold, innovative name, or simply name it after your members: Cathy, Kushal, and Lee's Social Action Forum, the Jobra Social Action Forum, the Midas Touch Social Action Forum, or any other name you like.

Once you've started your forum, define your action plan for this year. Keep it simple. It may be to help one unemployed person, a homeless person, or a beggar to find an income-earning activity and begin the climb out of poverty. Select the poor person you want to help, sit down with him or her to learn about his or her problem with earning an income—then find a solution for it.

I am planning to create a website where you can register your social action forum. On the website, you can describe your plan for the year, record your thoughts, mention the frustrations and excitements of your work, show the progress you are making, and display pictures relating to your project. It takes no special expertise, credentials, or resources to start a forum; all you need is the willingness and initiative to make a difference. If at the end of each year you submit an annual report on your forum and submit a new plan for the next year, your forum's registration will be extended for the coming year. At any time, anybody can visit the website of all the active forums and get in touch with them.

A social action forum can be built around any number of local problems and opportunities. Is there an abandoned lot in your neighborhood where garbage is piling up and disease is spreading? Start a forum for neighborhood improvement to transform the lot for some interesting purpose—a community garden, a playground, a recycling center, introducing something new in your neighborhood school, or anything else.

If you live in a developing country, the action program for your forum may be built around helping a beggar find a job or self-employment, getting a dropout to go back to school, helping a sick person find medical attention, or improving the sanitation or the water quality in your village.

Some social action forums may remain small but continue to do significant work. Others may grow bigger and bigger, and some may even become successful social businesses. An idea from one forum may inspire other forums to replicate the idea. A few forums may grow into major programs with the potential to transform entire nations. Some forums can have a global impact by developing innovative ideas to address a serious problem.

Aside from launching a social action forum, there are many steps that individuals can take to help promote the social-business idea. If you are a teacher or administrator at a school, college, or university, you could help launch a course to teach young business people about social business. If you are a member of a faith or civic group, you could help arrange a series of lectures, meetings, or conferences about opportunities for social business in your community. If you help to oversee or manage investment funds for a school, a pension fund, a faith organization, or any other institution, you can propose that a part of those resources be set aside to invest in social businesses. And, of course, if you are a business executive, you can explain to your CEO or board of directors the value of creating a social business and propose to create a social business by investing a part of the company profit with the consent of the shareholders.

Probably the most challenging and important aspect of this endeavor is likely to be designing social businesses. It will require all our creativity and imagination to come up with excellent business ideas that effectively address critical social objectives. One way to generate social-business ideas will be to hold business design competitions. Any organization or person can sponsor such a competition—a school, a foundation, a chamber of commerce, a corporation, an NGO, a church group, a civic group, an investment or venture capital fund, and so on. A social action forum could enter a competition or start a competition of its own.

I can picture local, regional, and even global competitions, with hundreds or thousands of participants vying to create the most practical, ambitious, and exciting concepts for social businesses. Prizes for the best business designs could include investing funding to finance the projects, or connections to social investors, social venture-capital providers, and lenders who might be interested in partnering to build the new businesses. All the proposals submitted could be published on the Internet to inspire the designers in the subsequent competitions or to provide ideas for entrepreneurs who want to start social businesses.

I have been promoting this idea of a social-business competition for the past several years, and now the Taiwanese magazine *Business Weekly* has actually announced such a competition. It has raised $1.5 million to provide seed money for the top ten submissions, which will be announced in November 2007. I am absolutely delighted about this initiative and look forward to attending the event at which the prizes will be presented.

New Frontiers for Foundations

Philanthropic institutions—especially the foundations launched by successful leaders in business—will find social business an especially appealing concept.

Throughout the twentieth century, foundations created by the premier entrepreneurs of the industrial age— John D. Rockefeller, Henry Ford, Andrew Carnegie—provided support for many of the world's most important charitable projects. In recent years, philanthropy has achieved new levels of visibility through the activities of some of the newest and largest foundations. In 2000, the founder of Microsoft and his wife launched the Bill and Melinda Gates Foundation, whose current endowment (March 2007) stands at $33.4 billion, the largest sum ever given to create a charitable foundation. Then, in June 2006, Warren Buffett, along with Gates among the three richest persons in the world (Mexican telecom mogul Carlos Slim Helú is the other), announced a plan to donate $37 billion from his personal fortune to the Gates Foundation, the largest single charitable gift in world history.

I believe the philanthropists of the future will be strongly drawn to social business. Because most major donors come from the business world, they will immediately understand that the social-business dollar is much more powerful than the charity dollar. Whereas the charity dollar can be used only once, the social-business dollar recycles itself again and again, *ad infinitum,* to deliver benefits to more and more people. Furthermore, philanthropists will be attracted to the idea of social business because it will allow them to leverage their business experience to tackle some of the world's most serious problems.

If Warren Buffett had asked for my advice, I would have advised him to use part of his money to create a social business whose mission would be to provide affordable, high-quality health insurance to the 47 million Americans without it. If Buffett himself—a business genius with decades of experience in the insurance industry—were involved in designing this social business, anybody can easily guess the outcome: The company would achieve a resounding success, and Buffett would be remembered in the history of American health care.

An End to Poverty

As understanding of social business spreads, and as more and more people take up the call to create social businesses, we can move closer and closer to achieving the ultimate goal: To relegate poverty, once and for all, to poverty museums.

Impossible? Not at all. There was a time when certain infectious diseases were thought to be unstoppable. They killed millions of people every year, and many people assumed they were an unchanging part of the human condition. Now, thanks to human creativity, scientific breakthroughs, and determined efforts by public health workers, some of those diseases have been virtually wiped out. The only way scientists can study them now is by examining samples of the microbes in carefully guarded laboratories. Why not strive to do the same with the disease of poverty?

This should be an objective to which people in every village, town, region, and country in the world commit themselves. It simply takes a few people to say, "Let's pledge to work together until the last poor person in our village has been lifted out of poverty." It takes a few more to make the same pledge about a city or county or local district. As this objective is achieved in one locality after another, the time will eventually come when the only way our children or grandchildren can understand what poverty *used* to be like will be by visiting the poverty museums.

When we look back at human history, it is clear that we get what we want—or what we fail to refuse. If we are *not* achieving something, it is because we have not put our minds to it. We are accepting psychological limitations that prevent us from doing what we claim we want.

At this moment, we accept the idea that we will always have poor people among us, that poverty is part of human destiny. The fact that we accept this notion is precisely *why* we continue to have the poor. If we firmly believe that poverty is unacceptable—that it should have no place in a civilized human society—then we will build appropriate institutions and policies to create a poverty-free world.

Poverty exists because we've built our philosophical framework on assumptions that underestimate human capacities. We've designed concepts that are too narrow—our concept of business (which makes profit the *only* viable human motive), our concept of credit-worthiness (which automatically eliminates the poor), our concept of entrepreneurship (which ignores the creativity of the majority of people), and our concept of employment (which relegates humans to passive receptacles rather than active creators). And we've developed institutions that are half-complete at best—like our banking and economic systems, which ignore half the world. Poverty exists because of these intellectual failures rather than because of any lack of capability on the part of people.

All human beings have the inner capacity not only to care for themselves but also to contribute to increasing the well-being of the world as whole. Some get the chance to explore their potential to some degree. But many never get any opportunity to unwrap this wonderful gift they were born with. They die with their gifts unexplored, and the world is deprived of all they could have done.

My work with Grameen Bank has brought me into close touch with the poorest of the poor. This experience has given me an unshakable faith in the creativity of human beings. None of them is born to suffer the misery of hunger and poverty. Each one of those who suffer this misery has the potential to be as successful a human being as anybody else in this world.

It is possible to eliminate poverty from our world because it is not natural to human beings—it is artificially imposed on them. Let's dedicate ourselves to bringing an end to it at the earliest possible date, and putting poverty in the museums once and for all.

Epilogue

"Poverty Is a
Threat to Peace"

—The Nobel Prize Lecture

DELIVERED IN OSLO, NORWAY, ON DECEMBER 10, 2006

Your Majesties, Your Royal Highnesses, Honorable Members of the Norwegian Nobel Committee, Excellencies, Ladies and Gentlemen,

Grameen Bank and I are deeply honoured to receive this most prestigious of awards. We are thrilled and overwhelmed by this honour. Since the Nobel Peace Prize was announced, I have received endless messages from around the world, but what moves me most are the calls I get almost daily, from the borrowers of Grameen Bank in remote Bangladeshi villages, who just want to say how proud they are to have received this recognition.

Nine elected representatives of the seven million borrowers-cum-owners of Grameen Bank have accompanied me all the way to Oslo to receive the prize. I express thanks on their behalf to the Norwegian Nobel Committee for choosing Grameen Bank for this year's Nobel Peace Prize. By giving their institution the most prestigious prize in the world, you give them unparalleled honour. Thanks to your prize, nine proud women from the villages of Bangladesh are at the ceremony today as Nobel laureates, giving an altogether new meaning to the Nobel Peace Prize.

All borrowers of Grameen Bank are celebrating this day as the greatest day of their lives. They are gathering around the nearest television set in their villages all over Bangladesh, along with other villagers, to watch the proceedings of this ceremony.

This year's prize gives highest honour and dignity to the hundreds of millions of women all around the world who struggle every day to make a living and bring hope for a better life for their children. This is a historic moment for them.

Poverty Is a Threat to Peace

Ladies and Gentlemen:
By giving us this prize, the Norwegian Nobel Committee has given important support to the proposition that peace is inextricably linked to poverty. Poverty is a threat to peace.

The world's income distribution gives a very telling story. Ninety-four percent of the world income goes to 40 percent of the population while 60 percent of people live on only 6 percent of world income. Half of the world population lives on two dollars a day. Over one billion people live on less than a dollar a day. This is no formula for peace.

The new millennium began with a great global dream. World leaders gathered at the United Nations in 2000 and adopted, among others, a historic goal to reduce poverty by half by 2015. Never in human history had such a bold goal been adopted by the entire world in one voice, one that specified time and size. But then came September 11 and the Iraq war, and suddenly the world became derailed from the pursuit of this dream, with the attention of world leaders shifting from the war on poverty to the war on terrorism. Till now over $530 billion has been spent on the war in Iraq by the United States alone.

I believe terrorism cannot be defeated by military action. Terrorism must be condemned in the strongest language. We must stand solidly against it, and find all means to end it. We must address the root causes of terrorism to end it for all time to come. I believe that putting resources into improving the lives of poor people is a better strategy than spending it on guns.

Poverty Is Denial of All Human Rights

Peace should be understood in a human way—in a broad social, political and economic way. Peace is threatened by an unjust economic, social and political order, absence of democracy, environmental degradation and absence of human rights.

Poverty is the absence of all human rights. The frustrations, hostility and anger generated by abject poverty cannot sustain peace in any society. For building stable peace we must find ways to provide opportunities for people to live decent lives.

The creation of opportunities for the majority of people—the poor—is at the heart of the work that we have dedicated ourselves to during the past thirty years.

Grameen Bank

I became involved in the poverty issue not as a policymaker or a researcher. I became involved because poverty was all around me, and I could not turn away from it. In 1974, I found it difficult to teach elegant theories of economics in the university classroom, against the backdrop of a terrible famine in Bangladesh. Suddenly, I felt the emptiness of those theories in the face of crushing hunger and poverty. I wanted to do something immediate to help people around me, even if it was just one human being, to get through another day with a little more ease. That brought me face to face with poor people's struggle to find the tiniest amounts of money to support their efforts to eke out a living. I was shocked to discover a woman in the village borrowing less than a dollar from the moneylender on the condition that he would have the exclusive right to buy all she produced at the price he decided. This, to me, was a way of recruiting slave labor.

I decided to make a list of the victims of this moneylending "business" in the village next door to our campus.

When my list was done, it had the names of forty-two victims who had borrowed a total amount of US $27. I offered US $27 from my own pocket to get these victims out of the clutches of those moneylenders. The excitement that was created among the people by this small action got me further involved in it. If I could make so many people so happy with such a tiny amount of money, why not do more of it?

That is what I have been trying to do ever since. The first thing I did was to try to persuade the bank located in the campus to lend money to the poor. But that did not work. The bank said that the poor were not credit-worthy. After all my efforts, over several months, failed, I offered to become a guarantor for the loans to the poor. I was stunned by the result. The poor paid back their loans, on time, every time! But still I kept confronting difficulties in expanding the program through the existing banks. That was when I decided to create a separate bank for the poor, and in 1983, I finally succeeded in doing that. I named it Grameen Bank, or Village Bank.

Today, Grameen Bank gives loans to nearly 7.0 million poor people, 97 percent of whom are women, in 73,000 villages in Bangladesh. Grameen Bank gives collateral-free income-generating, housing, student and micro-enterprise loans to poor families and offers a host of attractive savings, pension funds and insurance products for its members. Since it introduced them in 1984, housing loans have been used to construct 640,000 houses. The legal ownership of these houses belongs to the women themselves. We focused on women because we found giving loans to women always brought more benefits to the family.

Since it opened the bank has given out loans totaling about US $6.0 billion. The repayment rate is 99 percent. Grameen Bank routinely makes a profit. Financially, it is self-reliant and has not taken donor money since 1995. Deposits and own resources of Grameen Bank today amount to 143 percent of all outstanding loans. According to Grameen Bank's internal survey, 58 percent of our borrowers have crossed the poverty line.

Grameen Bank was born as a tiny homegrown project run with the help of several of my students, all local girls and boys. Three of these students are still with me in Grameen Bank, after all these years, as its topmost executives. They are here today to receive this honour you give us.

This idea, which began in Jobra, a small village in Bangladesh, has spread around the world and there are now Grameen-type programs in almost every country.

Second Generation

It is thirty years now since we began. We keep looking at the children of our borrowers to see what has been the impact of our work on their lives. The women who are our borrowers always gave topmost priority to the children. One of the Sixteen Decisions developed and followed by them was to send children to school. Grameen Bank encouraged them, and before long all the children were going to school. Many of these children made it to the top of their class. We wanted to celebrate that, so we introduced scholarships for talented students. Grameen Bank now gives 30,000 scholarships every year.

Many of the children went on to higher education to become doctors, engineers, college teachers and other professionals. We introduced student loans to make it easy for Grameen students to complete higher education. Now some of them have PhDs. There are 13,000 students on student loans. Over 7,000 students are now added to this number annually.

We are creating a completely new generation that will be well equipped to take their families way out of the reach of poverty. We want to make a break in the historical continuation of poverty.

Beggars Can Turn to Business

In Bangladesh 80 percent of the poor families have already been reached with microcredit. We are hoping that by 2010, 100 percent of the poor families will be reached.

Three years ago we started an exclusive programme focusing on the beggars. None of Grameen Bank's rules apply to them. Loans are interest-free; they can pay whatever amount they wish, whenever they wish. We gave them the idea to carry small merchandise such as snacks, toys or household items, when they went from house to house for begging. The idea worked. There are now 85,000 beggars in the program. About 5,000 of them have already stopped begging completely. The typical loan to a beggar is $12.

We encourage and support every conceivable intervention to help the poor fight out of poverty. We always advocate microcredit in addition to all other interventions, arguing that microcredit makes those interventions work better.

Information Technology for the Poor

Information and communication technology (ICT) is quickly changing the world, creating a distanceless, borderless world of instantaneous communications. Increasingly, it is becoming less and less costly. I saw an opportunity for poor people to change their lives if this technology could be brought to them to meet their needs.

As a first step to bring ICT to the poor we created a mobile-phone company, Grameen Phone. We gave loans from Grameen Bank to the poor women to buy mobile phones to sell phone services in the villages. We saw the synergy between microcredit and ICT.

The phone business was a success and became a coveted enterprise for Grameen borrowers. Telephone ladies quickly learned and innovated the ropes of the telephone business, and it has become the quickest way to get out of poverty and to earn social respectability. Today there are nearly 300,000 telephone ladies providing telephone service in all the villages of Bangladesh. Grameen Phone has more than 10 million subscribers, and is the largest mobile-phone company in the country. Although the number of telephone ladies is only a small fraction of the total number of subscribers, they generate 19 percent of the revenue of the company. Out of the nine board members who are attending this grand ceremony today, four are telephone ladies.

Grameen Phone is a joint-venture company owned by Telenor of Norway and Grameen Telecom of Bangladesh. Telenor owns 62 percent share of the company, Grameen Telecom owns 38 percent. Our vision was to ultimately convert this company into a social business by giving majority ownership to the poor women of Grameen Bank. We are working towards that goal. Someday Grameen Phone will become another example of a big enterprise owned by the poor.

Free Market Economy

Capitalism centers on the free market. It is claimed that the freer the market, the better is the result of capitalism in solving the questions of what, how, and for whom. It is also claimed that the individual search for personal gains brings collective optimal result.

I am in favor of strengthening the freedom of the market. At the same time, I am very unhappy about the conceptual restrictions imposed on the players in the market. This originates from the assumption that entrepreneurs are one-dimensional human beings, who are dedicated to one mission in their business lives—to maximize profit.

This interpretation of capitalism insulates the entrepreneurs from all political, emotional, social, spiritual, environmental dimensions of their lives. This was done perhaps as a reasonable simplification, but it stripped away the very essentials of human life.

Human beings are a wonderful creation embodying limitless human qualities and capabilities. Our theoretical constructs should make room for the blossoming of those qualities, not assume them away.

Many of the world's problems exist because of this restriction on who participates in the free market. The world has not resolved the problem of crushing poverty that half of its population suffers. Health care remains out of the reach of the majority of the world population. The country with the richest and freest market fails to provide health care for one-sixth of its population.

We have remained so impressed by the success of the free market that we never dared to express any doubt about our basic assumption. To make it worse, we worked extra hard to transform ourselves, as closely as possible, into the one-dimensional human beings as conceptualized in the theory, to allow smooth functioning of the free-market mechanism.

By defining "entrepreneur" in a broader way we can change the character of capitalism radically, and solve many of the unresolved social and economic problems within the scope of the free market. Let us suppose an entrepreneur, instead of having a single source of motivation (such as, maximizing profit), now has two sources of motivation, which are mutually exclusive, but equally compelling—a) maximization of profit and b) doing good to people and the world.

Each type of motivation will lead to a separate kind of business. Let us call the first type of business a profit-maximizing business, and the second type of business a social business. Social business will be a new kind of business introduced in the marketplace with the objective of making a difference in the world. Investors in the social business could get back their investment, but will not take any dividend from the company. Profit would be ploughed back into the company to expand its outreach and improve the quality of its product or service. A social business will be a non-loss, non-dividend company.

Once social business is recognized in law, many existing companies will come forward to create social businesses in addition to their foundation activities. Many activists from the nonprofit sector will also find this an attractive option. Unlike the nonprofit sector where one needs to collect donations to keep activities going, a social business will be self-sustaining and create surplus for expansion since it is a non-loss enterprise. Social business will go into a new type of capital market of its own, to raise capital.

Young people all around the world, particularly in rich countries, will find the concept of social business very appealing since it will give them a challenge to make a difference by using their creative talent. Many young people today feel frustrated because they cannot see any worthy challenge, which excites them, within the present capitalist world. Socialism gave them a dream to fight for. Young people dream about creating a perfect world of their own.

Almost all social and economic problems of the world will be addressed through social businesses. The challenge is to innovate business models and apply them to produce desired social results cost-effectively and efficiently. Health care for the poor, financial services for the poor, information technology for the poor, education and training for the poor, marketing for the poor, renewable energy—these are all exciting areas for social businesses.

Social business is important because it addresses very vital concerns of mankind. It can change the lives of the bottom 60 percent of world population and help them to get out of poverty.

Grameen's Social Business

Even profit-maximizing companies can be designed as social businesses by giving full or majority ownership to the poor. This constitutes a second type of social business. Grameen Bank falls under this category of social business.

The poor could get the shares of these companies as gifts by donors, or they could buy the shares with their own money. The borrowers with their own money buy Grameen Bank shares, which cannot be transferred to non-borrowers. A committed professional team does the day-to-day running of the bank.

Bilateral and multilateral donors could easily create this type of social business. When a donor gives a loan or a grant to build a bridge in the recipient country, it could create a "bridge company" owned by the local poor. A committed management company could be given the responsibility of running the company. Profit of the company will go to the local poor as dividend, and towards building more bridges. Many infrastructure projects, like roads, highways, airports, seaports, utility companies could all be built in this manner.

Grameen has created two social businesses of the first type. One is a yogurt factory, to produce fortified yogurt to bring nutrition to malnourished children, in a joint venture with Danone. It will continue to expand until all malnourished children of Bangladesh are reached with this yogurt. Another is a chain of eyecare hospitals. Each hospital will undertake 10,000 cataract surgeries per year at differentiated prices to the rich and the poor.

Social Stock Market

To connect investors with social businesses, we need to create a social stock market where only the shares of social businesses will be traded. An investor will come to this stock exchange with a clear intention of finding a social business, which has a mission of his liking. Anyone who wants to make money will go to the existing stock market.

To enable a social stock exchange to perform properly, we will need to create rating agencies, standardization of terminology, definitions, impact measurement tools, reporting formats, and new financial publications, such as *The Social Wall Street Journal*. Business schools will offer courses and business management degrees on social businesses to train young managers how to manage social-business enterprises in the most efficient manner, and, most of all, to inspire them to become social-business entrepreneurs themselves.

Role of Social Businesses in Globalization

I support globalization and believe it can bring more benefits to the poor than its alternative. But it must be the right kind of globalization. To me, globalization is like a hundred-lane highway criss-crossing the world. If it is a free-for-all highway, its lanes will be taken over by the giant trucks from powerful economies. Bangladeshi rickshaws will be thrown off the highway. In order to have a win-win globalization, we must have traffic rules, traffic police, and traffic authority for this global highway. The rule of "strongest takes it all" must be replaced by rules that ensure that the poorest have a place and piece of the action, without being elbowed out by the strong. Globalization must not become financial imperialism.

Powerful multinational social businesses can be created to retain the benefit of globalization for poor people and poor countries. Social businesses will either bring ownership to poor people, or keep the profit within poor countries, since taking dividends will not be their objective. Direct foreign investment by foreign social businesses will be exciting news for recipient countries. Building strong economies in poor countries by protecting their national interest from plundering companies will be a major area of interest for social businesses.

We Create What We Want

We get what we want, or what we don't refuse. We accept the fact that we will always have poor people around us, and that poverty is part of human destiny. This is precisely why we continue to have poor people around us. If we firmly believe that poverty is unacceptable to us, and that it should not belong to a civilized society, we would have built appropriate institutions and policies to create a poverty-free world.

We wanted to go to the moon, so we went there. We achieve what we want to achieve. If we are not achieving something, it is because we have not put our minds to it. We create what we want.

What we want and how we get to it depends on our mindsets. It is extremely difficult to change mindsets once they are formed. We create the world in accordance with our mindset. We need to invent ways to change our perspective continually and reconfigure our mindset quickly as new knowledge emerges. We can reconfigure our world if we can reconfigure our mindset.

We Can Put Poverty in the Museums

I believe that we can create a poverty-free world because poverty is not created by poor people. It has been created and sustained by the economic and social system that we have designed for ourselves; the institutions and concepts that make up that system; the policies that we pursue.

Poverty is created because we built our theoretical framework on assumptions which underestimate human capacity, by designing concepts which are too narrow (such as concepts of business, credit-worthiness, entrepreneurship, employment) or developing institutions which remain half-done (such as financial institutions, where the poor are left out). Poverty is caused by the failure at the conceptual level, rather than any lack of capability on the part of people.

I firmly believe that we can create a poverty-free world if we collectively believe in it. In a poverty-free world, the only place you would be able to see poverty is in the poverty museums. When schoolchildren take a tour of the poverty museums, they will be horrified to see the misery and indignity that some human beings had to go through. They will blame their forefathers for tolerating this inhuman condition, which existed for so long, for so many people.

All human beings have the inner capacity not only to care for themselves but also to contribute to increasing the well-being of the world as a whole. Some get the chance to explore their potential to some degree, but many others never get any opportunity, during their lifetime, to unwrap the wonderful gift they were born with. They die unexplored and the world remains deprived of their creativity, and their contribution.

Grameen has given me an unshakeable faith in the creativity of human beings. This has led me to believe that human beings are not born to suffer the misery of hunger and poverty.

To me poor people are like bonsai trees. When you plant the best seed of the tallest tree in a flowerpot, you get a replica of the tallest tree, only inches tall. There is nothing wrong with the seed you planted, it is only the soil-base that is too inadequate. Poor people are bonsai people. There is nothing wrong in their seeds. Simply, society never gave them the base to grow on. All it needs to get poor people out of poverty is for us to create an enabling environment for them. Once the poor can unleash their energy and creativity, poverty will disappear very quickly.

Let us join hands to give every human being a fair chance to unleash their energy and creativity.

Ladies and Gentlemen,

Let me conclude by expressing my deep gratitude to the Norwegian Nobel Committee for recognizing that poor people, and especially poor women, have both the potential and the right to live a decent life, and that microcredit helps to unleash that potential.

I believe this honor that you give us will inspire many more bold initiatives around the world to make a historical breakthrough in ending global poverty.

Thank you very much.

For Further Information

You may contact Professor Yunus
and the Grameen Bank at:

Professor Muhammad Yunus
Grameen Bank
Mirpur Two
Dhaka 1216
Bangladesh
Fax: 8802-8013559
E-mail: *yunus@grameen.net*
Website: *www.grameen.com*

Index

Index

Tim Campbell

Muhammad Yunus was born in Chittagong, a seaport in Bangladesh. The third of fourteen children, he was educated at Dhaka University and was awarded a Fulbright scholarship to study economics at Vanderbilt University. He then served as chairman of the economics department at Chittagong University before devoting his life to providing financial and social services to the poorest of the poor. He is the founder and managing director of Grameen Bank and the author of the bestselling *Banker to the Poor.* Yunus and Grameen Bank are winners of the 2006 Nobel Peace Prize.

PublicAffairs is a publishing house founded in 1997. It is a tribute to the standards, values, and flair of three persons who have served as mentors to countless reporters, writers, editors, and book people of all kinds, including me.

I.F. STONE, proprietor of *I. F. Stone's Weekly*, combined a commitment to the First Amendment with entrepreneurial zeal and reporting skill and became one of the great independent journalists in American history. At the age of eighty, Izzy published *The Trial of Socrates*, which was a national bestseller. He wrote the book after he taught himself ancient Greek.

BENJAMIN C. BRADLEE was for nearly thirty years the charismatic editorial leader of *The Washington Post*. It was Ben who gave the *Post* the range and courage to pursue such historic issues as Watergate. He supported his reporters with a tenacity that made them fearless and it is no accident that so many became authors of influential, best-selling books.

ROBERT L. BERNSTEIN, the chief executive of Random House for more than a quarter century, guided one of the nation's premier publishing houses. Bob was personally responsible for many books of political dissent and argument that challenged tyranny around the globe. He is also the founder and longtime chair of Human Rights Watch, one of the most respected human rights organizations in the world.

. . .

For fifty years, the banner of Public Affairs Press was carried by its owner Morris B. Schnapper, who published Gandhi, Nasser, Toynbee, Truman, and about 1,500 other authors. In 1983, Schnapper was described by *The Washington Post* as "a redoubtable gadfly." His legacy will endure in the books to come.

Peter Osnos, *Founder and Editor-at-Large*